Critical Theory and Film

Critical Theory and Contemporary Society

Series Editor

Darrow Schecter

ABOUT THE SERIES

Critical Theory and Contemporary Society explores the relationship between contemporary society as a complex and highly differentiated phenomenon, on the one hand, and Critical Theory as a correspondingly sophisticated methodology for studying and understanding social and political relations today, on the other.

Each volume highlights in distinctive ways why (1) Critical Theory offers the most appropriate concepts for understanding political movements, socio-economic conflicts and state institutions in an increasingly global world and (2) why Critical Theory nonetheless needs updating in order to keep pace with the realities of the twenty-first century.

The books in the series look at global warming, financial crisis, post–nation state legitimacy, international relations, cinema, terrorism and other issues, applying an interdisciplinary approach, in order to help students and citizens understand the specificity and uniqueness of the current situation.

Darrow Schecter,
Series Editor,
Reader in the School of History, Art History
and Humanities, University of Sussex, UK

BOOKS IN THE SERIES

- *Critical Theory and Film*: Fabio Vighi, Reader and Co-director of the Žižek Centre for Ideology Critique at Cardiff University, UK
- *Critical Theory and Contemporary Europe*: William Outhwaite, Chair and Professor of Sociology at Newcastle University, UK
- *Critical Theory, Legal Theory, and the Evolution of Contemporary Society*: Hauke Brunkhorst, Professor of Sociology and Head of the Institute of Sociology at the University of Flensburg, Germany
- *Critical Theory in the Twenty-First Century*: Darrow Schecter, Reader in the School of History, Art History and Humanities, University of Sussex, UK
- *Critical Theory and the Digital*: David Berry, Department of Political and Cultural Studies at Swansea University, UK
- *Critical Theory and the Contemporary Crisis of Capital*: Heiko Feldner, Co-director of the Centre for Ideology Critique and Žižek Studies at Cardiff University, UK

Critical Theory and Film

Rethinking ideology through film noir

FABIO VIGHI

BLOOMSBURY
NEW DELHI • LONDON • OXFORD • NEW YORK • SYDNEY

Bloomsbury Publishing India Pvt. Ltd
Second Floor, Building No. 4
DDA Complex LSC, Pocket C – 6 & 7
Vasant Kunj, New Delhi 110070
www.bloomsbury.com

BLOOMSBURY, Bloomsbury Academic India and the Diana
logo are trademarks of Bloomsbury Publishing Plc

First published in India 2019
First published 2012

This edition published with permission from Bloomsbury Publishing Plc,
50 Bedford Square, London, WC1B3DP, UK

British Library Cataloguing-in-Publication Data
A catalogue record for this book is available from the British Library.

Library of Congress Cataloging-in-Publication Data
A catalog record for this book is available from the Library of Congress

ISBN: 978-93-88912-26-6

2 4 6 8 10 9 7 5 3 1

Typeset by Newgen Imaging Systems Pvt Ltd, Chennai, India
Printed at Manipal Technologies Limited, Manipal

For Alice, Elena and Sofia

Contents

Introduction

Enlightening deceptions . . .

In the underrated film noir *Hollow Triumph* (1948, Steve Sekeley), also known as *The Scar*, the hero's repeated attempts to deceive his enemies eventually turn into fatal self-deception. Following an aborted hold-up against a casino run by the mob, John Muller (Paul Henreid), a compulsive criminal, goes into hiding to avoid the gangsters' vengeful fury. By chance, he discovers his double in the person of a Dr Bartok and promptly decides to change his identity by appropriating Bartok's life. The only difference between him and the doctor, he notes, is a long scar the latter has on his cheek. Muller, who has some medical knowledge, proceeds to cut a matching mark on his face guided by a photograph of his double. When he discovers that the photo he used had been wrongly processed, and that as a result he has incised the wrong cheek, he becomes understandably anxious. However, to his surprise, nobody notices the difference, so he proceeds to murder Bartok and take over his medical practice, even beginning an affair with Bartok's secretary Evelyn (Joan Bennett). Safe in his new identity, he believes to have escaped all trouble. However, two twists of fate await him. First, he finds out that the gangsters are no longer after him, which retrospectively makes the painful and risky identity change unnecessary. Second, in a shattering finale, he learns that Dr Bartok was a compulsive gambler who had run up huge debts with another unforgiving casino owner. When the new gangsters finally catch up with him, he gets his comeuppance, for there is no way of demonstrating that he is not the real Dr Bartok . . .

The many twists that typify classical Hollywood film noir as a rule reveal a subtle dialectical logic at work within the narrative. In *Hollow Triumph* this logic implies, in an exemplary way, that the more the subject tries to control and manipulate external events, the more he dupes himself, since he paradoxically turns into the very object of his manipulation. As if in a short circuit, the subject comes to coincide with the object, the target of his actions. Thus, Muller's assertive resolve to control reality, characterized by his sharp albeit amoral criminal intelligence, ironically culminates in self-framing, a gesture that makes him appear simultaneously as the subject and the object of his scheming. The only difference between himself and Dr Bartok is the position of a scar, which nobody notices. Like no other genre or canon, film noir consistently objectivizes subjectivity, depriving it of its hubris while nonetheless preserving agency as a necessary mark of human conduct. In standard noir criticism, such ironic twists whereby the agent, in his effort to affirm his identity against an objectively inimical universe, effectively sets up the conditions of his subjection and demise, are explained through a reference to fate: The hero is existentially at the mercy of a cold and meaningless universe. This, however, would be consolatory. My argument in this book is that such a reading should be refined by extracting its dialectical (and indirectly political) substance. Fate, in film noir, is not merely the implacable external force that deprives us of our freedom and turns us into puppets. A dialectical reading of noir shows how subjectivity and fate are linked by an umbilical cord, and that distinguishing between the two amounts to a perspectival error.

Conceiving of classical film noir in dialectical terms allows me to begin to redefine the overall weight and mode of appearance of ideology within film. More specifically, my analysis opens up the space for a 'critical counter-attack' on traditional Critical Theory via a reassessment of the theoretical justification of their uncomplimentary dismissal of the film industry. While 'critical theory' is today used as a generic term to define any theory with a critical edge, in this study I only consider the Marxist school of thought responsible for the emergence of the specific brand of theory devoted to the critical analysis of society and culture, namely the Frankfurt School. As is well known, the Frankfurt School (Frankfurt Institute for Social Research), especially with its most representative proponent Theodor W. Adorno, developed a damning critique of film from within its wider liquidation of the 'culture industry', which it regarded as pervasively ideological. Although Adorno differentiated between *film as artform* and *film as industry*, the cautious and sporadic attention he paid to the former is obscured by the emphatic, categorical dismissal of the latter. In truth, these two approaches to film are perfectly compatible, and should be mapped against Adorno's wider distinction between art and mass culture. As for the latter, he went as far as to write about the 'dictatorship of the culture industry' (Adorno 1992: 250), while cinema, the 'central sector of the culture industry' (Adorno 2001: 100) was emphatically linked with authority:

> The masks of the film are so many emblems of authority. Their horror grows to the extent that these masks are able to move and speak, although this does nothing to alter their inexorability: everything that lives is captured in such masks. [. . .] Whoever goes to a film is only waiting for the day when this spell will be broken, and perhaps ultimately it is only this well

> conceived hope which draws people to the cinema. But once there they obey. They assimilate themselves to what is dead. And that is how they become disposable. (Adorno 2001: 95)

Significantly, Adorno and Horkheimer began writing on film during their 1940s exile in Los Angeles, where they were directly and fully exposed to the might of the Hollywood machine. It was also in the 1940s that the retroactively named film noir saw its birth in Hollywood, rapidly consolidating its formulaic character. Taking its cue from this contingent historical encounter, my reading turns around the standard approach whereby Critical Theory is supposed to provide the framework within which to understand the ideological role of the film industry. Relying especially on Hegel's model of the dialectic, I argue that the study of film can help us disentangle the philosophical and political presuppositions of Critical Theory's distinctive dialectical method, thus pointing towards its inherent shortcomings. The critique of the 'culture industry' is undoubtedly Adorno's and Horkheimer's most influential and controversial concept. This book argues that the problem with such a concept is, simply put, that it misses a 'dialectical twist', despite the fact that it was coined by two convinced dialecticians. Adorno's assertion of an unbridgeable divide between critically effective *art* (essentially, modernist art) and industrially produced, debilitating *entertainment* does not capture in its entirety the complex, ambiguous and fundamentally contradictory nature of cultural production under capitalism. Even in those very few passages where Adorno seems less intransigent in his critique of the film industry, he is still adamant about its direct ideological function. See, for example, the following excerpt, penned in the 1940s with Hanns Eisler:

> Technology opens up unlimited opportunities for art in the future, and even in the poorest motion pictures there are moments when such opportunities are strikingly apparent. But the same principle that has opened up these opportunities also ties them to big business. A discussion of industrialized culture must show the interaction of these two factors: the aesthetic potentialities of mass art in the future, and its ideological character at present. (Adorno and Eisler 2005: liii)

My specific point here is that 1940s Hollywood film noir, a typical case of film-commodity, displays a stringent dialectical logic that remained completely unappreciated by those critical theorists, Adorno *in primis*, who turned dialectics into the paramount instrument for critical investigation.

While dissecting the cultural logic of capitalism, Adorno and Horkheimer omitted to articulate a rigorous analysis of those cultural products, such as

Hollywood films, that they regularly dismissed as 'infantile [. . .] regression manufactured on an industrial scale' (Adorno 2001: 178). Making use of Critical Theory's key methodological tool, namely dialectics, my general aim is to show how capital's drive to churn out cultural commodities can be fruitfully hijacked by theory and made to reveal the profoundly contradictory and potentially liberating tendency nestled at the core of the cultural commodity itself. To carry out my argument, I focus on film noir as a specific canon that acquired popularity precisely during the 'American years' of the Frankfurt School. Film, together with radio and magazines, was regarded by Adorno and Horkheimer as the authoritarian kernel of the culture industry. Its main ideological effect, in their view, was its contribution to the creation of the conditions for the thorough and irreversible debilitation of the rational faculties of the masses, effectively preventing any form of authentically critical reflection on the status quo. My take on film noir demonstrates that what this attitude prejudicially disqualifies is precisely a reflection on the film-commodity as the locus where the (theoretical) antidote to the logic of capital can be extracted.

It is well known that Adorno turned to aesthetics from a philosophical angle, in the attempt to find an anchoring point for his dialectical thought founded in negativity. Thus, while art is dialectical 'by making itself resistant to its meanings', similarly philosophy sticks to the negative 'by refusing to clutch at any immediate thing'. Although rooted in the concept, philosophy 'must strive, by way of the concept, to transcend the concept' (Adorno 2000: 15), a formula which in Adorno also captures the essence of art. Philosophy, aesthetics and negative dialectics are thus bound together by a double aim: To resist the irrationality of instrumental reason and, by the same token, transcend it. As Martin Jay put it, for Adorno the only purpose ascribable to art was 'the presentation of a foretaste of the "other" society denied by present conditions' (Jay 1996: 211). Art was thus conceived as a receptacle for a utopian dimension clad strictly in black (negativity). Conversely, the film industry came to represent an emblematic instance of the ideological triumph of instrumental rationality in a world dominated by technology. The ideological purpose of film as mass art in the age of technological reproduction was that of reconciling the masses with the status quo. Walter Benjamin, on the other hand, proposing a different take on technological reproduction (see Benjamin 1992: 211–44), believed in the subversive potential of cinema as the medium capable of sustaining a politicized art which would exert a direct influence on the masses. In this respect, he followed Brecht, who was also sanguine about the revolutionary potential of cinema (despite his personal frustration with the film industry).[1] Adorno and Benjamin kept disagreeing on the role of film until less than 2 years before Benjamin's death, when Benjamin concurred with his younger friend that the advent of the talkies had stifled the revolutionary potential of silent cinema.[2]

I suggest, however, that their contrasting stances were supported by a shared presupposition which, especially if considered from today's perspective, cannot fail to appear outmoded and somewhat naive, namely the belief in the subversive role that art/culture can play in relation to a given audience. What if Adorno's and Benjamin's *common* error resided precisely in this belief? What if, in other words, the radical potential of an artifact or cultural product can only be postulated in strict correlation with theory rather than as a direct effect on those who have access to it? From this angle, Adorno's strenuous defence of modernism as an aesthetic canon harbouring some form of resistance to the devastating commodification of culture that characterized the course of twentieth century, should also be partially reconsidered.[3] Is it not obvious that modernism too, however negative and resistant to meaning, was intimately and pervasively governed by the logic of late capitalism, and that therefore its defence as a last cultural bastion against the technology-fuelled, unstoppable capitalist wave risks sounding like a subtly, perhaps unconsciously disingenuous retreat from asking real questions about the core of capitalism? My entire argument relies on the premise that the crucial weakness of the Frankfurt School (and Western Marxism in general) resides in its decision to (dis)place Marx's critique of the political economy within the wider horizon of the critique of instrumental rationality, as if the latter was the true cause of modernity's degeneration.[4] The focus on *Kulturindustrie* was a consequence of that displacement. With this I do not mean to align myself with those critics who crudely dismiss culture as an insignificant by-product of economic determinants. On the contrary, the cultural dimension as I perceive it remains a key area of investigation if we are to understand the socio-economic context of our lives. However, it needs to be considered in connection with the theoretical tension hosted by cultural commodities such as films.

. . . As real as masks

The debate on whether film theory is dead or alive is a particularly pressing one in today's film studies, and has been so since at least 1996, when David Bordwell and Noël Carroll published their polemical volume *Post-Theory: Reconstructing Film Theory*. My dialectical outlook attempts to somewhat redefine the main premise behind such a debate. From my perspective, it is not so much a matter of arguing for or against the use of specific theoretical frameworks to decode the way film speaks to us, but rather to show how cinema, as a purely *fictional* domain, engages with the same basic structural dynamics that configure and define reality in its magmatic complexity. Bluntly stated, the overarching aim of my study is to reduce the distance that separates the discipline 'film studies' from the reality it reflects. This task implies shifting the focus away from the specificities of film and engaging directly with its conceptual power vis-à-vis the real. The underlying assumption is that cinema is intrinsically theoretical, inasmuch as its condition of signification is a recording of reality that hinges upon the replication of the fundamental laws that connect us to the world. As a fictional construct, film mirrors the fictional constitution of reality itself. It therefore works like a magnifying lens illustrating the mechanisms through which we can say that we exist.

In a remarkably accurate and concise definition, Warren Buckland (2009: 6) has written that 'film theory (like all theory) is a form of speculative thought that aims to make visible the underlying structures and absent causes that confer order and intelligibility upon film'. Without meaning to completely disengage from the study of film as a specialized cultural product, my wager nevertheless implies replacing the last word of the quotation ('film') with 'reality'. It seems to me that film theories would benefit enormously from relinquishing at least some of their discipline-specific concerns in order to be more daring in their investigation of film's direct connection with the real. For instance, film theory need not be anxiously attached to a terminology whose ever-increasing complexity and abstraction tend to deplete intellectual analysis. The fact that film theory has been in crisis since the 1990s should lead us to look for the main cause of such crisis in the waning desire to understand 'the underlying structures and absent causes that confer order and intelligibility upon' reality itself. Along these lines, Francesco Casetti surmises that one of the reasons for the weakening of film theory is 'the weakening of the social need for "explanation"' (2007: 39). This claim, I think, needs to be endorsed and radicalized: The progressive vanishing of film theory is ultimately one with the vanishing of Theory that has characterized postmodern thought at large, because what tends to be jettisoned today is not only the will to interpret the world but especially to re-signify thoroughly. In this respect, we can positively say that cinema today reflects its historical context.

As stressed by Casetti (1999), in post-war film theory the theme of the equivalence between cinema and reality was developed mainly, though in different ways, by three theorists: André Bazin, Pier Paolo Pasolini and Gilles Deleuze, all of whom used the equation film–reality to emphasize both the common structural constitution of the two notions as well as the cinematic potential to encode a non-symbolizable, implicitly subversive dimension of the real. From this angle, Pier Paolo Pasolini's heretical semiotics of the 1960s should be resurrected. The 'outrageous' character of Pasolini's claim, made against such authoritative semioticians as Umberto Eco and Walter Metz, hinged on the basic assertion that ultimately there is no difference between cinema and reality, in so far as *reality itself is intrinsically cinematic*, that is, structured around a particular interplay of fictions or symbolic (dis-)identifications.[5] The study of cinematic fictions would thus coincide with the study of reality. In Jacques Rancière's words: 'The real must be fictionalized in order to be thought' (Rancière 2006b: 38), or, to quote Alain Badiou: 'Beyond semblance there is the *necessity* of semblance, which has perhaps always constituted its real' (Badiou 2007: 51). Starting from the *necessity of semblance*, then, a film holds the potential to unravel for us something crucial about the semblance of reality, namely the way in which the latter comes into being and constitutes its meanings.

It is for this reason that I often refer to the psychoanalytic paradigm. Rather than making use of individual psychoanalytic concepts (mirror stage, gaze, suture, etc.) for the understanding of cinema, however, I prefer to show how cinema validates the fundamental psychoanalytic axiom (particularly decisive in Freudian–Lacanian theory) that the emergence of signification depends on a degree of repression, whose 'work' is detectable in those symptomatic formations that return to affect and distort signification itself. Cinema, like reality, confronts us with the necessity of what Lacan conceptualized as the 'swipe of symbolic castration', which implies our constitutive alienation in fiction. This book treats film dialectically inasmuch as films negotiate their symbolic status with a real which is repressed and yet constantly comes back, disturbing any fixed meaning we might wish to assign to a given narrative – exactly as it happens in ordinary reality. This leads to a definition of ideology which was intuited by the critical theorists of the Frankfurt School but not fully articulated: Ideology as the very division between an explicit text and its repressed underside, which makes its presence felt through symptomatic knots of radically displaced meaning. Film noir here is discussed precisely as a privileged field to grasp the dialectical function of these symptoms. To the question 'is there an emancipatory potential in film noir?', one should answer yes, provided we accept the detour of theory, that is, provided we submit noir to a thorough dialectical analysis.

Although I do not linger here on the various debates on 'film theory', my argument stems from the conviction that the cinematic interaction of images composes in itself a form of consciousness that, as it is the product of a constitutively alienating act of symbolization, lies in wait of being translated into theory. A radical film theory should always begin by acknowledging that filmic images deal with reality rather than with its pale imitation – not, however, because of their power to transcend the fictional domain, but precisely because the elementary fabric of reality, in so far as it is open to experience, is fundamentally fictional. Symbolic representation is the mode and condition of existence of reality itself, inclusive of its relation to what is unrepresentable. As a form of thought, then, cinema always thinks the real, for it is inextricably entangled with existence; conversely, reality can only be thought as an intrinsically cinematic form of appearance. In connection with Adorno's previously quoted passage on films as masks of authority, we should dialecticize his indictment and counterclaim that *reality itself needs masks* in order to appear and achieve given (though fragile) significations. In Hegel's dialectic, the speculative identity of thought and its object is predicated upon the *defect* of both: The intrinsic inconsistency (contradiction) that qualifies thinking *is* the inconsistency of substance, of the very object of thought. For this reason, masks are necessary, and at the same time adequate only to express their inadequacy. The main character of this book is the dialectical figure that discloses the correlation of thought, reality and film at the level of their common struggle to wear real masks.

A theoretical premise on Adorno's theme of the 'preponderance of the object'

The materialistic assertion that the object is constitutively preponderant in respect of thought's attempt to grasp it is undoubtedly the central notion in Adorno's dialectics, the hinge sustaining his entire theoretical edifice and much of Critical Theory's anti-dogmatic and anti-metaphysical aims. As such, it plays a strong role in Adorno's denunciation of the culture industry and, more specifically, of film. For this reason, it deserves full attention right from the beginning of this study. In *Negative Dialectics*, Adorno writes: 'It is by passing to the object's preponderance that dialectics is rendered materialistic. [. . .] Once the object becomes an object of cognition, its physical side is spiritualized from the outset by translation into epistemology' (Adorno 2000: 192). Defending the moment in matter that is non-identical with thought – that is, that thought only illegitimately transforms into a subjective, cognitive moment – Adorno effectively rejects any (Hegelo-Marxist) attempt at dialectically reconciling subject and object as intrinsically ideological. Contradiction and negativity (non-identity) mark the object of knowledge as much as the knowing subject, practical activity as much as theory, to the extent that no correspondence between the two terms of the dialectic can ever be envisaged. In this understanding of dialectics, subject and object

> are not positive, primary states of fact but negative throughout, expressing nothing but nonidentity. Even so, the difference between subject and object cannot be simply negated. They are neither an ultimate duality nor a screen

> hiding ultimate unity. They constitute one another as much as – by virtue of such constitution – they depart from each other. (Adorno 2000: 174)

Throughout this book, we shall see how, in his justification of negative dialectics, Adorno pays tribute to Hegel and yet denounces him as the thinker who eventually mortified the object in order to subsume all experience under subjective reason. In fact, Adorno seeks to rescue Hegel from what he regards as his entrenchment in a doctrine of affirmative, ultimately undialectical subjectivism. As he put it in the 1950s: 'no reading of Hegel can do him justice without criticizing him' (Adorno 1993: 145). For Adorno, the basic discrepancy at the core of the dialectical procedure concerns the incompatibility between the subject qua thought's compulsion to identify and the persistence of an objective dimension that exceeds and resists identification – and that is ultimately vindicated through the alliance between philosophy and aesthetics: 'Philosophy as a whole is allied with art in wanting to rescue, in the medium of the concept, the mimesis that the concept represses' (Adorno 1993: 123).

However anti-Hegelian in denying the speculative coincidence of subject and object, Adorno's dialectical method nevertheless follows Hegel in appreciating the coincidence of the *semblance* and the *truth* of thought: There is no difference between them, since there is literally *nothing beyond the semblance of what we think*. Thought coincides with its appearance, not with a supposedly deeper truth-content. As a logical consequence, and in keeping with Hegel's rectification of Kant's transcendentalism, Adorno argues that the only way for dialectical thought to begin its course is by directing its force against itself qua appearance: 'Aware that the conceptual totality is mere appearance, I have no way but to break immanently, in its own measure, through the appearance of total identity' (Adorno 2000: 5). What we have here is the acknowledgement that the dimension proper to dialectics is that of *appearance*, semblance, that is to say a flat surface where thought's compulsion to identify is constantly supplemented by its own immanent contradiction, its non-coincidence with itself. On this plane, where thought identifies objects and therefore *appears* as thought, the non-identity qua appearance which inhabits and fuels the dialectic is, in Adorno's words, the 'inevitable insufficiency' of thought itself, directly connected with 'my guilt of what I am thinking' (Adorno 2000: 5).

At this stage, we are able to conjure up a clear picture of how 'negativity', 'dialectics' and the theme of the 'preponderance of the object' come to intertwine in Adorno, conferring upon his philosophy an unresolved and irresolvable tension between materialism (the 'preponderance of the object') and an idealistic drive unwittingly caught between Kant's transcendental turn and Hegel's radical immanentism. With Hegel – and against the misplaced anti-Hegelian claims of most of his pages – Adorno holds fast to the conviction that '[i]dentity and contradiction of thought are welded together' (Adorno 2000: 6). However, his insistence on the priority of the object – the claim that the object of thought can never be fully subsumed under conceptual identity, as it leaves behind an 'indigestible' remainder of itself, an 'indissoluble "Something"' (Adorno 2000: 135), that is to say a 'hard kernel' that resists thought's urge to identify – is much more ambiguous. It is a sign of the Marxist legacy of his philosophy *and* it provides evidence that such materialism tends to relapse into the Kantian paradigm where a transcendental gap persists between the categories of thought and its object. Although Adorno does take issue against Kant's transcendentalist 'solution' of using the unattainable 'thing-in-itself' 'to spur cognition to untiring effort' (Adorno 2000: 175), one is compelled to surmise that Adorno's own endeavour of positing the identity of subject and object as a utopian goal is intrinsically Kantian for the same fundamental reasoning that Adorno uses against Kant. Adorno's theory of the preponderance of the object outside the domain of reason is thus intimately Kantian, despite it being presented, in Hegelian terms, as 'a moment in dialectics – not beyond dialectics, but articulated in dialectics' (Adorno 2000: 184).

It is worth reiterating that Adorno's entire philosophical enterprise is based on the conviction that *satisfaction with conceptuality equals conceptual fetishism*. The task of philosophy for him is precisely to extinguish 'the autarky of the concept' (Adorno 2000: 12) as that alone would allow us to perceive things for what they are. The defining mark of negative dialectics is that it forces the concept to turn against itself, towards the non-identity of thought, and from there it attempts to connect with the material surplus within the object of thought. Such a stance allows us to appreciate Adorno and Horkheimer's previous critique of the Enlightenment, where the latter was denounced as profoundly undialectical, in so far as it represented the progressive degeneration of thought into an instrumentalized ratio that, through its mastery over nature, ended up reifying all human existence.[6] In an evocative analogy, Adorno suggests that the emphasis on the subjective or conceptual moment turns into a prison for the subject, just like the protective armour of the rhinoceros, a consequence of its struggle for survival, is an 'ingrown prison' the animal tries in vain to shed; as an objective prison framing the animal, this armour may explain 'the special ferocity of rhinocerposes', which can be compared to the 'more dreadful ferocity of *homo sapiens*' (Adorno 2000: 180). And of course the analogy can be stretched further to Adorno's critique of the culture industry as precisely the locus where the armour of culture, which delimits the specificities of its fields, turns into an objective prison, fuelling a self-referential industry and stifling authentic cultural ambitions to connect with the social sphere.

It is not the aim of my enquiry to establish whether Adorno and Horkheimer's critical evaluation of the Enlightenment was theoretically and politically consistent, or whether it was irredeemably vitiated by a reliance on the negative that undermines the viability of any sociopolitical project. What I instead try to develop is a reflection on the dialectical impetus that sustains the critical thought of the Frankfurt School, and especially of Adorno. In turn, this reflection allows me to suggest a recalibration of the correlation between Critical Theory and film. For this purpose, I examine the crucial role played by negativity in Adorno's philosophical system. The aim of his negative dialectics (and the reason why he ultimately rejects Hegel) is to rescue the objective dimension as 'the experience of something that cannot be dissolved in consciousness' (Adorno 1993: 86), that is, that cannot be subsumed under identity thinking. Adorno is nevertheless aware that the latter embodies the very functioning mode of thought, without which thought itself would vanish. Given this awareness, Adorno can only lament not so much the compulsion to identify which qualifies thought, but *the waning of the experience of dialectical thinking* that characterizes the contemporary 'administered' society.

One should recognize here the strenuous commitment to contradiction and negativity that cuts across the entirety of Adorno's production. The agony of the world under total administration coincides with the historical agony of the dialectic, for only the dialectic can make us aware of the gap between thought and its object, thus inscribing a degree of freedom in our relation to the world. In Adorno's reasoning, Western civilization itself is marked by a self-destructive teleology whose affirmative progress is punctuated by the decline of the dialectic and the concurrent closure of thought around its abstracting and baleful identifying principle. It is against what he deems the impending catastrophe that will materialize as a consequence of the unstoppable impoverishment of dialectical thinking, that Adorno brandishes the notion of negative dialectics as the persistent sense of contradiction and non-identity that may save us. A well-known passage from the introduction of *Negative Dialectics* reads: 'a cognition that is to bear fruit will throw itself to the objects *à fond perdu*. The vertigo which this causes is an *index veri*' (Adorno 2000: 33). The New, against the barbaric tide of instrumental reason, can only materialize if dialectical thinking is recuperated as the central dimension of thought, beyond thought's typically functional mode of identification. The vertigo Adorno refers to is the necessary condition for the experience of truth and freedom. It is, however, a somewhat paradoxical condition, since it coincides with the at least minimally traumatic (undialectical) experience of thought's separation from itself.

But is there still room for this non-affirmative dialectics in today's world? In his classic *Late Marxism: Adorno, or the Persistence of the Dialectic*, Fredric Jameson argued that, indeed, we are in urgent need of the return of a dialectical mode of thinking centred on Adorno's motif of the negative, maintaining that Critical Theory itself should be understood as characterized by the persistence of this motif, that is, *the thought of the founding, inerasable contradiction of thought*. In a world permeated by affirmative culture – or, in Marxian terms, by the omnipresence of value – the critical theorist should continue painstakingly to reveal the dialectical truth by highlighting the immanent negativity or lack of foundations of this affirmative ethos. What is at stake in this effort is the search for a philosophical strategy whereby thinking itself could be conceived as disengaged from its poisonous compulsion to identify, and instead be apprehended as open to a series of stunning reflections *lacking* the necessity of a relation to an immediate goal and a logical object. Adorno is very precise in stressing the 'tangential' quality of this type of thinking, which would not jettison identification for the sake of the object. In *Negative Dialectics* we read: 'The analysis of the object is tangential to the rules of thinking. Thought need not be content with its own legality; without abandoning it, we can think against our thought, and if it were possible to define dialectics, this would be a definition worth suggesting' (Adorno 2000: 141). Although Adorno repeatedly tells us that reason becomes irrational where it hypostatizes abstraction, thus losing sight of the principle of incommensurability of the object, at the same time he knows that theory must operate, as it were, on the 'line of fire', at the junction where it dissociates from its positivity without disintegrating into a permanent relapse into chaos.

The risk of *cupio dissolvi* is, to be true, implicit in Adorno's position, which for all its theoretical complexity and sophistication is far from immune to the temptation of utopian romanticism. However, this risk is counterbalanced by the awareness of the need for a degree of identification in thinking, albeit of a supposedly radically different nature. When, for instance, he criticizes the barter principle as 'the reduction of human labour to the abstract universal concept of average working hours' and thus as 'fundamentally akin to the principle of identification', Adorno nevertheless immediately reminds us that 'if we denied the principle abstractly – if we proclaimed [. . .] that parity should no longer be the ideal rule – we would be creating excuses for recidivism into ancient injustice' (Adorno 2000: 146). Later, he puts this in clearer terms: 'Dialectically, cognition of nonidentity lies also in the fact that this very cognition identifies – that it identifies *to a greater extent*, and *in other ways*, than identitarian thinking'; critiquing the latter, then, ultimately means that 'identity does not vanish but undergoes *a qualitative change*. Elements of affinity – of the object itself to the thought of it – come to live in identity'

(Adorno 2000: 149, my emphasis). It is here that we find the central aporetic tension of Adorno's dialectics, and more generally of Critical Theory: On the one hand, the necessity to liberate thought from its iron cage of abstract and immediately available equivalences; on the other, the deeply felt though somewhat disavowed realization, tinged with melancholy, that such a liberated thought would not be able to survive a second outside its cage.

Apropos this tension, it is crucial to observe that the *qualitative change* in identity thinking that cognition of non-identity would yield is not further qualified by Adorno, thus inevitably striking one as a rather suspect theoretical leap. Adorno tellingly insists that 'the ideal of identity must not simply be discarded. Living in the rebuke that the thing is not identical with the concept is the concept's longing to become identical with the thing. This is how the sense of nonidentity contains identity' (Adorno 2000: 149). Again, one feels obliged to notice the overlap between the romantic/utopian roots of Adorno's thought (the longing for unmediated reconciliation which dwells within the practice of negative dialectics) and the inability to offer any suggestion, no matter how tentative, as to what a potentiated 'identity thinking' – one where 'elements of affinity' between thought and its object 'come to live in identity' – might actually imply in concrete sociopolitical terms. In other words, the critical and political weight of Adorno's concept of negative dialectics is supported by the external reference to a strictly speaking non-dialecticizable utopian goal. For all its subtlety, Adorno's reasoning does not manage to conceal how its crucial anchoring point lies outside rather than inside the dialectical process. More precisely, it is anchored in an idea of messianic futurity where reconciliation, and thus the prospect of the abolition of ideology and alienation, effectively coincides with either death or a vague allusion to a wholly different, enhanced type of identity.

It is therefore apparent that Adorno attempts to resolve the aporetic tension arising from his defence of the preponderance of the object by positing a utopian identity *à venir*. While his central injunction is that thought must not mortify the object of thought by placing it under classifying categories, at the same time – while holding fast to the impossibility of true cognition – he opens up the theoretical space for a longing directed at the 'identity to come', however impossible and indeed sacrilegious it would be to try and qualify the latter any further. From this angle, it could be argued that Adorno, as it were, 'has his cake and eats it': He writes hundreds of riveting pages protesting against a modern thought that has congealed and self-destructed by abolishing the gap between itself and the object, while at the same time hinting at the possible reconciliation of subject and object albeit in a utopian, strictly unrepresentable future; he pursues 'the inadequacy of thought and thing' (Adorno 2000: 153) while safeguarding the moment of their adequacy by displacing it onto an ever-elusive temporality to come. What is suspect about this intellectual venture is what we might describe as the sublimating ruse that secretly sustains it: Negative dialectics and the critical dimension it opens up is strictly dependent on the 'promise of happiness' (reconciliation) which, in *Aesthetic Theory*, Adorno mentions in connection with a dictum by Stendhal (see Adorno 1999: 311 and 136).[7] Here we should point out how, in Adorno, dialectical mediation does not culminate, as it does in Hegel, in the paradox of its *speculative identity* with an unmediated objective surplus of the dialectical process; instead, it is simply rendered impotent by the 'preponderance of the object', which pre-exists thought and with which thought reconciles only in a non-speculative utopian perspective (which is why Adorno eventually consigns his dialectic to an aesthetic realm where the longed for liberation of thought can achieve a clearer determination). The difference with Hegel is crucial. While in Hegel the unmediated material surplus coincides with the process of dialectical mediation in its formal totality ('Spirit *is* a Bone'), in Adorno the material surplus thwarts such coincidence making the dialectic utterly inconsistent, that is, negative. What Adorno misses is the finesse of the Hegelian thesis according to which the identity of thought with itself – thought's dialectical consistency – is guaranteed precisely by its ultimate coincidence with its opposite, a 'raw piece' of unmediated real that eludes it radically.[8]

With regard to the call for a redoubling of the function of thought, Adorno's dialectic has often been linked with a convergence towards postmodern variations of 'weak thought', inasmuch as it would appear to promote a sense of the finitude and fragility of Being which seems to preclude access to a genuinely creative theoretical wager. For all its caustic audacity, Adorno's defence of non-identitarian thinking is based on an existentially motivated conception of freedom which can be questioned on the ground of its disdain for anything related to human and historical categories such as 'proximity, home, security'. The following passage reflects this position of proud detachment which, however militant it may sound, cannot but strike us as intimately duplicitous:

> What differs from the existent will strike the existent as witchcraft, while thought figures such as proximity, home, security hold the faulty world under their spell. Men are afraid that in losing this magic they would lose everything, because the only happiness they know, even in thought, is to be able to hold on to something – the perpetuation of unfreedom. They want a bit of ontology, at least, amidst their criticism of ontology – as if the smallest free insight did not express the goal better than a declaration of intention that is not followed up. (Adorno 2000: 33)

In relation to the above quotation, one could point out that the 'declaration of intention' that *cannot* be followed up is Adorno's, for otherwise what would be the alternative to the 'perpetuation of unfreedom' brought about by identity thinking? To be sure, one should retain Adorno's insistence on the notions of spell and magic as coincidental with security: Any thought figure of security is nothing but its form of appearance. However, problems emerge once we try to decipher the meaning and function of the 'free insight' into that which 'differs from the existent'. What is this insight? Is it another figure of thought (perhaps available only to 'enlightened' intellectuals)? Does it imply an existential position? A political one? Or does it belong exclusively in the aesthetic dimension? And does it lead to an alternative ontology or does it remain suspended? In short, here we get a glimpse of the limitations of Adorno's otherwise compelling dialectical method with its notion of the radical otherness or heterogeneity of the object. My contention is that what is missing is, first of all, the qualification of the 'free insight' into non-identity as a traumatic one, which of course would immediately cast a different light upon the tendency of thought to seek an 'ontological cover'. Unless Adorno posits the instance of disconnection from the compulsion to identify as inherently *traumatic*, his virile injunction to 'see through' the witchcraft of identity thinking risks sounding as an empty call. To put it in the language of psychoanalysis, Adorno seems to reject the symbolic status of subjectivity, which Lacan regards as a kind of 'universal date of birth' of the subject: There is no such thing as a subject without the swipe of symbolic castration; that is to say, subjectivity (and thus consciousness) is strictly coincidental with our becoming alienated in the Other (the symbolic order, the law, ideology, etc.). Secondly, the weakness of Adorno's negative dialectic – especially apparent from the standpoint of the historical deadlock of contemporary theory – resides in his failure to provide a concrete insight into the potential progression from the spell of the autarky of thought that demarcates ontology to figures of thought representing an enhanced, even liberated rational dimension. If thought, as Adorno famously puts it, is the *servant of nonbeing* (of the ineffable surplus in the object) – that is, it is driven by its constitutive distance from the otherness of the object – what does it mean to think beyond the regressive condition of identity thinking? As one can see (even intuitively, in fact), the positing of an abyssal gap between thought and the materiality of the object – which would only be bridged on condition that thought redefines itself radically – is constantly at risk of turning into quicksand for any thinking that might aim at providing coordinates for future emancipation. For all its mordacity and speculative boldness, Adorno's critical theory is in danger of melting into what has been labelled a 'melancholy philosophy', where the link between what is and what is not – between the subject and the object-addendum – is given merely as a desideratum.

What matters mostly to Adorno and his brand of critical theory is, as we have seen and shall develop throughout this study, the denunciation of the perpetuation of identity thinking, a criticism levelled from the starting point of the assurance of the object's preponderance. My claim is that such criticism is not necessarily consigned to thought as an incentive to think the new, but instead risks remaining an ultimately inconsequential 'utopian light' which finds its scope either within the realm of art, or in the concrete yet suspicious experience of bodily pleasure.[9] Attempting to rectify such a stance, I will argue, in conjunction with a reflection on cinema, that the dialectical method embraced by the early Frankfurt School Critical Theory falls short of a decisive reflexive twist which can be recovered via Hegel. To put it in Adorno's terms, the vertigo of the encounter with the object of thought in its excessive, non-identical and therefore indigestible quality needs to be translated into a daring vision of a future constellation which might replace the stale and anodyne universe of value in which, more and more realistically, we are at risk of disappearing in. Critical Theory's argument against identity thinking is of course more than relevant today, and yet in itself it is no longer sufficient. Film, intended as the cultural commodity liquidated by Adorno as regressive and integral to the ideological straitjacket of the administered world, offers us a chance to reassess Critical Theory's dialectical method.

Notes

1 Brecht had been bitterly disappointed by Georg W. Pabst's 1931 film version of his *Threepenny Opera*, to the extent that the disagreement between the two led to a famous lawsuit. For a comparison of play and film, see Elsaesser (2004: 311–29).

2 In a letter of 9 December 1938, Benjamin wrote to Adorno: 'I see more and more clearly that the launching of the sound film must be regarded as an operation of the film industry designed to break the revolutionary primacy of the silent film, which had produced reactions that were difficult to control and hence dangerous politically' (Adorno and Benjamin 1999: 295).

3 Incidentally, I believe that Adorno was fundamentally right in reproaching Benjamin for his lack of dialectical mediation. At the same time, however, he did not fully understand the importance of Benjamin's focus on the figure of the dialectical image. Benjamin, more clearly than Adorno, had located the symptomatic potential of cultural commodities.

4 From within the wider critique of instrumental rationality, of course, capitalism and communism appear as sharing the same basic fault. On this point, I endorse Slavoj Žižek's insight that 'instrumental reason *as such* is capitalist, grounded in capitalist relations', while communism failed because it was 'the inherent capitalist fantasy – a fantasmatic scenario for resolving the capitalist antagonism he [Marx] so aptly described'. In other words, communism is seen by Žižek as 'a subspecies of capitalism, an ideological attempt to "have one's cake and eat it", to break out of capitalism while retaining its key ingredient' (i.e. a specific type of productivity, which in communist societies was expected to be unlimited as a consequence of the elimination of exploitation, profit, private property, and so on) (Žižek 2001: 19). In correlation to this, we should add Žižek's other insight about the 'absolute *scandal* of the Frankfurt School. How could a Marxist thought that claimed to focus on the conditions of the failure of the Marxist emancipatory project abstain from analysing the nightmare of Really Existing Socialism?' (Žižek 2006: 127). Elsewhere, he adds: '"Stalinism" [. . .] was thus, for the Frankfurt School, a traumatic topic apropos of which it *had* to remain silent – this silence was the only way for them to retain the inconsistency of their position of underlying solidarity with Western liberal democracy, without losing their official guise of "radical" leftist critique. Openly acknowledging this solidarity would have deprived them of their "radical" aura, [. . .] while showing too much sympathy for the Really Existing Socialism would have forced them to betray their unacknowledged basic commitment to Western liberal democracy' (p. 44). What seems to be missing from this analysis, however, is the initial theoretical premise endorsed by Žižek himself: Had Adorno developed a stringent critique of Stalinism, this would have been sustained precisely by the reference to instrumental rationality qua wider transcendental horizon of such critique (capitalism and communism being, for the Frankfurt School, two negative effects of the same cause).

5 'Cinema is identical to life, because each one of us has a virtual and invisible camera which follows us from when we are born to when we die' (Pasolini 1967: 609; see also Pasolini 1995: 252).

6 In a passage that seems to have emerged from his 1947 work with Horkheimer, Adorno states: 'The circle of identification – which in the end identifies itself alone – was drawn by a thinking that tolerates nothing outside it; its imprisonment is its own handiwork. Such totalitarian and therefore particular rationality was historically dictated by the threat of nature. That is its limitation. In fear, bondage to nature is perpetuated by a thinking that identifies, that equalizes everything unequal. Thoughtless rationality is blinded to the point of madness by the sight of whatsoever will elude its rule' (Adorno 2000: 172). Here, one can immediately notice what the key difference between Adorno and Hegel (and Lacan) is: While in Adorno's dialectics the object in excess of subjectivity is *not* produced by the subject but it pre-exists it, in Hegel, and Lacan, it is nothing but the result of the subject's own identificatory processes.

7 It is worth noting that in both instances Adorno refers to art's *promesse du bonheur* (incidentally, a dictum wrongly ascribed to Stendhal who in fact coined it in relation to beauty; see Finlayson 2009) as a promise that has to be broken in order to be effective: 'Because all happiness found in the status quo is an ersatz and false, art must break its promise in order to stay true to it' (Adorno 1999: 311); 'Art is the ever broken promise of happiness' (p. 136). This dialectical recasting of the notion of commitment in art (art must be negative in order to remind us of its potential to capture 'happiness') typifies Adorno's strategy of sublimation.

8 Hegel's theme of the coincidence of opposites can be appreciated in psychoanalysis through Lacan's couple 'big Other' and '*objet a*'. To function as a consistent symbolic framework, the big Other must overlap with, or collapse into, a meaningless remainder of the very process of symbolization it embodies, namely *objet petit a(utre)*, the recalcitrant 'small other' that resists symbolization, thus triggering fantasy, desire and enjoyment. Along the same Lacanian lines, in order to function, ideology needs to come to coincide, at some point, with its opposite, that is, the raw Real of *jouissance*. These 'equivalences' are at the heart of Žižek's Hegelo-Lacanian theoretical edifice.

9 Unlike Horkheimer, who tended to ratify the Marxian thesis that happiness should be conceived as social happiness and therefore as something immanent in human labour, Adorno held that the idea of collective happiness was dangerously close to ideological distortions of reality. As he put it in a famous aphorism, *Es gibt keinen richten Leben im falschen* ('Wrong life cannot be lived rightly', see Adorno 2005a: 39). On the other hand, in various parts of his work, he states, more or less directly, that happiness is intimately connected with bodily pleasure, whether as part of an aesthetic experience or literally in sexual terms. For instance, in *Minima Moralia* we find the following claim: 'He alone who could situate utopia in blind somatic pleasure, which, satisfying the ultimate intention, is intentionless, has a stable and valid idea of truth' (Adorno 2005a: 63). The defence of (heterosexual) pleasure (*Lust*), in so far as it defies functionality and instrumentality, is a recurrent theme in Adorno, and frequently appears in the form of a lost experience: 'As the arrangements of life no longer allow time for pleasure conscious of itself, replacing it by the performance of physiological functions, de-inhibited sex is itself de-sexualised' (Adorno 2005a: 169). This negative understanding of sexuality as integrated in bourgeois life will become a dominant theme in Adorno, as in the essay 'Sexual Taboos and Law Today', where we read: 'sexuality, turned on and off, channelled and exploited in countless forms by the material and cultural industry, cooperates with this process of manipulation in so far as it is absorbed, institutionalized, and administered by society. As long as sexuality is bridled, it is tolerated.' On the one hand, Adorno laments that sex has been commodified and thus desexualized and neutralized, turned into 'a kind of sport', by the 'sex industry'; on the other hand, he still holds on to what society cannot accept about sexuality: 'Whereas sexuality has been integrated, that which cannot be integrated, the actual spiciness of sex, continues to be detested by society' (Adorno 1998: 72–3). Regardless of the sociological value of Adorno's critical remarks, what matters to me here is to highlight Adorno's defence of the non-conceptual dimension in sexuality.

1

The dialectic's narrow margin: Film noir between Adorno and Hegel

Self-limitation in film noir

One of the well-known paradoxes of film noir is that it emerged out of a synthetic combination of Hollywood's industrially produced, mainstream cinema and the artistically minded, modernist European sensibility. Among others, James Naremore (1998: 40–95) argues that American film noir brings together in an unprecedented way the techno-ideological might of Hollywood and the artistic and intellectual sophistication that by then was largely dominant in Europe under the generic term 'modernism'. The standard historicist argument is that film noir came to represent an intriguing amalgamation of Hollywood's traditional, monolithic cinematic style and the European artistic legacy:

> The affinity between noir and modernism is hardly surprising. In the decades between the two world wars, modernist art increasingly influenced melodramatic literature and movies, if only because most writers and artists with serious aspirations now worked for the culture industry. When this influence reached a saturation point in the late 1930s and early 1940s, it inevitably made traditional formulas (especially the crime film) seem more

> 'artful': narratives and camera angles were organized along more complex and subjective lines; characters were depicted in shades of gray or in psychoanalytic terms; urban women became increasingly eroticized and dangerous; endings seemed less unproblematically happy; and violence appeared more pathological. (Naremore 1998: 45)

This oft-recited line of thought essentially registers the American culture industry's hegemonic ability to incorporate a heterogeneous and recalcitrant artistic tendency, which nevertheless is supposed to have remained surreptitiously active and implicitly subversive within the Hollywood system. What this view tends to overlook, however, is the consideration that the structural limitations imposed by Hollywood on European 'art cinema' might have been decisive not only in the creation of noir, but especially in helping those modernist aspirations to find a mode of expression that could also strengthen rather than merely weaken and dilute them.

This argument is based on the well-known Hegelian paradox, on which I will return later, concerning the necessary encryption of the infinite within a finite context: True (infinite) depth of meaning is not to be found in the supposition that limitless combinations and synergies of significations are possible, but, on the contrary, it depends on an encounter that clearly delimits the potentially endless proliferation of a given notion. The intrinsic wealth of noir, its extraordinary cultural resonance within film as a whole but also within other disciplines,[1] is therefore strictly correlative to its historical encounter with a boundary, a rigid structural framework that paradoxically allowed it to flourish, to express itself fully. It is not merely that Hollywood and the European tradition suddenly came into dialogue with each other, and that the chance encounter produced a framework (noir) where these traditions can be seen as smoothly 'speaking to each other', exchanging their respective cultural legacies. Rather, the emergence of noir works as a tremendously persuasive example of how indispensable a frame is for a given potential to expand. I claim that the 'Hollywood frame', the set of rigid conventions Hollywood so explicitly embodies (particularly inflexible during the so-called Golden Age), was essential to the birth of noir in the 1940s – and, in a way, it also retroactively reveals how the European tradition itself, in its best, most inspired manifestations, was already the expression of a distinct act of framing, of self-limitation, rather than the result of unencumbered artistic or experimental opening out. What is important to add at this stage, especially in connection with noir, is that the act of framing which allows a given potential to actualize itself is never fully successful. In more general terms, reality appears to us not only because its potential infinity is subjected to a limit, but because something within the delimiting frame, oddly enough, seems to elude the frame's compass. In psychoanalytic (Lacanian) terms, we would say that every symbolization of reality, in itself necessary, produces an enigmatic surplus of sense (the Real), which persistently disturbs the symbolic space, threatening its consistency and our relative 'peace of mind'.

It is through this awareness that we are able to explain the typically noir-ish effect of what I would call 'the hole within the frame': Somewhere within the diegetic space, the frame itself has redoubled, *it has reproduced itself in inverted form*, thus creating the typically paranoid feeling that the (noir) character, in his effort to control reality, is actually being controlled, watched by an invisible gaze. This tension between the necessity of the frame and its internal redoubling – the passage from the frame (which we use in order to 'capture', make sense of reality) to the frame within the frame (from which reality, as it were, looks back at us) – does not simply embody an exciting cinematic trope, but provides us with the elementary mechanism behind the formation of sense, the mechanism explaining how reality itself comes into being. The first great merit of film noir is to make such mechanism explicit, in all its ambiguity: Reality 'holds up' for the noir subject provided he manages to avoid that reality's enigmatic, not–fully symbolized, feature (as a rule embodied by the femme fatale) turns into a gaze, in so far the latter is homologous to the hole or gap in reality's fabric that threatens to swallow him. The noir hero knows well that there is a narrow margin, a minimal difference, between the configuration and internal consistency of reality and its disintegration. The dialectical point, of course, is that the hole or crack that undermines reality in its symbolic constitution, bringing forth its fundamental meaninglessness, is the subject itself – the subject in over-drive, defined by the intrinsic excess of desire.[2]

If the above considerations are plausible, then our discussion of noir risks taking us almost to the opposite end of Adorno's well-known reprimands against the culture industry's totalitarian penchant for neutralizing and homogenizing all authentic inspiration and critical potential therein contained. Similar to that of Adorno, Fredric Jameson's defence of high modernism is based on the view that modernist art as a rule offered significant elements of resistance against the voracious appetite of the culture industry, its intrinsic ideology and the economic logic it projected upon artistic creativity. (Here we should remind ourselves that the relationship between modernism and film qua harbinger of modernity was highly ambiguous even when approached from within the modernist camp. As a quintessential product of modernity, film was eschewed by such modernists as Wyndham Lewis and T. S. Eliot, who regularly ridiculed the new medium, denying it any artistic value or cultural force. On the other hand, literary modernists like James Joyce, Antonin Artaud and Virginia Woolf saw in film the potential for a progressive encounter between modernism and mass modernity.) Although both Adorno and

Jameson are wary not to ascribe to high modernism the status of a pure aesthetic condition unaffected by structural (economic) relations, they nevertheless view the advent of mass culture in the first half of the twentieth century as a manifest threat against the aesthetic and critical capacity of art.

With this in mind, it would perhaps be appropriate to rethink the basic coordinates of the usual debates of the 'mass/popular/entertaining (American) culture vs. elitist modernist (European) art' kind.[3] Rather than lament the involution and loss of the work's artistic value under the co-optative logic of late capitalism, or, conversely, blindly proclaim the democratic appeal of popular culture, it is critically more incisive to explore those manifestations of the culture industry where the formal, internal logic of what is produced more palpably speaks *against* its economic function. If subjected to theoretical scrutiny, a cultural commodity often turns out to be much more complex than its exchange value might indicate. It is not, then, merely a matter of praising the modernist quality of film noir,[4] for we should primarily acknowledge that noir is a Hollywood phenomenon through and through, the name given to a type of cultural commodity that was mass produced in the studios exactly like Westerns or melodramas, irrespective of the difficulty encountered in defining it.[5] Film noir, I argue, offers the ideal terrain to develop what we might call an immanent critique of cultural commodities of the filmic kind – a critique that searches, first and foremost, for signs of the dialectical composition of the commodity itself.

Let us briefly consider one of the films noirs that more subtly explores the relationship between modernism and mass culture, namely Fritz Lang's widely acclaimed *Scarlet Street* (1945) – on which I will also return later, albeit from a different angle. For the time being, we shall observe how Lang – perhaps the prototype of the émigré European director in Hollywood – depicts the connection between the artwork and its mass consumption. Chris (Edward G. Robinson) is a humble, undistinguished clerk in 1930s' New York who in his free time enjoys painting, secluded in the bathroom of his flat. Neither his philistine wife nor his friends are able to appreciate the quality of his work, which, since it does not conform to their unsophisticated understanding of pictorial realism, they deem odd and even ludicrous. The paintings, to which Chris himself does not attach any specific artistic significance (he paints as a hobby), are eventually appropriated by a young couple, Kitty (Joan Bennett) and Johnny (Dan Duryea), who are unmistakably characterized as vulgarians, models of the new mass-consumer type: Kitty is an empty-headed young woman thoroughly desensitized by the amount of rubbish she consumes (including 'cultural junk', as underlined by her obsession with the 'Melancholy Baby' tune she plays again and again on the phonograph), while Johnny is a reptile-like, repugnantly cynical crook with petit-bourgeois aspirations.

By mistaking Chris for a famous painter, they see in his work only a potential source of financial gain. No attempt is made to comprehend the artwork aesthetically; instead, the latter is automatically turned into exchange value, an object of consumption to be sold and profited from.

It is easy to read into this plot the Adornian critique of mass culture as a diabolical corruptor of genuine art. Each character, except the sophisticated art critic who recognizes the significance of Chris's paintings, is an ordinary American citizen displaying a remarkable insensitivity towards culture and an equally notable uniformity of bad taste, trapped in a homogenized environment where anything remotely cultural is conceived as either a commodity or a hobby. However, the distance between Lang's film and Adorno's disparaging assessment of mass culture remains considerable, measurable as it is by the simple consideration that Chris himself, the painter and unwitting creator of modernist works, is neither an artist nor an intellectual by any stretch of the imagination, but rather a stereotypically benumbed member of mass society, just like the rest of the characters. What sets him apart, then, has nothing to do with social consciousness; on the contrary, his difference emerges as a classic instance of what psychoanalysis has labelled the 'return of the repressed', an unconscious libidinal impulse, triggered by repression, which here first finds its outlet in the sublimated domain of art, while later it turns into blind homicidal fury (Chris's assassination of Kitty). On this point – the theme of the 'objectively unconscious' dimension of art – we find an element of contact with Adorno's aesthetic theory, and yet the possibility of a Hollywood film retaining such a speculative value is unthinkable for Adorno. In Lang's film, the encounter between modernism (Chris's paintings) and a 1930s' mass modernity already dominated by cultural regression (mindless pop music, shallow radio programmes, hobbies in one's 'free time' etc.) does not only sanction the triumph of the culture industry, but also yields an ambiguous image of unconscious defiance which, however embalmed in negativity and despair, inscribes a minimal discrepancy within the anonymous sameness of modernity. My specific claim is that a dialectical analysis of noir ought to focus on such discrepancies in order to underscore not their insubordinate difference from the ideological closure that typifies the cultural apparatus in which they are conceived, but rather their *speculative coincidence* with it.

Let us briefly return to the issue of the European influence on film noir. While from a historicist angle it is perfectly satisfactory to claim that the symbiotic relationship between the European legacy and Hollywood 'generated an intriguing artistic tension' (Naremore 1998: 48), at the same time, I suggest that reflections concerning this symbiosis take a more openly dialectical configuration. How exactly did the encounter between two antagonistic conceptions of film happen to give rise to noir? Perhaps it is too generic to ratify such encounter as one of mutual influence, while it remains simplistic to claim that Hollywood unilaterally absorbed and redeployed the talent of many European émigrés directors, writers, musicians and film technicians,[6] who therefore would have had to conform to the tight rules of the American film industry, sacrificing at least part of their artistic or even political aspirations. Indeed, part of the thesis of this book is built on the dialectical reversal of this claim. As anticipated, I argue that the exhilarating novelty incarnated by film noir materialized because, rather than stifling the talent flocking in from the old continent, the technical and ideological constraints imposed by the Hollywood studio system *allowed it to fulfil its potential.* If such a claim seems misplaced at this early stage of the analysis, then the least one can propose is that contact with Hollywood imposed on most of these émigrés a healthy recalibration of their artistic experimental penchant: Talent was forced to take less conspicuous – and less conscious – forms of expression, *and as a consequence it flourished.*

One should pause here to reflect on the dialectical quality connoting the emergence of the noir phenomenon, in so far as noir can and should be regarded as an original 'category of thought': Film noir did not come about as the result of a conscious decision made against other external standards or demands, but its birth as a cinematic form of consciousness can be characterized as the result of *film's encounter with its own immanent self-limitation.* Film noir, in other words, appeared in the early 1940s on account of the inner dynamism of film as a particular mode of thinking, its unfolding fuelled by a series of internal stumbling blocks such as the clash between Hollywood and the European modernist tradition. Of course, this logic is generally applicable to any significant development of the cinematic medium. In fact, from a dialectical angle, any noteworthy form of film-related consciousness comes forward through the encounter with an inherent limit, rather than as a mechanism of seamless progress.

As anticipated, the Hegelian dialectic tells us that subordination to an external limit should not immediately be referred to a condition of coercion, but, on the contrary, it may foster freedom, facilitating self-realization. Why? Not because awareness of the limit can be conducive to its overcoming, but because the presence of an external, 'objective' limit (of artistic freedom of expression, for instance) often overlaps with an 'enabling self-limitation', that is, with a boundary internal to my subjectivity that allows me to achieve self-identity and thus act freely. The perception of an external obstacle thwarting my potential is thus more often than not an illusion masking the fact that the concrete realization of my potential needs a degree of self-limitation, a framework within which to assert itself. In order to be able to exercise freedom, I must be embedded within a self-enclosed unit of sense, a background or framework which, simply put, confers meaning upon my actions. While in my everyday life I do not perceive this background, its presence is absolutely crucial if I am to engage in any sort of (creative) activity. Any form of linguistic expression, for instance, needs the invisible support of all the introjected linguistic rules that we have learnt and that now mechanically, without us being aware of them, allow us to express ourselves (if we started thinking about grammar rules every time we talk or write, we would bungle everything). Similarly, my freedom as a citizen relies on a complex, often undetectable disciplining network of laws and habits that create the space for my subjective freedom. Sports provide particularly good examples here: In football (soccer), for instance, the unique, unrepeatable contingency of a given passage of play (say, leading to the scoring of a goal) secretly redoubles not only into the unconsciously introjected rules of the game, but also into the acquired (through repetition, i.e. culturally) mechanisms of physical motion required to play football. Spontaneity and naturalness, for Hegel, are therefore misnomers, for they always necessarily hinge on some automatic, mechanically attained experience of self-limitation. We might be elated at the thought that we are acting spontaneously, following our natural inclinations, but in fact any such experience is sustained by an unreflective, unconscious mechanism of self-constraint which provides the background discipline necessary for our actions.

My overarching wager with regard to film noir is that subordination to the externally coercing apparatus of Hollywood must have coincided, for a number of European émigré directors/film people, precisely with the experience of self-limitation qua productive mechanism leading to creative expression. Although the internal limit was already there, the sudden, somewhat shocking encounter with the 'Hollywood machine' and its strict rules and working schedules must have been healthy, paradoxically functioning against the stifling of inspiration, providing a tangible framework within which to exercise one's freedom of expression. This is why I am tempted to reverse the usual argument that film noir, although born in Hollywood, was actually a product of a typically European artistic sensibility (German expressionism, French surrealism, modernism in general, etc.). Rather, I suggest that without the *specific* and *explicit* institutional discipline imposed by Hollywood (for we should not forget that European cinema has also always been institutionally, i.e. ideologically, mediated), we would not have film noir today. If this is the case, then, we might ask what it is that makes film noir and not, say, the Western, more worthy of our dialectical analyses. Can we not detect the same paradox of the coincidence of limit and creative freedom in other cinematic styles or genres? The answer is disarmingly simple: yes. However, more clearly than in other cases, noir conveys, whether we look at it as form or content, the odd yet dialectically captivating coincidence of the confined, limited, self-enclosed space of cinematic representation and the radically contingent, open-ended, non-teleological dimension pertaining to film as an innovative category of thought. The focus of most of this book falls on the exploration of the noir universe as an exemplary case of Hegel's dialectical unity of opposites. Within the term *film noir*, the notion *film* (the *genus* that overdetermines all specific film-forms) will be unravelled as coincidental with the contingency of *noir* (a particular *species* of film). Indeed, film noir is Hegelian through and through; my contention is that, as far as film is concerned, it should be regarded as the home of the dialectic.

Given the above framework, my main theoretical argument will revolve around the role played by negativity within the noir universe. The danger to avoid in thinking film as a dialectical process is the postulation of a logic of positive resolution of antagonisms and appropriation of differences. As suggested, Hollywood did not merely absorb, digest and quietly capitalize on the wealth of human and cultural resources that was fleeing Nazi Europe, turning difference and otherness into sameness. Such a statement would deny film noir any real originality, reducing it to its vulgar commodity value. Contrary to any simplistic supposition of appropriation of difference, the contact between Hollywood's gargantuan film factory and the European tradition generated in noir an original film-form that combines narrative closure and stylistic codification with the foundational imperfection pertaining to the notion 'film' in so far as it is intended as a category of thought. One way of clarifying the dialectical logic pertaining to this unique amalgamation of contrasting features is by indulging in a brief digression on the relationship between dialectics and excrements. As it happens with every dialectical process, in our case Hollywood did attempt to greedily ingest the object it stumbled upon (the European tradition largely brought in by the émigrés film people). This act of appropriation/ingestion, however, should be more precisely defined as an act of *sublation* (Hegel's *Aufhebung*) in the sense that it did leave some traces of its taking place. More precisely, it was qualified by the concomitant externalization of a metaphorically speaking excremental excess that, while remaining a determination of Hollywood, also functioned as Hollywood's inherent contradiction, its constitutive stain or mark of incompleteness. In Hegelian parlance, film noir allows us to appreciate how the oft-discussed gap between Hollywood and European cinema is already internal to Hollywood precisely as its constitutive excess. The outcome of the dialectical process whereby Hollywood sublates the European tradition was a type of film-making that encompasses, perhaps uniquely in the history of cinema, the very tension between film as a specific way of thinking and representing the world, and its inherent contradiction: A perfectly balanced conflation or overlapping of *closure* and *fragmentation*, *conventionality* and *innovation*, *ideology* and *defiance*, *coherence* and *ambiguity*, *repetition* and *novelty*. Ultimately, Hollywood's film noir provides evidence of how the culture industry, in its dialectical development, is not simply an inexorable system that destroys and assimilates every difference that crosses its path (Adorno's schematic position). Rather, it makes us aware of the fact that there is no conscious mastering agent at the helm of the insatiable dialectical development of thought, since the act of *assimilation* paradoxically overlaps with that of *excretion*, producing difference and contingency, and concluding its cycle by releasing such contingent element so that it can be analysed and theorized.[7]

The noir panorama beyond spectatorship

In 1955, Raymond Borde and Etienne Chaumeton published the first, pacesetting book on film noir, retroactively sanctioning the birth of what they preferred to name a cycle or a series rather than a genre.[8] The title of their book was *Panorama du film noir (1941–1953)* and one of its merits is to have immediately recognized as the main trait of the noir universe its pervasive negativity and defiance, well represented by familiar features such as its cruel or oneiric atmosphere, sleazy or perverse eroticism, violence and oppressive sense of death. In the two critics' own succinct account: 'Film noir is a film of death, in all senses of the word' (Borde and Chaumeton 2002: 5). To refine their analysis, Borde and Chaumeton (2002: 5–13) identify attributes that point towards the implicitly subversive character of the newly developed canon – attributes that have by now become widely accepted in the critical literature on the subject. For instance, they immediately notice the kind of ontological significance that film noir assigns to crime. They observe that fictional representatives of the law are frequently portrayed as characters of dubious morality, while the central figure of the private detective is even more decidedly placed 'midway between order and crime'. The criminal, on his part, is presented as odd, excessive, and yet ambiguous and often attractive, a far cry from the unequivocal 'Scarface-type thug' of pre-noir films. Conversely, the hero is physically ordinary, ethically dubious, rarely a model of decency and moral integrity: 'he's often the masochistic type, his own executioner [. . .] someone who gets tangled up in dangerous situations, not so much through a concern for justice or through cupidity as through a sort of morbid curiosity.' Along these lines, apart from her being lethal to others, the femme fatale 'is also fatal unto herself'. Finally, the two critics notice how filmic action tends to be strangely opaque and incoherent, depriving the audience of the habitual reliance on narrative consistency and concomitant sense of emotional identification. Here, I want to mention one small but indicative example among many: The fog scene at the end of Anthony Mann's *Raw Deal* (1948), when Joe Morse (Dennis O'Keefe) makes his way towards the apartment of pyromaniac mobster Rick Coyle (Raymond Burr) to finally execute his personal revenge. Cinematographer John Alton (born Johann Altmann), famous for his extreme photography and camera angles, suddenly plunges the hero into a surreal, dreamy landscape, introducing a somewhat bewildering subjective shot of an anonymous boy on skates who first bumps into one of the mobster's men patrolling the area, and then into the hero himself. There is more than a mere attempt at creating tension here: As already announced in other parts of the film where the frame was left in almost total darkness, in these fog-dominated shots we perceive *suspense* quite literally as a subtle yet powerful *suspension of meaning*, a disconnect from narrative development.

The above observations lead us to the following question: Is there a way to reflect on the subversive potential of noir without rehashing the by now worn out description of the various defiant aspects of this type of filmmaking, regularly branded as 'Hollywood's dark side' (Naremore 2002: xxi)? Interpretations based on such description indeed abound. Their common feature is the attempt to translate into positive knowledge the structural imbalance perceived as distinctive of the noir canon. This is achieved primarily through specific approaches that, however, share a more or less tacit agreement on the necessity to historicize (contextualize) classic film noir. We can distinguish between three main historicist approaches: (1) *Formal*, normally emphasizing the influence that expressionism and surrealism have had on the typical visual features of noir (unusual camera angles, contrasted lighting, play of shadows, etc., as in the cinematography of the aforementioned John Alton); (2) *Sociological*, placing noir within the context of the corruption of American cities, post–World War II poverty or the emancipation/subjugation of women and concomitant denting/triumph of male identity; (3) *Philosophical*, mainly linking noir with the existential sensibility inherited from France or from the anti-empirical, transcendental strand in the American philosophical tradition. These approaches have the precise aim of explaining the noir phenomenon through informed references to context while generically acknowledging its disruptive quality as variously experienced and appropriated by audiences.

In respect of spectatorship, the discourse on noir is still by and large informed by the old assumption that audiences respond to these films through 'a shared feeling of anguish or insecurity' in so far as the trademark of noir is '*the state of tension created in the spectators by the disappearance of their psychological bearings*. The vocation of film noir has been to create *a specific sense of malaise*' (Borde and Chaumeton 2002: 13).[9] This critical template is particularly evident in feminist film theory. Laura Mulvey, for instance, famously drew on film noir as an ideal example of the way in which film generates patriarchal anxiety vis-à-vis woman (see Mulvey 1992), while Elizabeth Cowie has highlighted the perversity involved in identifying with the male character attracted to the dangerous femme fatale (see Cowie 1993). More recently, Michele Aaron has argued that film noir is directly connected with the spectators' masochistic pleasures.[10] In my view, however, and as it will become apparent in the course of the book, spectatorship theories are by definition problematic, all the more obviously today when audiences are becoming increasingly aware of the type of cinematic enjoyment they choose for themselves. Thus there seems to be a chasm between the oft-noted claim that film noir (potentially) unleashes conflictual or subversive sentiments in the spectator, and the extraordinary fascination it exerts on our postmodern sensibility, which, to quote a famous title from Fredric Jameson, feeds the cultural logic of capitalism.

In fact, when considering the question of noir's impact on audiences, I would suggest that the current postmodern euphoria about the noir canon may serve to instruct us about what noir always was, namely a commodity. Noirified enjoyment of whichever kind (innocent, sadistic, masochistic, etc.) has always been, in essence, a *commodified* form of enjoyment, which by definition tends to sap rather than stimulate one's critical thinking. First we enjoy it unproblematically, and then, perhaps, given the right conditions, we think about it. Although Adorno and Horkheimer's liquidation of the film industry is based precisely on this insight (film is a commodified form of enjoyment), at the same time it is also limited by it, for it fails to dialecticize the object-film *beyond* audience consumption. In the famous 1936 letter to Walter Benjamin, where he takes issue against his friend's notion of aura, Adorno writes:

> the idea that a reactionary individual can be transformed into a member of the avant-garde through an intimate acquaintance with the films of Chaplin, strikes me as simple romanticization. [. . .] You need only have heard the laughter of the audience at the screening of this film [Chaplin's *Modern Times*] to realize what is going on. (Adorno and Benjamin 1999: 130)

The very fact that Adorno needs to stress this point is telling, since it suggests that his criticism of film is based exclusively on considerations concerning spectatorship (as, indeed, his later partial re-evaluation of experimental cinema will be). When, in the same letter, he reproaches Benjamin's critical method for neglecting dialectical mediation, we could therefore deduce that Adorno is inadvertently commenting on his own approach to film: While prescribing '*more* dialectics' to Benjamin, he himself fails, with regard to film, to accomplish the 'dialectical penetration of the "autonomous" work of art, which transcends itself by virtue of its own technical procedures into a planned work' (p. 131) – though, of course, he would have argued that films cannot be classified as autonomous works of art. Much of my analysis in this volume is built around the argument that it is now necessary to move beyond spectatorship theory tout court, precisely to avoid falling into the pitfalls of generic cultural and sociological criticism.

Going back to the 'sense of malaise' mentioned by Borde and Chaumeton in respect of film noir, I therefore doubt whether it was ever there (in the movie theatres) in the first place. It is my conviction that the disruptive quality of noir can only be adequately rendered by delivering the analysis from issues of spectatorship in order to bring it to converge, instead, on theorizations of narrative and stylistic representation specific to the cinematic medium. If, as I believe, there is a subversive potential to noir, this should be retrieved via the intervention of a critical thought keen to unravel in the cultural artefact the foundational dynamics of its textual organization, which can be ascribed to neither spectatorship nor historical context alone. More to the point, my exploration of film noir draws on dialectical thought as conceptualized by Hegel and later articulated in that distinctive tradition, midway between philosophy and sociology, known as Critical Theory. I will attempt to make such theorizations apparent by focusing primarily, though not exclusively, on a number of B-noirs such as Richard Fleischer's *The Narrow Margin*, a low-budget production shot in 1950 and released in 1952.[11] First, however, I will turn to Adorno's 'Hollywood years' (from 1941 till 1949).

Adorno goes to Hollywood

A European émigré in Los Angeles at the time of the commercial explosion of the retroactively named noir canon, Adorno was the most distinguished representative of the first generation of critical theorists working under the aegis of the so-called Frankfurt Institute for Social Research, informally known as the Frankfurt School. It is widely acknowledged that his position towards the film industry (as well as towards the other new cultural media of the twentieth century such as radio and television) was as acerbically unflattering as his stance on popular (or popularized) music, especially jazz. One of Adorno's most lapidary declarations indicative of the above stance is the following caustic remark from *Minima Moralia* (a text that, with *Dialectic of*

Enlightenment, *The Authoritarian Personality* and *Composing for the Films*, he penned during his Californian exile): 'every visit to the cinema leaves me, against all my vigilance, stupider and worse' (Adorno 2005a: 25). What interests me about the unlikely couple 'Adorno and film'[12] is something that has yet to be attempted, namely the exploration of the significance that the theoretical foundations of Adorno's dialectical thought might have for an approach to film noir aimed at redeeming the critical impact of a commodity historically nestled at the heart of the burgeoning culture industry. Let us recall that by 1944, the year they completed the chapter on the culture industry included in the *Dialectic of Enlightenment* (published in German in 1944 and in English translation in 1947), Adorno and Horkheimer, at the time exiled in Los Angeles, had acquired vast knowledge of the Hollywood studio system through a number of contacts they had within the 'Germanic émigrés' circle gravitating around the film industry. It is noteworthy that first Horkheimer and then Adorno were persuaded to move to Los Angeles from New York by their mutual friend and prolific director Wilhelm ('William') Dieterle, who had been working in Hollywood since the early 1930s (see Claussen 2008: 166).[13]

Adorno's most reliable 'Hollywood informer', however, was probably Fritz Lang, the prominent Austrian director who had emigrated to California in 1934 after completing a string of vitally important films in Weimar Germany.[14] Testament to the intimate nature of their friendship is the fact that in their Los Angeles years, Adorno, Horkheimer and Lang had began addressing each other (and their respective partners) with animal nicknames such as 'Hippopotamus' (Adorno) and 'Badger' (Lang), apparently in order to jokingly mark their 'independence from degenerate mankind'. Adorno and Lang remained good friends even after they both returned to Germany, as testified by the 30 letters they exchanged from 1949 to 1967 (see Claussen 2008: 163–4). My question here, however, is not a philological one. From my theoretical perspective, what seems striking in relation to this contingent yet extraordinary intellectual milieu – with Adorno, Horkheimer and Lang (but also Bertolt Brecht, Thomas Mann, Hanns Eisler and many others) meeting and exchanging ideas in and around Hollywood, where most of these intellectuals who had fled Nazism were employed – is that, to put it simply, despite all the available information he had, Adorno effectively opted not to apply his dialectical method to the concrete analysis of Hollywood films such as, for instance, those made by his friend 'the badger'.

Suffice it to recall that although Lang was critical of Hollywood, to the extent that at one point he set up his own production company (Diana Productions), he nevertheless acquired a prominent position of power within the studio system. While it is more than plausible that Lang supervised Adorno and Horkheimer's corrosive pages on the film industry that would appear in the

Dialectic of Enlightenment,[15] we should not forget that by 1940 he had already 'conquered' Hollywood by mastering Hollywood's favourite genre, the Western, with such films as *The Return of Frank James* and *Western Union*, both made in 1940 for the 20th Century Fox. Also, before the end of the war Lang had completed his anti-Nazi tetralogy,[16] and in 1944 and 1945 two of his most overtly psychoanalytic films (*The Woman in the Window* and *Scarlet Street*, respectively) had appeared.[17] It is highly unlikely that Adorno had not seen these influential noirs (or 'crime melodramas', as they were known then), or had not had a chance to hear Lang discuss them – which makes his silence on these popular yet complex modernist works rather deafening.

To appreciate the potential for dialectical analysis hosted by Lang's aforementioned noirs, let us recall an article written by French film critic Philippe Demonsablon and published on the *Cahiers du Cinéma* in 1959 with the explicit title 'The Imperious Dialectic of Fritz Lang' (English translation in Jenkins 1981: 18–25). Here, the intellectual vibrancy that qualifies Lang's cinema – a cinema that transforms images into ideas, according to Andrew Sarris's famous definition (see Sarris 1968: 64) – is directly connected with a narrative procedure that privileges 'the accumulation of contraries' until it reaches the point of saturation, which in turn calls for the film's final resolution. The thesis that 'the most urgent sense of creation [in Lang] is expressed by the dialectical movement' (Demonsablon in Jenkins 1981: 18) could well have been explored by Adorno (or other fellow critical theorists) had he opted to use his dialectical method of enquiry not only to rebuke the culture industry as a deleterious capitalist (superstructural) macro-phenomenon, but also to analyse in detail some of its actual products. Here, we must immediately note that, beyond his many scathing remarks on film as a mass-produced medium, Adorno actually retained a certain degree of hope in film as an artistic form.[18]

In his 1966 essay 'Transparencies on Film', his most consistent foray into the seventh art,[19] he defended an avant-garde type of cinema inasmuch as it was not supported 'by the power of capital, technological routine and highly trained specialists' (Adorno 2001: 178). More precisely, he argued in favour of films that privilege awkwardness and improvisation,[20] as well as a subjective perspective bordering on the unconscious and rejecting objectivity and realism.[21] Despite all this, however, Adorno concluded his essay on a pessimistic note, sanctioning the impossibility for cinema to carry 'purely aesthetic values' due to its ineludibly objective character: 'The photographic process of film, primarily representational, places a higher intrinsic significance on the object, as foreign to subjectivity, than aesthetically autonomous techniques; this is the retarding aspect of film in the historical process of art' (Adorno 2001: 181).[22] This insight was not new. In 1934, Adorno had visited the Babelsberg studios in Potsdam, later describing the experience in a letter to Walter Benjamin: 'reality is always constructed with an infantile attachment to the mimetic and then "photographed"' (Adorno and Benjamin 1999: 131). The mimetic realism inscribed in the filmic medium, and capitalized on by the film industry, in Adorno's view liquidates individuation, imagination, expressivity, as well as any genuine difference from the norm, thus cementing ideology. As we have it in the *Dialectic of Enlightenment*:

> The whole world is made to pass through the filter of the culture industry. [. . .] The more intensely and flawlessly [filmic] techniques duplicate empirical objects, the easier it is today for the illusion to prevail that the outside world is the straightforward continuation of that presented on screen. [. . .] Real life is becoming indistinguishable from the movies. The sound film, far surpassing the theater of illusion, leaves no room for imagination or reflection on the part of the audience, who is unable to respond within the structure of the film, yet deviate from its precise detail without losing the thread of the story; hence the film forces its victims to equate it directly with reality. (Adorno and Horkheimer 1997: 126)

The argument that mass-produced cinema 'confiscates the imaginary' is at the heart of Adorno's dismissal of cinema's intrinsic realism – a thesis that he develops *against* the defence of mimetic realism that we find, for instance, in the writings of his friend Siegfried Kracauer (especially in his *Theory of Film: the Redemption of Physical Reality*, first published in 1960). Let us recall that in an article dating back to 1926, Horkheimer had already indicted technology (photography, telegraphy and the radio) for having brought people too close to the world, to the point that this proximity was now desensitizing people as to the real misery and sufferings of the world itself (see Horkheimer 1978: 19). This criticism is, of course, inherent to many a current within avant-garde cinema. To appreciate the flavour of Adorno's stance, one has only to think of such film-makers as Jean-Luc Godard, Jean-Marie Straub and Danièle Huillet, and Guy Debord; or (specifically in Adorno's case) Alexander Kluge,[23] Michelangelo Antonioni and experimental film-maker/composer Mauricio Kagel.[24] The point is that Adorno's critique can easily be developed from a cinematic perspective. However, my intention here is to proceed in the opposite direction, that is, not by showing the filmic potential of Adorno's dismissal of the film industry, but by unravelling how the film industry itself, as it were, can provide some surprising insights into Adorno's critical (dialectical) thought.

While Adorno's analysis is theoretically consistent, it seems to me that by veering towards the appreciation of sheer 'aesthetic values', it misses the crucial dialectical point about the *inherent contradiction* of mass-produced films, and more generally of the entertainment industry. This is all the more surprising when in 'Transparencies on Film' we find the following remark, which would appear to suggest the viability of such dialectical method for the investigation of works conceived within the culture industry:

> In its attempts to manipulate the masses the ideology of the culture industry itself becomes as internally antagonistic as the very society which it aims to control. The ideology of the culture industry contains the antidote to its own lie. No other plea could be made for its defence. (Adorno 2001: 181)

This is no small insight, and would certainly deserve more sustained investigation from Adorno himself. Instead, he ends his piece by re-emphasizing the reactionary nature of film within the culture industry in so far as the latter 'is not the art of the consumer but rather the projection of the will of those in control onto their victims' (p. 185).

My general argument is based precisely in the claim that the culture industry is internally antagonistic. In this respect, as a whole, Adorno's position on film is not particularly insightful. In his most unbiased writings on cinema, like 'Transparencies on Film', it is apparent that he is not only looking for ways of disrupting the formulaic character of mainstream cinematic production, but he is actually asserting something about the very nature of cinematic communication: To be subversive, or emancipatory, film must try to push the boundaries of the symbolic, connect with the 'surplus' of meaning that qualifies any act of communication. While this is to be subscribed, one should also stress the opposite strategy: The symbolic, precisely because highly organized, always produces a surplus of sense that can be located dialectically. Given the specific context of the Hollywood studio system of the 1940s and 1950s, film noir offers us the ideal filmic product against which to measure the intrinsic non-identity (to use Adorno's terminology) of cultural commodities whose success depends, typically, on their ability to transform or recycle any potential critical instance into (ideological) enjoyment. In a nutshell, I explore film noir with a view to demonstrate that, using Adorno's own words from the above quotation, 'the culture industry [Hollywood] contains the antidote to its own lie'. This is the immediate aim of my dialectical analysis of noir.

On a different level, I claim that such analysis allows us not only to unravel the critical and creative capacity hosted by the noir canon, but also to grasp the extent to which it is Adorno's specific understanding of the dialectic that leads to his failing to develop a redeeming criticism of cultural commodities such as films. In fact, by its very theoretical nature, Adorno's negative dialectics eschewed the in-depth investigation of cultural products that presented themselves as 'vulgar' commodities. With reference to crime films, all Adorno had to say was that filmic representations of tragic or asocial personalities had a precise ideological function: That of assuaging and even eradicating the tendency to revolt within late-capitalist societies.[25] Similarly, he rejected any auteurial propensity within the film industry, on the grounds that it simply provided a liberal deviation or exception tailored to reaffirm even more devilishly the ideological message. For instance, in *Dialectic of Enlightenment* we read: 'Whenever Orson Welles offends against the tricks of the trade, he is forgiven because his departures from the norm are regarded as calculated mutations which serve all the more strongly to confirm the validity of the system' (Adorno and Horkheimer 1997: 129). Along the same lines, rehearsing a perceptive point he had already made to Benjamin,[26] in *Composing for the Films* (written with Hanns Eisler), he emphasizes his dislike for 'pretentious grade-A films' within the industry:

> Mass production of motion pictures has led to the elaboration of typical situations, ever-recurring emotional crises, and standardized methods of arousing suspense. [. . .] As in many other aspects of contemporary motion pictures, it is not standardization as such that is objectionable here. Pictures that frankly follow an established pattern such as 'westerns' or gangster and horror pictures, often are in a certain way superior to pretentious grade-A films. What is objectionable is the standardized character of pictures that claim to be unique; or, conversely, the individual disguise of the standardized pattern. (Adorno and Eisler 2005: 16)

All things considered, the danger in Adorno's stance is that his critical inclination to liquidate the film industry as a whole runs the risk of being anti-dialectical, as it fails to confront the elementary principle of dialectical thinking, namely the imperative of locating the negative not only where negativity is fully embraced and solicited, but *especially* where it is foreclosed and/or converted into its opposite. Hollywood's film noir presents us with a wonderful opportunity to accomplish the latter type of analysis.

The negative and the whole

Adorno's critical method, already fully operative in *Dialectic of Enlightenment*, is structured around a dialectic that emphatically draws its critical consequence from the prominence it assigns to negativity. It is a method where intellectual mediation (or reflection) is legitimized by the critic's awareness that it will never achieve its aim – it will never manage to fully grasp and condense the object of thought within a stable concept. In short, the negative is Adorno's antidote against totality, which he equates with ideology. While

I wholeheartedly endorse Jameson's view that the negative resonance of Adorno's dialectic is very much worth preserving in a time of increasing atrophy and indeed closure of critical reason,[27] my approach orients itself toward rescuing a type of dialectical mediation based on the Hegelian axiom of the coincidence of totality and contradiction. The method of analysis I aim to advance is one where the negative is eventually shown as foundational in both the subjective and objective dimensions of thought, to the extent that the concept of totality qua identity of thought with its object, much vituperated by Adorno, is shown as being correlative to, and inseparable from, the negative itself. This can be clarified precisely in connection with the critical survey of cultural commodities such as commercial films.

A dialectical critique of so-called mainstream cinema (in our case, Hollywood's film noir) should not confine itself to denouncing the intrinsically irrational ossification of reason under the conditions imposed by capital on the culture industry (Adorno and Horkheimer's position in the *Dialectic of Enlightenment* and elsewhere). Rather, it seems much more productive to conceive of dialectical criticism as beginning from the quite modest claim that, in order to function, thought by definition must rely on identificatory processes – something which, incidentally, Adorno himself, despite all the emphasis he placed on non-identity and liberation from 'totalitarian thinking', had to concede.[28] Then, in a second move, the principle of identification between thinking subject and object of thought is shown as being predicated upon an underlying instance of negativity that pervades the entire dialectical movement and expresses itself through inerasable contradictions. The point is therefore not to abandon Adorno's thesis on the primacy of the negative in dialectical criticism, but to illustrate how this deep-seated negativity itself is nothing but *the other side of the whole* – or, put differently, the underside that accompanies, like a shadow, any cognitive process of identification. One should therefore take literally, against Adorno's intention, the latter's famous anti-Hegelian claim that 'das Ganze ist das Unwahre' (the whole is the untrue)[29]: It is untrue in so far as it *coincides* with its moment of irreducible contradiction – a reading which effectively brings us back to Hegel. It is not that the whole can only be given as a utopian realm whose realization is infinitely deferred and therefore untrue, but that, quite differently, the necessary wholeness of thought in thinking its objects is constitutively marked, or stained, by its negativity.

The concept of 'negative dialectics' was developed by Adorno in his 1966 volume of the same name, though it originates in his early thought, where it was conveyed by different expressions such as 'principle of non-identity' and 'logic of disintegration'.[30] Susan Buck-Morss has used an effective simile to define its meaning, comparing it to quicksilver: 'negative dialectics' means that the concept slips away the moment you think you have grasped it (Buck-Morss 1977: 186). Indeed, the predominance of a moment of recalcitrant negativity in Adorno's anti-metaphysical thought is first and foremost testament to Adorno's abhorrence at the prospect of his thought freezing into a set meaning, grasping itself in a concept, thus allegedly reproducing a fetishized, hypostatized 'copy' of itself. More generally, it is the measure of Critical Theory's distance from the optimistic drive of orthodox dialectical materialism. Adorno and fellow critical theorists were committed to non-identitarian thinking against what they regarded as the dogmatic fallacies not only of Marxism but especially of bourgeois idealism. The purpose remained that of subverting the status quo. As concisely put by Buck-Morss: 'Only by keeping the argument circling in perpetual motion could thought escape compromising with its revolutionary goal' (1977: 187). Such was, for Adorno, the significance of dialectics, and for this reason it had to privilege the moment of non-identity, disjunction, fragmentation – in a word, negativity – over that of totality and wholeness. Subject and object, consciousness and substance, were destined never to meet, each perpetually moving in opposite directions so as to avoid lethal entrapment in either the concept or the lack of it, which eventually amounted to the same thing: 'The whole point of his [Adorno's] relentless insistence on negativity was to resist repeating in thought the structures of domination and reification that existed in society, so that instead of reproducing reality, consciousness could be critical' (Buck-Morss 1977: 189).

The aim of Adorno's negative dialectics, then, was to lay bare reason's non-identity with social reality, while exposing the impossibility of the categories of consciousness ever catching up with material nature. As it became increasingly apparent from Adorno's own writings, reconciliation between subject and object, and thus the overcoming of the critical/negative moment, was consigned to a utopian realm accessible only via 'true art' (only sporadically conceived as film)[31] and never available in social reality. The goal of Adorno's branch of dialectics was therefore to prevent thought's identification with the given, at the cost of theory relinquishing all links with concrete revolutionary situations. Thus, it could be argued (as it has been argued)[32] that Adorno's dialectical method, whose main task was to avoid thought's reification, unwittingly and paradoxically fell into the pitfalls of reification, reduced to a fetish by its own staunch opposition to conceptual fetishism.

In *Aesthetic Theory*, his last, unfinished and posthumous book, Adorno confirmed his philosophical insights into the necessary negativity of dialectics. Artworks for him are composed of a subjective and an objective side that are inextricably enmeshed and destined to never coincide. When considering the various ways in which the subject–object relationship can be understood in aesthetic terms, Adorno vies for the epistemological view that the constitution of a work of art depends on how the object (ultimately, matter itself) is subjectively mediated, though he sees such mediation as a thoroughly immanent affair which in the end dissolves the traditional, fixed categories of objectivity and subjectivity. He specifies: 'In the artwork the subject is neither the observer nor the creator nor absolute spirit, but rather spirit bound up with, preformed and mediated by the object' (Adorno 1999: 166). The work is by definition both objective and subjective, in so far as the objectivity of the materials used to make it are dialectically injected with subjective impulses, which themselves take on an objective, alienated form. In Adorno's words: 'The artwork becomes objective as something made through and through, that is, by virtue of the subjective mediation of all its elements' (p. 168). The central point at stake here is that the subjective moment does not belong to the artist or the receiver of the work; instead it is lodged in the autonomous expression of the work's own language, in its specific context, as a *latent* force materializing 'a social relation that bears in itself the law of its own reification: Only as things do artworks become the antithesis of the reified monstrosity' (p. 167).

Emancipated from the artist's intention and resistant to interpretation, 'true art' for Adorno embodies, in a negative and therefore implicitly critical form, the antagonistic nature of social relations. Since, according to him, social relations under capitalism are hypostatized into false identity, art has a chance to become the antithesis of society, and only as such can it play a progressive role. However, the expression of such antithesis at the same time works as a reminder of the liberating reconciliation to come. It is by giving body to an instance of critical negativity that art simultaneously manages to envision utopia qua resolution of the difference between subject and object. What interests me in Adorno's aesthetic theory is precisely the dialectical outlook that turns subjective mediation into an objective, 'self-alien' moment:

> It is virtually the seal of objectification that under the pressure of its immanent logic the [subjective] conception is displaced. This self-alien element that works contrary to the purported artistic volition is familiar, sometimes terrifyingly so, to artists as to critics. (Adorno 1999: 170)

In Adorno's theory of art, the objective moment of the artwork is by definition subjectively mediated, but at the same time, any creative intervention can only be given as dislocated, self-alienated and therefore *thoroughly objectified*. Hence, inevitably, we arrive at the paradoxical definition of subjective creativity as a concretion of radical difference, of otherness, that is, *objectivity* (and vice versa) – which, as Adorno ponders, gives the notion of 'genius' a significance that is totally divorced from its standard equation with the idea of the 'spontaneously creative subject' (pp. 170–2).[33]

With my investigation into film noir, I intend to verify the presence of this dialectical knot, or short circuit, between subject and object not only in purely philosophical terms (subjective creativity bound up with what already exists, i.e. the object qua matter), but especially as a feature that inheres in both the narrative structure and the stylistic dimension of the noir universe.[34] Adorno himself would seem to encourage such an approach, for instance, when he claims that 'dialectics does not give any instructions for the treatment of art, but inheres in it' (Adorno 1999: 140). If my analysis of film noir manages to bring to light specific structural dynamics that are ascribable to Adorno's concept of negative dialectics, then we are admittedly entitled to argue that film noir embodies what was neglected by Adorno and Critical Theory, namely a short circuit within film *qua object of mass culture*. In other words, the moment film noir is shown to give body to that dialectical configuration described by Adorno as specific to art, it inevitably discloses Adorno's failure to engage critically with (at least this expression of) popular culture. It is my conviction, however, that such failure would tell us more about the brand of dialectics embraced by Adorno than about his alleged haughty disdain for popular culture as such. His dismissal of the Hegelian thesis on the speculative identity of subject and object inevitably lead Adorno to a priori reject as ideology all those products that the culture industry explicitly paraded as products for mass consumption. These were cultural commodities such as film noir – and more generally anything churned out by Hollywood – that retained the appearance of a consistent and unbreakable totality precisely on account of their being commodities.

It is here, at the heart of his negative dialectics, that we should look for the cause of Adorno's criticism of mass-produced popular culture. To understand Adorno's approach to the culture industry, we need to scrutinize his dialectical method vis-à-vis Hegel's. Ultimately, Adorno's critique of Hegel's idealism rests on a feature of his thought that he shared with the general hubris of postmodernism: The failure to appreciate how in Hegel every affirmation of identity or totality simultaneously amounts to the highest avowal of difference, negativity or exception.[35] Even more pointedly, every attempt to engender a totalized field, fully consistent with itself, can be regarded as the aim of Hegelian dialectics only in so far as it coincides with its inherent failure. A positive, fully mediated totality in Hegel is by definition *coincidental* with a 'non-mediated' remainder of contingent externality that eludes the dialectical spiral. The most concise formulation of such coincidence can probably be found in the 'Phrenology section' of the *Phenomenology of Spirit* where Hegel (1977: 185–210) argues that 'Spirit is a bone': Spirit, indicating the highest, most complete totality of dialectical mediations, is identical with an inert 'piece of reality' that resists the dialectical tide, excluded from sublation. In so far as it is the result of mere mediating activity, Spirit is unable to sustain itself as a rational edifice, which is why it needs the support of some external, alien element that cannot be dialectically integrated and 'digested'. The most exemplary dialectical paradox thus consists in the identity of the totalizing principle with the radical inconsistency of what it refers to. Hence the significance of Hegel's notion of *speculative* identity between subject and object: It is an identity based on an instance of non-recognition whereby the subject ultimately posits its identity with what cannot be caught or recognized in its own mediating activity, with a particular piece of contingent reality of which, as it were, 'there is no trace in the mirror'. The subject is always-already 'out there', in the realm of objectivity, in the form of an uncanny material leftover whose 'immunity' to the subject's reflective activity is simultaneously the condition of possibility of reflection as such, that is, the prerequisite for the subject's ability to perceive the domain of objects. If Spirit *is* a bone, then Subject *is* the foreign body that cannot be caught in the dialectical loop.

The implication of all this is of course that the speculative identity between subject and object is predicated upon an instance of traumatic negativity: If the subject were able to capture its own self-externality, it would explode, it would cease to exist a set of specific subjective features. The identity (and thus sanity) of the subject is preserved by its inability to recognize itself 'in the mode of objectivity', that is, as a strictly speaking meaningless objective element part of the external substance. The same logic is at work in the famous passage of the preface to the *Phenomenology of Spirit* where Hegel claims that everything hinges on grasping the True not only as Substance but also as Subject. What he means is precisely that it is necessary to grasp the speculative identity between the two; the subject is true in so far as its 'lack to itself', its non-reflective exception, is also what defines substance. Here is the crucial passage:

> The disparity which exists in consciousness between the 'I' and the Substance which is its object is the distinction between them, the *negative* in general. This can be regarded as the *defect* of both, though it is their soul, or that which moves them. That is why some of the ancients conceived the *void* as the principle of motion, for they rightly saw the moving principle of the *negative*, though they did not as yet grasp that the negative is the self. Now, although this negative appears at first as a disparity between the 'I' and its object, it is just as much the disparity of the substance with itself. Thus what seems to happen outside of it, to be an activity directed against it, is really its own doing, and Substance shows itself to be essentially Subject. (Hegel 1977: 21)

To give a quick filmic example of this coincidence of substance and subject as an overlapping of an alien surplus of sense (negativity), let me go back to Lang's American cinema (thereby highlighting again the influence that it could have had on Adorno's dialectic). Lang's first Hollywood film, *Fury* (1936), gives us the perfect opportunity to examine Hegel's thesis. We are first introduced to an average American guy named Joe Wilson (Spencer Tracy), who works hard to save some money and marry Katherine Grant (Sylvia Sidney). His life changes when, on the way to his fiancée, he is stopped and arrested on insubstantial evidence for the kidnapping of a child in the small town of Strand. While Joe is in prison awaiting the result of preliminary investigations, rumours about the captured kidnapper spread across the small town, and a mob quickly gathers around the county jail demanding immediate justice, threatening to take the law in its own hands. As even the sheriff cannot contain the angry crowd, the prison is eventually set on fire and Joe is presumed dead. The way in which Lang depicts the gathering of the lynching mob and the chilling eruption of violence is remarkable in capturing with utmost precision the excess of obscene *jouissance* that supplements the ordinary lives of bourgeois citizens in small town America. We are confronted with a quasi-carnivalesque situation where, as in Bakhtin's well-known theorization, the rule of the law is momentarily suspended. The mob's incendiary fury is rendered as sheer enjoyment, reflecting the frequent episodes of lynching that took place in the United States at the time.[36] In Hegelian terms, what we face here is a poignant representation of the 'defect' of substance, the necessary surplus of sense that accompanies and threatens to derail substance qua socio-symbolic framework (in Lacanian terms, 'the big Other'). The truly Hegelian step, however, is the one that follows this exemplary cinematic representation of the excess/defect (i.e. negativity) of substance, establishing the speculative identity between the latter and the subject. Let us recall the final part of the above quotation from the *Phenomenology of Spirit*: 'what seems to happen outside of it, to be an activity directed against it, is really its own doing, and Substance shows itself to be essentially Subject'. The twist in Lang's film is that, after the jail is burnt down, the main character, Joe, shows up, albeit as a very different person. We discover he had managed to escape through a hole in the prison wall caused by an explosion, and when he reappears in front of his two astounded brothers, he is determined to exact his revenge against the townsfolk. With the help of his brothers and a conscientious District Attorney, he carefully masterminds the trial of 22 individuals who took part in the lynching. These are found guilty of murdering him and are sentenced to death, until Joe's final repentance, sudden arrival in court, and confession of his responsibility in setting up the trial.

The finesse of Lang's dialectical narrative construct consists in presenting this enraged, vindictive Joe Wilson as the obscene side of the same character we had been introduced to at the beginning of the film. In masterminding the conviction of the people who had tried to lynch him, he has to pretend to have been killed by them; in other words, his revenge is built on a blatant lie that can cost people their lives. Following Hegel, we can say that while his activity only seems to be directed against the social substance (here represented by the townsfolk and its ideals), it actually overlaps with it, thus showing substance to be essentially subject. As Joe's girlfriend puts it, he is no different from them, since they share the same 'defect', the same disgusting, obscene *jouissance*. Here we have a chance to specify the nature of the overlap of substance and subject. What is speculatively identical is the inconsistency that inhabits both terms, the main implication being that substance itself, the ultimate framework of sense encompassing all entities (the Absolute, Jacques Lacan's 'big Other', etc.), is characterized by a self-splitting, a distortion, an inherent division that defines it completely. In *Fury*, substance is presented as the quintessentially American community of Strand: A perfectly self-enclosed bourgeois microcosm. And the film's central Hegelian claim is that the obscene excess/distortion of this social substance is equivalent to the subject in its radically finite, fragile, fundamentally destabilized mode of appearance.

What the film does not develop, however, is a crucial implication of this insight, namely, to put it bluntly, that the overlapping inconsistency under scrutiny *is also the site demarcating a radically emancipatory potential*. Although Lang seems to be pointing in the opposite direction – eventually forcing Joe back within the wider boundaries of good old American democracy (see his final speech, undoubtedly the weakest, least convincing point of the film), and by the same token punishing/humiliating the townsfolk – we are still entitled to argue that the double explosion of fury we witness in this film also accounts for an event that embodies potential liberation from the bourgeois social order. The least we can do when watching *Fury*, then, is detect in the overlapping negativity of substance and subject the traces of a failed revolutionary potential. Following Walter Benjamin's lesson, we should think of a revolutionary intervention as a redemptive repetition of an unsuccessful or distorted past event that nevertheless managed to expose the 'crack' within the positive social order. Despite the liberal contempt voiced by the film for the obscene deflagration of populist violence, such violence is nevertheless symptomatic in marking the place of a botched revolutionary chance.

Ontology of self-deception in film noir

Self-deception is a key feature of Hegel's dialectic. To the common criticism that self-deception in Hegel resolves itself in the subject's final passage from a limited, particular position to that of universality, whereupon it embraces substance, I oppose the following interpretation as neatly presented by Slavoj Žižek:

> The properly Hegelian answer to this [the above] criticism is that *there is simply no such 'absolute subject'*, since the Hegelian subject is *nothing but* the very movement of unilateral self-deception, of the *hubris* of positing oneself in one's exclusive particularity, which necessarily turns against itself and ends in self-negation. 'Substance as Subject' means precisely that this movement of self-deception, by means of which a particular aspect posits itself as the universal principle, is not external to Substance but constitutive of it. (Žižek 1999: 76)

Paradoxically, Adorno fully endorsed the emphasis on the subject's constitutive disjointedness, though he tended to use it as an argument *against* the totalizing scope of idealism rather than as the measure of the disjointedness of substance. Thus, Adorno's and the whole Frankfurt School's reading of 'substance as subject' follows a different logic from the one exposed above. The main difference consists in their positing a moment of freedom from alienation. In the Frankfurt School tradition, Hegel's motto is understood as representing the identity between the subject's self-deception, that is, alienation, and substance as an ideological construct, that is, 'alienated substance', the realm of 'unfreedom'. This is indeed the theoretical insight that allows the Frankfurt School (one thinks not only of Adorno but also of Marcuse here) to hold on to the notion of a non-alienated, liberated concept of substance: If this is what 'substance as subject' means, then the subject has a chance to recognize in substance the cause of its own alienation in order to, at least potentially (or in a utopian perspective), proceed to fight it in the name of a future non-alienated relationship with nature. Self-deception is therefore not intended as a necessary precondition for subjectivity to emerge, but as a consequence of the ideological weight of substance. As such, it can and should be challenged. In the reading of Hegel that I privilege, on the other hand, self-deception is ontological, which leads to the obvious question: Where is freedom to be found if there is nothing but deception? What Adorno and the Frankfurt School of Critical Theory have left unexplored is how, in Hegel (particularly in the 'logic of essence'), freedom is extracted from necessity, which then leads to the affirmation of the identity between substance (objective logic) and subject (subjective logic). What has always been alien to the Frankfurt School is something that lies at the heart of Hegel's *Logic*, namely *necessity* as the affirmation of a *contingent* (free) subjective choice: All the freedom we have is the freedom to retroactively impress a content-specific symbolization on reality.

We will have many an opportunity to go back to this point at later stages of the book. For the moment, let us turn to cinema and observe that, at the narrative level, one of the definitive signs of a great film noir is precisely *its full avowal of the hero's self-deception*. Let us just think of quintessential noirs such as Billy Wilder's *Double Indemnity* (1944) or Jacques Tourneur's *Out of the Past* (1947), often regarded as the two most representative works of the canon. In the first, we encounter the paradigmatic noir case of masculine deception vis-à-vis woman as the film's hero, insurance salesman Walter Neff (Fred MacMurray), falls into the murdering scheme of femme fatale Phyllis Dietrichson (Barbara Stanwyck) from the first moment he catches a glimpse of her half-naked body (more precisely, of her anklet, which functions as a perfect example of what Lacan famously baptized as *objet a*, the object-cause of desire) in her decadent Los Angeles home. Incidentally, the voice-over from the gullible salesman – who at the start of the film retells the story in flashback as he is about to die – has the precise effect of reminding us of his idiotic self-deception ('I killed him for money and for a woman. I didn't get the money. And I didn't get the woman'). In the second example, the above situation is pushed to the limit, with Jeff Bailey (Robert Mitchum) eventually going as far as to endorse, in what appears to be a suicidal gesture, his lethal obsession with devious femme fatale Kathie Moffat (Jane Greer). It is no surprise that, making use of Lacan's theory of sexual difference, Žižek considers *Out of the Past* as 'perhaps the crucial *film noir*' on account of the Mitchum character's identification with the excessive, unbearable dark side of woman (Žižek 1992: 66). The fact that the Mitchum character, despite having had plenty of warnings apropos Kathie's heartless cynicism, does not reject the destructive potential inscribed in this femme fatale, is dialectically significant because it allows us to locate the negative kernel of the (Lacanian as well as Hegelian) subject.[37]

A slight variation on this tragic noir theme is staged by Robert Siodmak's *Criss Cross* (1949), where Steve Thompson (Burt Lancaster), still in love with his fickle ex-wife Anna (Yvonne DeCarlo), is drawn into the Los Angeles underworld and, after a series of double-crossings, ends up killed next to Anna, who embodies to perfection the ephemeral substance of the noir object of desire. Throughout the film, she seems within reach of the obsessive male hero, who keeps telling himself that 'everything [between them] will be alright', and yet she regularly slips away, tormenting him by fuelling his imagination. No doubt Siodmak portrays her as a selfish woman, who eventually, in fact, ruins the two men who love her; however, we find also a degree of sympathy in the way she is depicted (not a frigid femme fatale but sexually driven; a victim of her husband), which ultimately serves the purpose of increasing her ambiguity in relation to the hero's desire. The final scene is typical of this ambiguous logic: Already badly wounded, the Lancaster character manages to reach Anna, certain that they can now escape together, finally reunited. However, the moment she realizes that hoodlum and ex-lover Slim Dundee (Dan Duryea) is on their tracks, she does not hesitate to pack her bags, preparing to leave on her own ('How far could I get with you?'). When she crosses the threshold of the house, though, we hear a car arriving, and a few seconds later, we see Anna rushing back to Steve. Slim follows her in and eventually kills them both – only then, dead, in each other's arms, are they finally together. The point to highlight is that the narrative leaves her return suspended, portraying her gesture as not only motivated by fear but also by a somewhat repressed sense of guilt. The fact that she dies next to Steve, even throwing herself onto him before Slim shoots, would seem to reinforce the ambiguity of her character, which, of course, only heightens her status as sublime object-cause of desire.

We ought to remark that the obverse of this classic noir situation is also true. Instead of presenting us with a purely deceptive and destructive image of femininity, a number of films noirs focus on the troubled conscience of their femmes fatales. While the result for the male hero does not change (he keeps being duped by woman), the emphasis falls more heavily on the complexity of feminine psychology. In Robert Wise's excellent *Born to Kill* (1947), his first noir, the protagonist Helen Brent (Claire Trevor) is a woman deeply divided between the security offered by her wealthy but ordinary fiancé and the dangerous excitement incarnated by the disturbingly self-confident, brutal, near-psychotic Sam Wilde (Lawrence Tierney). The film is particularly successful in drawing upon the unresolved ambiguity of the woman's sexual allegiances. The character's inner tension lasts until the very final scene, when her sudden awakening from self-deception simply comes too late: Both she and her lover get their comeuppance, offering us the figuration of a subjectivity drenched in unredeemable contradictions. In this noir, it is clear that woman is fatal unto herself because, as it were, she is 'deceptive unto herself'. The same unredeemable contradiction defines the Barbara Stanwick character in Robert Siodmak's *The File on Thelma Jordon* (1950). Here the femme's deception of assistant D. A. Cleve Marshall (Wendell Corey), for the purpose of committing a crime (the killing of her rich aunt), is marred by her falling in love with him. Although this does not stop the Stanwick character from carrying out her evil plan, built on the most cynical exploitation of Cleve's love for her, right at the end of the film we witness the moment of redemption: As Thelma is driving off to a new life with her partner in crime Tony Laredo (Richard Rober), unexpectedly, as if overwhelmed by guilt, she attacks him causing the car to veer off the road and roll into a ditch, where it goes up in flames.[38] This moment of moral salvation is captured nicely in the next scene, when, at the hospital, seconds before passing away, Thelma utters her last words to Cleve: 'you don't suppose they could let only half of me die?' While there is no redemption for Cleve, who loses both wife and job for his illicit relationship with Thelma, the femme fatale is here shown as an emotionally conflicted woman whose negative side is to some extent counterbalanced by her sense of guilt.[39] In all these films, self-deception is presented also as a feminine trait.

Within these parameters, a classic noir like Rudolph Matè's *D.O.A.* (1950) also deserves a mention. Edmund O'Brien plays happy bachelor Frank Bigelow who embarks on a business trip only to find himself entangled in a hellishly intricate situation without having anything to do with any of the circumstances.[40] He is poisoned, kidnapped, shot at and forced to kill just because, as part of his job, he had notarized a bill of sale for some material (iridium) that had been stolen without him knowing. The classic Hitchcockian topos of 'the man who knew too much' is here developed to a vertiginous complexity, with the hero deceived not by a ruthless woman or an evil organization but rather by fate, as his dying words confirm: 'All I did was notarize a bill of sale.' Ironically, it was not the hero who, unknowingly, 'knew too much', but the piece of paper he had left behind (the evidence of the sale), thus presenting once again the scenario of a radically split subjectivity where the core of the subject is externalized in, literally, alien matter. This is, then, the extreme result of the fairly common noir scenario where someone is the bearer of a threatening message without being aware of it. My inability to access the knowledge I carry (and, by contrast, the Other's ability to perceive it as potentially lethal) is key to the definition of the split (duped) subject of psychoanalysis. As such, it is one of the features of film noir that should be regarded as implicitly critical of today's dominant (hegemonic) notion of a pacified, frictionless subjectivity, whereby individuals are supposed to be able to read and learn from each other's knowledges and attitudes with a view to reaching spiritual maturity – when it is all too obvious that such configuration of subjectivity fits to perfection the (consumerist) ideology of late capitalism.

In film noir, another variation on the topos of the subject who 'knows too much' is represented by the figure of the innocent witness, normally a bystander who minds his own business and nevertheless gets entangled in some infernal criminal scheme. Take for instance Norman Foster's superb *Woman on the Run* (1950), which begins with a man, casually walking his dog at night, who all of a sudden is unwittingly exposed to a murder scene taking place inside a car. From that moment on his life turns into a living hell, since as eye witness he is chased everywhere by the killer. The interesting detail about this film is the insight it gives us in relation to the chased character's private life. We learn that for years he had been in a very unhappy marriage, so impersonal a relationship that his own wife had little knowledge of his tastes, talents and general preoccupations, including a heart condition which forced him to take a given medication on a daily basis. Here, therefore, the knowledge embodied by the character is effectively redoubled, and as such it becomes truly constitutive of subjectivity: While he knows that he knows too much in the eyes of the killer, he nevertheless ignores that the unwanted knowledge he embodies since becoming the witness of a murder has triggered a process of sublimation in the eyes of his wife. As she sets out looking for her husband, she discovers parts of his life (for instance, how admired he was by other people) that literally turn him again, for her, into a love object. As with all cases of real passion, the loved one is not merely an individual with whom to have a meaningful and mutually productive partnership, but instead an other endowed with a certain 'gift' that he or she is unaware of possessing.

With this in mind, emphatic cases of split subjectivity and self-deception can be found in a number of B-noirs such as (to mention but a few) *Fear in the Night* (Maxwell Shane, 1947), where one of the weakest heroes in the whole noir series is hypnotized and then manipulated into committing a murder (the couple 'hypnosis' and 'murder' returns in Otto Preminger's *Whirlpool*, 1949)[41]; *The Man Who Cheated Himself* (Felix E. Feist, 1950), the story of Lt Ed Cullen (played by Lee J. Cobb), who organizes the cover-up of a murder committed by the cynical femme he has fallen for, and then keeps sticking to the plan until his final downfall, despite knowing all too well what is coming; *Nocturne* (Edwin L. Marin, 1946), a deceptively ordinary noir, hardly ever mentioned in the many volumes on the subject, in which hard-boiled detective Joe Warne (George Raft) embarks on a potentially self-destructive journey to capture the killer of a lady's man whose death had been archived as suicide – he persistently frames the wrong woman, until the final confession of the male killer; or again, perhaps the most extreme of all these cases, *So Dark the Night* (Joseph H. Lewis, 1946), the story, set in France near Paris, of a famous detective who struggles to unravel a mysterious series of assassinations only to finally discover that *he* was the murderer.

In all of the above films – inevitably an insufficient selection in the immense noir reservoir – what is truly irresistible about the depiction of the subject is his proclivity to be duped by events to the extent that such deception is eventually presented as *ontological*, that is to say coincidental with the subject's own condition of being in the world. The difference with the classical detective story comes immediately to the fore: While in the latter the subject's desire to restore a coherent symbolic universe eventually triumphs, in noir the subject typically remains stuck to a disturbingly elusive fantasy scenario that fascinates him to the point of paralysis, ultimately reducing subjectivity to a meaningless and empty framework correlative to a senseless drive.

Despite what we might be lead to believe by the typically fast-paced noir narrative, what emerges under the guise of an active subject (usually, but not always, the detective) is a passive, powerless bystander whose fascinated gaze corresponds to the basic inconsistency in the universe of sense that he beholds and that threatens to swallow him, depriving him of the elementary coordinates of his identity.[42] Think for example of the exceedingly convoluted yet inspired *Crack-up* (Irving Reis, 1946), where the main character, art critic George Steele (Pat O'Brien), is manipulated by a crooked art collector who literally replaces parts of his consciousness with unconscious hallucinations by injecting him with doses of a potent 'truth serum'. No wonder no one, not even his girlfriend, believes him when he describes the unconscious scenarios he thinks have actually taken place (such as, in the film's key scene, a train accident he claims he was a victim of). The central intuition of *Crack-up*, not developed yet at the heart of the narrative, corresponds to the psychoanalytic insight that the truth about the subject lies in the fundamentally alienated, foreclosed core of his unconscious 'text'. More generally, the noir subject is condemned to radical alienation, often in the form of a senseless attachment to a world that, for the very reason of this attachment, appears equally senseless. In the aforementioned *So Dark the Night*, for instance, the proverbial 'crack' in reality's orderly texture (a series of mysterious murders that cause havoc in a peaceful rural community) is perfectly coincidental with the detective's spellbound gaze, to the extent that the object of such fascination is none other than the detective himself (he was the killer qua cause of reality's disintegration).

The dialectical flavour of the typically noir brand of self-deception cannot be missed: While reality in film noir emerges only because of the intercession of the character who investigates it, simultaneously the objectively given external world twists the subject's mediation to the extent that, at a certain point, the latter becomes uncannily aware not only that things are not what they seem, but also, and more crucially, that the nightmarish world around the character is (literally) one with his or her own personal nightmare. In the opening scene of Anatole Litvak's *Sorry, Wrong Number* (1948), Leona Stevenson (Barbara Stanwyck) is shown in her lavish New York apartment as she tries to reach her husband on the phone. Accidentally, though, she gets connected to someone else's phone call – she enters another's fantasy, and a very secret one at that. The conversation she overhears is about a murder which two men are arranging for that very evening. Understandably shocked, the woman dutifully alerts the police: An unknown person, somewhere in New York, is about to be killed. As the complex plot unfolds via a series of suspenseful flashbacks, however, it becomes clear that the person under threat is none other than the film's protagonist. Bedridden on account of a regressive heart condition, eventually Leona Stevenson is forced to face the *other's* nightmare *as her own*. In Hegelian terms: The defect of substance (the inerasable antagonism that disturbs the world's balance, i.e. in our case crime) coincides with the place occupied by the subject (the Stanwyck character was, as we discover, both active agent and passive object in a tortuous plot involving deep-rooted conflict both in class and sexual terms).

We might be able to better appreciate the dialectical significance of Litvak's film by comparing it with acclaimed masterpieces such as Alfred Hitchcock's *Rear Window* (1954), Michelangelo Antonioni's *Blow-up* (1966) and Francis Ford Coppola's *The Conversation* (1974). All these works share the standpoint of a more or less passive subject witnessing a crime – an explosion of negativity or, in Lacanian parlance, *jouissance* – that while tearing apart the apparently peaceful fabric of society at the same time reflexively captures the out-of-jointness of the subject itself qua spectator. The crucial aspect to notice is that in all these films the subject is first presented as a detached observer who by chance comes across the scene of a crime. The films' lead characters are all positioned externally with regard to the witnessed scene, in the specific sense that they believe they have nothing to do with it. But what these films implicitly denounce is precisely the ideological stance behind such declaration of autonomy from an objective reality experienced as other – as concerning others. By the end of these narratives, in fact, such presupposition has been demolished: The characters are drawn into the picture (literally in *Blow-up*), objectified by their implacable fascination with the murder scene, to such an extent that their life is suddenly put at risk. These are undoubtedly among the clearest filmic avowals of Hegel's speculative idealism: They demonstrate that there is no such thing as a subjectivity un-dialectically detached from the presumed objectivity of the world. Quite on the contrary, they emphatically show how the core of the subject – its objectivized/alien hub – is always-already connected with the world in so far as it stands for the world's surplus/lack of sense, its irredeemable antagonism. The marriage of subject and object is indeed a negative affair, in that it can only be celebrated as a coincidence of lacks. The lesson of these films is clear: Any 'ideological sin' is founded upon the hubris of a subject who believes himself or herself to be a detached, objective spectator. Of course, for this very reason we are never free from ideology. Or rather, freedom comes in the paradoxical form of those unbearable instances when the speculative identity between us and the world becomes real – as indeed suggested in the above films.

On this evidence, I insist that we should move away from the standard and tedious spectatorship issue of the audience's response to the story, or the latter's manipulation of the former, and instead call attention to the dialectical nature of manipulation or reflexivity within the film narrative. We should, in other words, apply the Hegelian lesson: The problematic distance between myself and the object-film (on account of which spectatorship theories exist) is coincidental not only with the gap or dislocation within my own subjectivity (due to the split introduced by the unconscious), but also with the internal deficit of film itself, its impossibility, as it were, *to fully coincide with itself.* The fact that spectators are deceived (often willingly, of course) while watching the plot unfold is decidedly less relevant, for a dialectical analysis of film, than observing how film emerges as the battleground where the constitution or destitution of meaning is decided. The whole point is that – if we apply to the cinema Adorno's implicitly psychoanalytic view that a work of art by definition 'secretes' a surplus of meaning that it cannot control[43] – film qua artwork is by definition bound to acquire an 'objectively alien' status with regard to its own symbolic structure. And the noir universe offers us the chance to observe the alien/excessive core of film in full flow, in so far as it is correlative to an encounter of lacks: The ontological void of the subject meets a deeply disjointed representation of objective reality. A convoluted plot proceeds forward, often at vertiginous speed, by virtue of the basic disconnection between objective reality and the knowledge or perception that one (or more) of the characters has of it. That is the very formula of detection, of course. What is distinctively noir, however, is how this tension culminates in the awareness that reality's ontological lack (of meaning) – its unredeemable 'turbulence' as regularly ascribed to the noir universe – defines nothing but the place of the subject, the place where the subject fulfils its negative potential (through drive and *jouissance*). If there is a theoretical formula that captures the essence of noir, perhaps it is the following: The ultimate senselessness of external reality (i.e. the 'crack' within reality's symbolic fabric) overlaps with the subject's self-defining fixation on such senselessness.

Norman Foster's little known yet commendable *Kiss the Blood Off My Hands* (1948) can be mentioned as another neat example of this overlap between symbolic substance and subject in film noir. Burt Lancaster plays Bill Saunders, an American survivor of a Nazi camp who struggles to make ends meet in London immediately after World War II. He kills a man in a pub fight, escapes and gets entangled in a series of misadventures that bring to light the hardships of post-war life in the English capital. The film effectively draws on two central themes: Bill's emotional instability, caused mainly by the war and resulting in his inability to control his almost animalistic physical strength, and the background portrayal of a city stricken by poverty and swarming with illegal activities. The key to understanding the dialectical connection between the two themes is not, however, the usual reference to context, which would suggest the rather banal observation that Bill's psychological fragility and proclivity to get into trouble originates in his traumatic participation in the war. Much more fruitful, theoretically speaking, is to consider the speculative identity of opposites as tidily framed by this storyline: The negative core of subjectivity, captured in its decentred, almost psychotic essence (Bill), is speculatively identical with the fundamental antagonism which defines the objective background (post-war London). More to the point, the 'theoretical beauty' of this film, and its conclusively noir statement, lies in the way it shows how the subject is nothing but the very *splitting* that prevents subjectivity from ever achieving a positive status that would be free of contradiction, while simultaneously defining external reality, inasmuch as the otherness of the latter is always-already constitutive of the former.

The opening scene is in this sense exemplary: Bill's single punch that kills a man whose only mistake was lack of friendliness provides a concise definition of the excess of the subject, the alien substance that throws subjective identity out of kilter, and that at the same time 'cuts a hole' within objective reality, belying its presumed balance. Precisely because Bill did not intend to kill, his proto-psychotic rage is utterly self-defining, the mark of his subjectivity (as confirmed by many other such explosions of rage within the film). Such splitting at the heart of his self is also the main source of fascination for the female character, played by Joan Fontaine, who until the very end is unsure as to whether she should trust such a volatile man. But the key point here remains the overlap of negativity that, paradoxically, retains the potential to redefine the subject's position vis-à-vis the symbolic network of society. Rather than merely increasing Bill's vulnerability, as a superficial reading would indicate, the killer punch with which the film begins radicalizes his alienation in his social context, producing a subjective condition akin to what Jacques Lacan called *separation*.[44] The subject now experiences his symbolic order as utterly foreign and inimical, characterized by a strange desire (to punish him) that shatters any preconceived notion of balance and order. (This fracture within the order of sense, or surplus of *jouissance*, is rendered with wonderful clarity in the sadistic scene where Bill is sentenced to hard labour and flogging. He is tied by hand, feet and neck to a torture device and then whipped ruthlessly, while a bureaucrat sat at a desk coolly ticks off the 18 lashes.) True, the Lancaster character is now forced to hide, and at the same time becomes prey to those who, having witnessed his act, can testify against him. However, precisely as a 'living dead' – as utterly alone and excluded in an already harsh society – he has a chance to refashion his identity from scratch by way of his 'miraculous' encounter with the Joan Fontaine character.[45]

At this stage, we should not overlook the *productive* role of the above dialectical logic. Aside from embodying the explosive site of negativity, such logic is strictly dependent on film intended as a symbolic unit of sense.

Without a minimum of symbolic consistency, any emphasis on negativity would be meaningless, a mere tautology (this is, I believe, the risk run by Adorno's negative dialectics). Film noir offers us a paradigmatic case of cinema's generic ability to hijack the negative core of representation in order to generate forward movement (i.e., a narrative) literally out of nothing. The narrative reliability of film noir, structured around a well-known series of conventions, is dependent upon a continuous interplay of meaning and suspension of meaning, which effectively corresponds to the manipulation of contradiction – or, in Hegelian terms, to an instance of 'tarrying with the negative'.[46] At the dialectical heart of noir we find precisely the identity of a symbolic totality (the logical consistency of the story) with its correlative self-relating negativity.

The Narrow Margin and double visions

To expand on the above, I shall continue my exploration of the relationship between film and dialectics by looking at what is often regarded as one of the best B-noirs ever made, Fleischer's *The Narrow Margin* (1952). In this claustrophobic tale – the last and deservedly most famous of the noirs made by Fleischer at the beginning of his career with legendary studio RKO – the action is kick-started by a classic situation of mistaken identity which, however, is revealed only at the end of the story. Two police detectives, Walter Brown (Charles McGraw) and Gus Forbes (Don Beddoe), have been given the perilous job of escorting a dead gangster's wife from Chicago to Los Angeles by train, so that she can testify against her husband's accomplices. The dark-haired moll (Mrs Neill, played by Marie Windsor) is a key witness in a grand jury probe, and also possesses a pay-off list linking gang members to the Los Angeles Police Department. Det. Brown's partner gets killed before they even get on the train, while the rest of the story takes place inside the interstate express heading for Los Angeles, with Det. Brown having to fend off the mob's repeated attempts to kill Mrs Neill. The unexpected twist, towards the end of the film, uncovers the degree to which, right at the beginning, the hard-boiled detective had been duped: The seductive and barefaced woman he was risking his life to protect was not Mrs Neill but none other than a fellow policewoman whose role was (allegedly) that of testing the detective's resilience to being corrupted by the mob. The real Mrs Neill was the woman who had introduced herself as Ann Sinclair (Jacqueline White), the innocent-looking blonde the cop had befriended on the train. By the time the gangsters realize they were also after the wrong woman, it is too late: Det. Brown saves the gangster's wife thanks to a last-ditch effort and, at the end of the journey, triumphantly escorts her to the Los Angeles grand jury.

The intellectual fascination that this 'train thriller' exudes is entirely retroactive, since the final revelation about the woman's mistaken identity suddenly casts a long shadow over the whole story, inducing us to reconsider the actual identity and motivations of most of its characters. The forward movement of the train is, as it were, counterbalanced by the backward movement we make to try and ascertain the true scope of the story. Why was the detective deceived by his superiors? Was it just, as it seems, to test him against potential corruption, or was he used as a pawn to divert the mob's attention onto the wrong woman? Or – even more insidiously – was the police department in Los Angeles trying to help the mob get rid of the gangster's real wife on the strength of her possessing information about corrupted cops? The complexity and ambiguity of this low-budget noir is, on second thought, truly breathtaking, which is another reason why a dialectical analysis of its narrative seems more than justified. Fleischer's key working tool here is *reframing*, both in formal and narrative terms, as well as metaphorically: Not only is the film characterized by a series of technically very accomplished shots focusing on reflections (especially, as we shall see, using the train's windows), but the action itself is slowly revealed as being contained within another, wider frame, whose true compass we struggle (and the film struggles) to make sense of. Put differently, the narrative reality unfolding before our eyes in strict chronological continuity is exposed as a distorted fiction contained within another frame, whose real boundaries remain somewhat obscure, if not impenetrable. This generates that quintessentially noirish feeling of paranoia which consists in the subject experiencing the socio-symbolic world around him (the 'paternal metaphor', the Law) not as a balanced and reassuringly neutral entity but rather as profoundly perturbed, inconsistent, pervaded by a desire that he cannot fathom.[47]

First, we should consider that the term of contradiction introduced by the initial (and retroactively disclosed) instance of self-deception is articulated around the classic noir feature of feminine elusiveness. The immediate cause around which the narrative unfolds is a woman (Mrs Neill, wife of the dead gangster) who pretends to be a different woman, thus effectively establishing herself as a double. The second and deeper cause, as we shall see, is the incriminating list of names allegedly in possession of the above woman – names of gangsters that she is supposed to hand in to the District Attorney in Los Angeles. With regard to femininity, it is worth noticing that both women in this story operate in disguise, a detail that redoubles the very reference to the figure of the double. The final twist reveals that the stereotypical moll played by Marie Windsor was actually on the side of the law, despite bickering (or rather pretending to bicker) with the detective from the start to the point of her killing, while the real Mrs Neill was the blonde mother who pretended to be the fictitious Ann Sinclair. Even the latter's young son would seem to confirm the deceptive register of the tightly woven storyline when, upon meeting Det. Brown on the train, mistakes him for a gangster. In short, *every identity in this film is redoubled*, and everyone is blinded as to the real identity of the other.[48] It is as if this action film had been secretly endowed with an invisible distorting mirror which, from beginning to end, amplifies its elementary narrative connections, introducing from within a subtle yet pervasive element of disjunction. Although we are clearly dealing with classical narrative cinema – or more specifically with what Deleuze named the sensory-motor schema of the movement image – at the same time it would not be far-fetched to detect in it a cinematic quality that threatens to implode the outward consistency of this typical action thriller.

It is fairly easy to refer back the central topos of the feminine double (incidentally, the two women never meet and are never shown in the same shot) to the standard deployment of sexual difference on which most noirs are construed: The dark, dangerously sexy lady is presented as the opposite (the other side) of the maternal blonde, and this clear-cut split is correlative to the conflicting male's (Det. Brown's) relationship to Woman as such. Duty here subtly clashes with sexual attraction (another classic noir *topos*), as it transpires from some of the heated exchanges between Det. Brown and the 'dark lady'. In a revealing close-up, for instance, Det. Brown unceremoniously tells her to stop complaining, adding: 'My partner's dead and it's my fault. He's dead and you're alive', after which he briefly pauses, runs his gaze down her body dressed in a sexy negligee, and whispers a sexually charged, deeply symptomatic 'some exchange . . .' Later, after a close escape, he reassures her that she is still unknown to the pursuing gangsters as luckily she is not the only woman on the train – to which she replies, with a seductive look firmly impressed on her face: 'but I'm the only woman who won't sleep tonight'; once again, though, Det. Brown's sense of duty kicks in as he quickly retorts 'I know a woman who won't sleep for many nights, Mrs Forbes' (his dead partner's wife). What ultimately transpires from these exchanges is somewhat counter-intuitive: The insistent reference to the call of duty does nothing but increase the fantasy of promiscuity.

We could legitimately argue that despite his readiness to adhere to his assignment, the hard-boiled detective is attracted to both women in different ways, and the fact that he ends up with the maternal blonde – who at the breakfast table worries about his nerves and orders the waiter not to bring him any coffee – is symptomatic of his choosing what he regards as the safer option. However, the validity of this choice is far from obvious, well beyond the detective's awareness, since we discover that the brunette was simply playing at the moll, while it was the innocent-looking blonde who had been married to a hoodlum. Thus, the most patent instance of unresolved tension in the film (the film's dark underside) materializes in this classic image of the feminine double, which retains its ambiguity intact until the end. The detail not to miss is that after the Marie Windsor character is 'bumped off' by the gangsters, who eventually manage to break into her hiding place on the train, not only the detective but everyone else in the film – thus, in a way, the film itself – unexpectedly lose interest in this character. Her sudden disappearance marks the beginning of the end of the detective's nightmarish chase, and yet at the same time it burns a hole in the story. This disappearance of the Lady, though central to many a film noir, is rarely taken to such extremes.[49]

To fully appreciate the weirdness of the effect caused by this abrupt disappearance, one should compare it with the standard situation of the same kind as dramatized in such works as Alfred Hitchcock's *The Lady Vanishes* (1938). In the latter, another 'train thriller', an elderly lady named Miss Froy (May Whitty) vanishes during a return journey to England from a fictional Central European country. Iris (Margaret Lockwood), who had befriended her just prior to her disappearance, is of course shocked to hear that other passengers on the train claim to never have noticed Miss Froy. Later, however, it is revealed that the old lady was a British spy and was being held prisoner in another compartment. The charm of Hitchcock's film derives from the narrative ambiguity concerning the actual identity of Miss Froy, who, however, eventually returns, albeit in a totally unexpected role. In Fleischer's film, on the other hand, the enigmatic identity of the lady is uncannily redoubled into a bewildering figuration of lack by the way the film negotiates its own internal symbolic structure: Not only is she revealed as a totally different person from the one she was initially identified as, but she is also *a lady who vanishes tout court*, without any room for character redemption (while redemption was available to Miss Froy). For this reason, the film that comes to mind apropos a similar representation of feminine elusiveness, though staged in a much more self-conscious manner, is a modernist masterpiece like Michelangelo Antonioni's *L'avventura* (1960), where Anna (Lea Massari) not only disappears from the story but her very absence is also, eventually, forgotten, generating the uncanny picture of a subjectivity so flimsy and insubstantial as to coincide with its absence.[50]

These considerations allow us to argue an important point in relation to the structural organization of the filmic text under scrutiny. Though it could be argued that the vanishing of the lady in *The Narrow Margin* corresponds to a conspicuous narrative inconsistency due to either the typical opaqueness of film noir as already identified by Borde and Chaumeton (2002: 11–12), or the restrictions on film length imposed by the studios, which often resulted in the erasure of explanatory scenes deemed of secondary importance, we are nevertheless entitled to maintain that, dialectically speaking, such inconsistency is absolutely legitimate. Why? Because it is precisely after the abrupt liquidation of the Marie Windsor character that the narrative re-establishes a degree of balance in terms of sexual tension – the very tension that had threatened and at the same time propelled the plot from its inception. If this is the case, then the elimination of the policewoman disguised as a moll corresponds to a quintessential case of filmic repression: The detective (and with him the film qua symbolic structure), represses the side of femininity he was unconsciously most attracted to; however, it is evident that the basic sexual inconsistency persists in the alluded relationship with the gangster's widow. Mrs Neill's words of reassurance to the detective (that as soon as she discovered her husband's 'true identity' – once again, an ambiguous identity – she immediately interrupted the relationship) do not quite succeed in eliminating this tension, but rather alert us once more to potential deception.

The 'redoubling of woman' is, of course, a standard narrative strategy in film noir. Examples are countless, and in the great majority the antagonism of sexual difference embodied by such 'double visions' is eventually completely disavowed, which is precisely why it should be regarded as essential. We find a classic case of such disavowal in Bruce Humberstone's *I Wake Up Screaming* (1941), a noir set in New York and generally mentioned in connection with the character of the disturbingly unbalanced detective Ed Cornell, played brilliantly by Laird Cregar. Perhaps more interesting, however, is the relationship that the male hero (a rather hackneyed sport promoter named Frankie and played by Victor Mature), entertains towards the two blonde sisters Vicky and Jill (respectively played by Carole Landis and Betty Grable). After turning Vicky, an ordinary waitress of extraordinary beauty, into a celebrity, the young woman leaves him to become a film starlet in Hollywood. The night before her departure, however, she is found murdered. What follows is the detective's obstinate attempt to pin the murder on Frankie, while Frankie turns his attention to Jill, Vicky's sister, eventually establishing with her that 'normal' relationship he could not have with Vicky. The subtlety and ideological ruse of the film lies in the way the male gaze shifts, almost imperceptibly, from Vicky to Jill[51]: The impossible relationship with Vicky qua object of desire (the cause of Frankie's desire from the beginning of the film) is replaced by the absolutely viable, ordinary relationship with Jill, the Betty Grable character. The gap of sexual difference – nicely epitomized by the double twist whereby Frankie uses his social standing to seduce Vicky, and then Vicky uses Frankie to achieve fame – is effectively obliterated by the final emergence of the perfectly ordinary couple (Frankie and Jill), in a similar way to how the emergence of the 'happy couple' concludes many noirs such as, to mention a well-known specimen, *Gilda* (Charles Vidor, 1946). As *the* noir melodrama, incidentally, *Gilda* fully vindicates, perhaps more than any other film of the canon, the corrosive power of sexual difference, despite his ending. The impossibility of the relationship between Gilda (Rita Hayworth) and Johnny Farrell (Glen Ford) – the central theme of the film – is embodied by a third character, namely the sadistic Mundson (George Macready). Mundson's role is crucial in bringing back together the two ex-lovers, enjoining them to fight with each other again while perversely observing the spectacle. Even more symptomatic is the reappearance he makes towards the end of the film, after his presumed death, for his return spoils the likely reconciliation between Gilda and Johnny. Though there is a happy ending – provided by the real liquidation of Mundson by 'Uncle Pio' (Steven Geray), the washroom attendant and amateur philosopher – such an ending does not manage to even minimally obfuscate the prominence of the gap of sexual difference that *Gilda* is built around.

Going back to *I Wake Up Screaming*, it is in connection with its trite finale that we should reconsider the Laird Cregar character of the overweight, unsettling detective who moves awkwardly in and out of the shots leaving huge shadows behind him. Although the film's ideological construct turns him into a psychopath whose determination to frame Frankie derives from his long-running obsession with Jill (as he confesses before committing suicide, he hates Frankie out of jealousy), it is precisely his deeply troubled fixation on Jill that gives the lie to the phony theme of the 'triumph of the ordinary couple'. (Incidentally, it turns out that the murder was committed by another unhinged character, the porter of the building where the sisters lived). Thus, the figure of the dangerously antisocial detective (typically, on the side of the law yet undermining it) hides nothing less than the negative core of both subject and social order, a negativity firmly repressed yet also unmistakably endorsed by the film. In respect of this negativity, the truth about the 'frictionless' relationship between Frankie and Jill should be located in the note Frankie wrote for Vicky just before she was killed: 'now you must disappear'. Although he did not kill her, what was truly unbearable for Frankie was the persistence of (the typically noir) woman qua locus of an excessive, threatening, potentially destructive enjoyment. Only after her disappearance could he engage in the 'successful' liaison with Jill.

We find another pair of memorable sisters, this time indeed twin sisters (Terry and Ruth), in Siodmak's hugely successful *The Dark Mirror* (1946).

Again, in spite of the alleged intellectual ambitions of the film (its often celebrated self-reflexive dimension),[52] the story is structured around the elementary question of the (at least partially) repressed correlation between the male gaze and the redoubled image of these identical sisters (both played by Olivia De Havilland). When a man is found dead in his apartment, one of the twins is identified as the culprit, but since we are dealing with identical sisters, who also provide alibis for each other, the police are unable to determine which of the two is the guilty party. A psychologist (Dr Scott Elliott, played by Lew Ayres) is hired to unravel the mystery. Predictably, he falls in love with one of them, Ruth, who (again, predictably) turns out to be the 'normal' one. He begins a relationship with her, while Terry is eventually unmasked as the manipulative and psychotic sibling who had killed out of jealousy. It is easy to detect here one of the basic ideological operations at work in noir: The radical ambiguity of femininity is broken down into two discreet units, the 'good' (normal, balanced, modest) and the 'bad' (scheming, overambitious, psychologically disturbed) girl – with the former eventually emerging as the ideal partner for man. Despite its ideological character, Siodmak's film does not completely forsake its real stakes. The final words of the psychologist to Ruth are revealing and symptomatic: 'Why are you so much more beautiful than your sister?' The very fact that he is able to 'see beauty' in her and not in her sister is indicative of the act of repression that runs through the entire film, suggesting how desperate he is to establish a viable rapport with the non-threatening sibling. The best example of this ambiguity comes with the scene close to the end when Terry, who believes Ruth to be dead, pays a visit to Dr Elliott pretending to be her sister. After he tells her he knows her real identity, she asks him, defiantly, whether 'he is sure he knows which one he kissed'. Although the doctor replies that he is absolutely certain, the question hits a raw nerve – even more so in the next scene, at the sisters' apartment, when Terry takes on Ruth's personality, as if she was possessed by her (in a way that reminds us of Norman Bates's impersonation of his mother at the end of *Psycho*). Only when the real Ruth suddenly appears from the room next door, revealing that the whole scene as well as her death had been staged, does Terry break down, smashing the mirror where Ruth's image is reflected. Although at the narrative level clarity as well as moral order is restored, with the good sister prevailing over the murderess, the fundamental enigma about femininity (well beyond the scientific issue of the twin sisters' overlapping personalities) remains central until the very end, with the final shot of Ruth's enigmatic expression after Dr Elliott's aforementioned question.

Another paradigmatic redoubling of woman is staged by Lewis Allen's *Appointment with Danger* (1951), which begins as a typical post-war propaganda film, with the voice-over praising the patriotic spirit of the US postal system. But of course there is much more to it. Alan Ladd plays Al Goddard, an icy, insensitive police detective who goes undercover to infiltrate a gang planning a one million dollars hold up to a post-office van. The central character, however, is a nun named Sister Augustine (Phyllis Calvert), who has witnessed a murder and is given police protection. Her humanizing influence on detective Goddard is instantaneous. The other woman in the film (though her part is small) is femme fatale Dodie (Jan Sterling), the boss's woman, whom it seems the Ladd character has a short affair with (we only see them dancing in her room at one point). In short, woman is divided between nun and prostitute, in line with the old 'male chauvinist' trick. The key point is, once again, sublimation: Almost à la Buñuel (see for instance *Viridiana*, 1961) woman is elevated to the status of the impossible/unavailable nun, while the Lady predictably loses her centrality within the narrative. In fact, the latter leaves the scene when she discovers that the Ladd character is not a member of the gang but an infiltrated policeman. She becomes anonymous, and is quickly forgotten by the detective. What should be evidenced here is the narcissistic strategy governing the male gaze, since his position as incorruptible representative of the law is correlative to the fantasmatic status of his relationship with the beautiful nun qua object of desire. The nun then gets it absolutely right when she tells him: 'If a woman were to ever love you as much as you love yourself, it would be the greatest romance in history.' A great film noir line if ever there was one.

Back to *The Narrow Margin*. What also stands out as a sign of radical dislocation within Fleischer's storyline is the knowledge possessed by the real Mrs Neill (the blonde woman). The moment Det. Brown intimates to her that she is in danger as she is being mistaken for the gangster's wife, she replies by confessing her true identity, and then proceeds to explain to him that the moll actually works for the police, even adding that he is being tested against corruption. How come she possesses all this knowledge (a knowledge normally reserved to the voice-over narrator)? Why would the police disclose to her information that might have jeopardized the entire operation? A woman who indeed *knows too much*, Mrs Neill is here confirmed in a role that cannot fail to appear suspicious, well beyond her seemingly neutral fictional persona. Not only is she not what she appears to be (the non-existent Ann Sinclair), but even her true identity (Mrs Neill), as it were, does not seem to coincide with itself. Despite the standard happy ending, subjectivities here remain redoubled, that is, traversed by a profound internal inconsistency. In fact, *The Narrow Margin* is characterized by an unresolved structural tension that accompanies the unfolding of its plot from start to end, capturing with accuracy the most intriguing feature of the noir canon. There is indeed a narrow margin, a minimal gap, between the film's overall logical consistency – encapsulated in its chronological continuity, narrative tightness and happy ending – and the negativity in which it is embedded. It is what, to borrow Adorno's own terms, we could call 'the film's non-identity': Although everything eventually falls into place, and the film can be enjoyed as a gripping action movie, a closer look reveals the presence of a deep fracture which remains visible and identifiable once the main twist is given a chance to retroactively 'rewrite' the story.

Once again, it is crucial to insist on the centrality of the twist. As with all best noirs, we come across a key moment that literally changes the (film's) past, to the extent that the most fruitful way to appreciate it would be to watch the film a second time. If we do that, we suddenly see things we were unable to see on first viewing, almost as if we had changed our viewing perspective and small details now appeared in a different light (a smile is suddenly infused with a different meaning, a line or dialogue takes on a completely unthought-of nuance etc.). The features of *suspense, unmasking* and *pre-narrative event*, which in an inspirational essay Ernst Bloch (1988) had identified as the three most integral conventions of any detective story, here serve precisely a meta-narrative purpose: To show that *the world is ontologically enveloped in self-deception*, that nobody is at home in it, and that eventually the act of detection – of searching for a hidden meaning or cause – can only end up in the revelation of its utter meaninglessness. Bloch refers to Sophocles' *Oedipus Rex* as the archetypal story of self-deception that afflicts the detective and metaphorically human beings tout court. Oedipus relentlessly hunts for the man who committed the crime which led to the plague of Thebes just like a modern detective would look for a criminal. Eventually, however, he discovers that *he is the object of his search*, the man he wants to unmask. The crime that triggered the search was nothing but his own crime. As in the previously mentioned *So Dark the Night*, the detective and the criminal turn out to be the same person.[53]

The issue of deception is not limited to narrative content but concerns also the stylistic dimension of *The Narrow Margin*. Typically in Fleischer,[54] the use of reflexive devices (mirrors, windows etc.) is obsessive and therefore, if we give credit to the celebrated psychoanalytic insight, essential. (Even Adorno agreed with this insight – perhaps more than he actually meant – when in *Minima Moralia* he stated: 'In psycho-analysis nothing is true except the exaggerations', Adorno (2005a): 49.) The first point to make is that Fleischer's subtle employment of redoubling screens has little to do with the standard attempts to convey character ambiguity, psychological depth or narcissism. Fleischer's noirs as a whole do not care much about the characters' inner turmoil but are rather interested in creating narrative tension through context and action. It would seem that the theoretical significance of the use of reflections (especially juxtaposed ones) in *The Narrow Margin* is that they force an opening between not so much the appearance and the reality of a character (suggesting the character's duplicity, for instance) but rather between appearance and appearance. That is to say, mirrored images here bring out the *inconsistency of appearances in so far as they appear* – regardless of whether they are mirrored or not. It is not a matter of either hinting at the 'true face' of a given character or situation, or to break down someone's presumed moral integrity, or even to evoke the proverbial 'abyss of subjectivity'.[55] Instead, the aim is to expose the status of reality itself in its depthless fictional evanescence, as a fleeting appearance and nothing more. What these mirror shots manage to embody is the central theme of the film: The virtual dimension of reality, its constant redoubling itself into another reality. They are therefore fully concordant with a narrative that depicts human existence as a short, claustrophobic journey tragically mired in self-deception. As noticed by Nino Frank (1946: 14) in what is reputed to be the first article on the genre, noir characters are 'puppets'. Here, the status of these puppets is not only epitomized by the figure of the duped detective (his idiotic expression the moment he is told that he had been protecting the wrong woman is truly unmissable), but is also successfully conveyed by form, that is to say, mainly by the mirror shots of characters and objects as they appear on the train's window screens.

To be precise, the film makes use of two types of reflections, the standard one through mirrors, and the less obvious, more sophisticated one through windowpanes. The latter type often creates uncanny juxtapositions of what is outside and inside the train, first and foremost reinforcing the feeling of entrapment. This is particularly evident towards the end of the film with a number of shots incorporating the gangsters' black car following the train. What is remarkable about a couple of these shots expertly playing with juxtaposed images has to do with the position of the camera: Not only placed inside the train looking out, but also outside the train looking in. The effect is truly uncanny, in the sense that it reinforces the feeling that what appears to be real, and really dangerous (the gangsters' car, whose ominous presence buttresses the sense of entrapment and thus the film's underlying metaphor of the illusory essence of life), is itself a reflection, a ghostly appearance and nothing else. This is confirmed, in narrative terms, when the threat represented by this car suddenly and unexpectedly evaporates as the vehicle is intercepted by the police. What we thus perceive in the series of reflected juxtapositions on glass is a visual reminder of the nightmarishly inconsistent status of reality itself, which throughout the film is conveyed as a sense of inexorable claustrophobia. What we see outside the train is just another image destined to be wiped out.

It is then clear that the train's windowpanes do not mark the dividing line between the fictional and the real, the deceptive and the authentic; instead, they support the central trope of the film, that is to say the film's subtle insistence on the presentation of reality as a fragile and utterly fictional space. Even more pointedly, we could argue that these reflections capture nothing less than the very essence of cinematic art, in so far as they are 'merely' *images projected onto a blank screen.* At this level of analysis, and particularly with regard to the key scene which is discussed below, *The Narrow Margin* lends itself to be accessed as a self-reflexive work commenting on cinema's ability to grasp (and constantly reflect) the fictional status of reality. In embodying to perfection the displaced truth about narrative content (its deep internal divisions), style here becomes autonomous from the plot.

What comes to mind apropos the haunting images reflected on the train window is Deleuze's argument about the rise of a new type of cinematic image immediately after World War II, namely the time-image. This new image, Deleuze argues, emerges from the ashes of the dominant classical narrative cinema which was based instead on the movement-image, that is, on the close correspondences among context, affection, action and reaction. At a certain historical point, especially with the advent of Italian neorealism, cinema begins to present us with characters who are simply unable or unwilling to react to given optical situations, or with the proliferation of disconnected spaces and chance relations: 'It is here that situations no longer extend into action or reaction in accordance with the requirements of the movement-image.' We witness the emergence of pure optical (and sound) situations, whereby a scene might be characterized by a gaze no longer followed by a reaction to what is seen: 'The situation no longer extends into action through the intermediary of affections. It is cut off from all its extensions, it is now important only for itself, having absorbed all its affective intensities, all its active extensions' (Deleuze 2005: 261).

The most exemplary manifestation of the time-image offered by Deleuze is undoubtedly the 'crystal-image'. This corresponds to a double-sided cinematic image where the actual part (the part logically inserted into the narrative) is caught in a kind of perpetual and unbreakable relationship with its virtual side:

> It is as if an image in a mirror, a photo or a postcard came to life, assumed independence and passed into the actual, even if this meant that the actual image returned into the mirror and resumed its place in the postcard or photo, following a double movement of liberation and capture.

Focusing especially on mirror shots, Deleuze argues that, in the crystalline circuit he has in mind (to exemplify he quotes scenes from films by Ophüls, Losey, Welles and Zanussi), the reflected image is virtual in relation to, for instance, the actual character, but it is allowed to acquire an actuality of its own that literally 'leaves the character with only a virtuality and pushes him back out-of-field' (Deleuze 2005: 68). Influenced by Henri Bergson's concept of time, Deleuze claims that in this indissoluble relationship between actual and virtual, or transparent and opaque, we are encouraged to catch a glimpse of the abyssal and fundamental dimension of time as expressed in film (see Deleuze 2005: 76–80). Without meaning to develop the argument in the direction of cinema's relation to time, it nevertheless seems appropriate to underline the virtual dimension captured by some of the mirroring shots in *The Narrow Margin*. The degree of formal autonomy they achieve in respect of the narrative context is indicative of the subtle aesthetic complexity of this film, despite the fact that it never ceases to retain its specific status as a 'good old' action movie based on a rational ordering mechanism epitomized above all by continuity. While there is no conscious search for a vision that might disrupt narrative continuity (as there is in the European art cinema that Deleuze's analysis by and large privileged), the autonomy achieved by some of these reflexive shots manages to express modernist concerns from within the general framework of classical Hollywood cinema. One way of translating this in dialectical terms is by emphasizing, borrowing Deleuze's terms, the coincidence of the objective and the subjective dimensions of noir: The 'over-objective conceptions of the Americans', that is, a cinema dominated by continuity and narrative closure, is actually correlative to a disruptive break, the very break that Deleuze tended to associate with European cinema's artistically conscious attempt at reaching 'a mystery of time, of uniting image, thought and camera in a single "automatic subjectivity"' (Deleuze 2005: 53).

The use of juxtaposed images is particularly intriguing in the scene where Det. Brown rescues Mrs Neill (the real one) and shoots dead 'the man with the fur coat', the gangster who had previously killed his fellow detective. The technical trick is once again remarkable in itself. Mrs Neill is in her compartment, under threat by the hoodlum who wants the list with the names of the fellow gangsters that she is supposed to take to the grand jury. Det. Brown is outside but cannot intervene as Mrs Neill would be killed instantly. As the train stops at a station, he captures some 'moving images' of what is taking place in the adjacent compartment in the form of reflections on the windows of a train that pulls up on the parallel track. Then the parallel train comes to a complete halt and the image becomes clearer, even more so as the light is turned out, reproducing the effect of projection within a cinema theatre. In order to be certain of shooting at the gangster and not at Mrs Neill through the closed door, Det. Brown watches carefully the movements the two make through the reflection on the windowpane. Then to isolate the gangster as a target, he shouts at Mrs Neill to fetch the list of names the gangsters were after (though she had already told him that she had sent this list to the District Attorney by post before travelling), and when she moves away, he confidently pulls the trigger.[56] It can be seen how by literally 'coordinating the fiction', even manipulating it, the detective for the first time in the film is actually in control of the story, assuming here a role that can be compared to either that of the director or that of the spectator. What is certain is that he literally directs the plot into a specific direction (where of course, in line with the edifying ending of the great majority of these classic noirs, good triumphs over evil). However, the remarkable aspect here is that this action which determines narrative closure acquires its significance precisely because it is played out as an intricate ploy of mirrored images. What we have is, in a way, the perfect dialectical coincidence of totality and lack, closure and openness: In order to achieve its conclusion as a self-fulfilled narrative, as a story, the film needs the particular 'event' represented by the emergence of these insubstantial images, which in fact are at its pivotal core – not only its core as a specific film, but also in so far as they embody reflexivity per se, the core of the medium (cinema).

This dialectical aspect whereby the essence of film, its reflexivity, is redoubled into an image, should not be underestimated as a noir feature. Such redoubling of reflexivity (film qua medium redoubled into image) does not merely challenge and destabilize any preconceived representation of external reality as a self-sufficient, fixed given, but also, and more importantly, it embodies the obverse of the closed totality represented by the consistent noir narrative. What it confirms above all is that any cognitive experience of reality needs a reflexive passage through the other: Just like for Det. Brown, who sees the conclusion of his nightmare in the moving picture on the screen in front of him, so does reality emerge for us literally through what is other from us, that is, through an outward movement seeking a stable anchoring point in the symbolic domain. The power of cinema is that of making us aware of this vital reflexive dimension *as constitutive of reality itself*. The theme of the dialectical correlation between reality and image is also developed by Fleischer in connection with the theme of the fundamental precariousness of subjective identity. In *The Narrow Margin* faces and identities are deceptive, substantially void, since the plot is centred on the impossibility of seeing/identifying the face and true identity of Mrs Neill. In one nice shot in the train station, for instance, the gangsters recriminate that they were not able to see the face of the girl, but at that very moment, the girl herself walks past behind them in soft focus. The interesting point about visual deception is of course available to us only retroactively: It is not simply that they miss her by a 'narrow margin', but that even if they had seen her, they would *not* have seen her, since the woman in question was not the real Mrs Neill but the policewoman in disguise. In *Follow Me Quietly*, Fleischer's previous work, this procedure is even more radical, with the police reconstructing the life-size dummy of a serial killer whose face, however, nobody had seen or could remember, thus forcing the police inspector to leave the dummy with an eerily blank face.

With regard to the use of window reflections, it is interesting to note how another 'train thriller' of the period uses exactly the same shot as a catalyst for narrative resolution. The film in question is Tourneur's *Berlin Express* (1948), generally considered inferior to his previous *Out of the Past* and yet teeming with wonderfully crafted scenes. The ideological/didactic character of this unusual noir, mostly shot on location in post–World War II Frankfurt and Berlin, is easy to locate – and ridicule. At the same time, however, we should note the strong reliance on, again, deception, to the extent that the uplifting educational value of the film should be contrasted with its illusive dimension, which remains its most significant aspect. While on a security train to Berlin, German diplomat and peace activist Dr Bernhardt (Paul Lukas) is killed when a bomb goes off in his compartment. Four witnesses to the murder are subsequently questioned. These represent neatly the allied forces in 1948 Berlin: American agricultural expert Robert Lindley (Robert Ryan), British schoolteacher James Sterling (Robert Coote), former member of the French resistance Henri Perot (Charles Korvin) and Lt. Maxim Kiroshilov (Roman Toporow), a grumpy Russian soldier. It is soon discovered that the man killed on the train was an unfortunate decoy for the real doctor, who is nevertheless kidnapped in Frankfurt railway station by an underground group of neo-Nazis who oppose Bernhardt's attempt to bring the allied forces to negotiate a way forward for a united Germany. Thus, the team of four set off working together to find the real doctor in the devastated streets of post-war Frankfurt.

After the first instance of deception through mistaken identity (Dr Bernhardt's), which is identical to the stratagem used in *The Narrow Margin* in respect of Mrs Neill, we witness a number of similar situations centred on the ambiguity of physical appearances. There is, for instance, the sequence involving a clown, who is first seen working for the neo-Nazis, but is then knocked out by a German man intent on helping Dr Bernhardt's cause (although he also had initially appeared in disguise); the latter puts on the clown's attire and, before being unmasked and killed, manages to save the Robert Ryan character from certain death. The final and most unexpected twist, however, concerns the identity of the French component of the group, who is revealed to be German and a member of the underground gang. When, back on the train travelling towards Berlin, the latter is about to strangle Dr Bernhardt, a clear reflection of the murder scene appears on the window of the adjacent compartment, where the Robert Ryan character (the American) is busy seducing Lucienne Mirbeau (Merle Oberon), Dr Bernhardt's French diplomatic secretary (and benign femme fatale). The dynamics concerning the mirror shot are exactly the same as those in Fleischer's film: The key scene in the adjoining compartment is portrayed on the windowpanes of a train running parallel to the one where the action takes place. This reflection of course allows the American to run to the doctor's rescue, while eventually the man under false identity is gunned down by the Allied police patrolling the security train.

All the above emphasis on deception and subterfuge gives us a film that is not only ideologically driven in pushing the humanistic rhetoric behind the occupying forces' coordinated control of post-war Germany, but also one that instils a pervasive sense of precariousness right at the heart of the narrative. It is not only the film's balanced humanism that achieves universal poignancy, but even more so its visual ambiguity, which is closely related to what is without a doubt the film's most enthralling image, that of the bombed out urban landscape of post-war Frankfurt (and eventually also Berlin). Paradoxical as this may sound, one should watch *Berlin Express* together with Roberto Rossellini's *Germania Anno Zero* (*Germany Year Zero*, 1948). The fact that they were shot on location at roughly the same time is testament to their being indelibly marked by a similar sense of loss and uncertainty. While Rossellini's film explicitly embraces this loss (the 'year zero' of post-war Germany) as the only way out of a dark predicament, Tourneur's proverbial taste for bleak atmospheres provides a perfect contrast to his film's overt didacticism. Again, I claim that we should see this apparent contrast (pervasive instability vs ideology/humanism) as an emblematic case of speculative identity of opposites.

A detour on ideology

As it can be gauged from the above discussion, my analysis of film noir makes use of Adorno's endorsement of the negative in order to advance a critique of his dismissal of classical narrative/popular cinema as a regressive aspect of mass culture. In a recent essay on Edgar Ulmer's classic B-noir *Detour* (1945), Paul Cantor has highlighted the strong affinities between the hidden message of Ulmer's film and Adorno's critique of American society as the home of the culture industry. Cantor's detailed analysis brilliantly unravels Ulmer's implicit pessimism and polemical verve towards a society that he, as a German émigré director, was experiencing as increasingly alienating. *Detour* is effectively crammed with suggestions that Ulmer's real aim was to portray America, and specifically Hollywood, as the land of shattered dreams, in a way that recalls closely Adorno's famous invectives against the culture industry in *Dialectic of Enlightenment*, and specifically against Hollywood itself as a 'fountain of illusions' (Cantor 2007: 144). *Detour* can legitimately be seen as representing a surprisingly faithful cinematic exemplification of Adorno's cultural criticism as directed especially against the American way of life. Although there is no way to know whether there actually existed a direct connection between Ulmer, Adorno and Horkheimer, Cantor concludes that their common critique of American society 'grew out of the same intellectual and cultural milieu', and ultimately connotes the elitist view of European intellectual mandarins vis-à-vis American popular culture. While I tend to share Cantor's underlying argument on the correlation between the critical/subversive spirit of film noir and Adorno's Critical Theory, my aim with this book is altogether different. I attempt to move beyond issues of historical contextualization to address instead, through film noir, questions concerning the theoretical constitution of Adorno's specific brand of critical theory and dialectical thought.

My study of noir contests Adorno's generic rejection of industrially produced cinema as merely and implicitly 'ideological' to show that, if freed from the constraints of a cinematic theory moulded by questions of auteurship and spectatorship, and instead consigned to a dialectical theory of the object-film, the discourse on noir can lead to a critique of reality tout court. The great merit of film noir is that it holds on to negativity without jettisoning its speculative identity with totality. Critics who praise the dark side of noir as a rule forget to include in their analyses how the deeply fractious, even nihilistic core of the noir universe is firmly situated within a closed universe of sense.[57] Although undoubtedly a concession to censor and market alike, the narrative conclusiveness of classic film noir should not be seen as a betrayal of its authentically negative, subversive core. Rather, such sense of ideological closure and representational wholeness is by definition the necessary obverse of negativity; without taking it into account, any appreciation of subversion would risk being grossly misplaced. We should perhaps reread through a Hegelian lens Walter Benjamin's famous maxim from the *Theses on the Philosophy of History* that 'There is no document of civilization which is not at the same time a document of barbarism' (in Benjamin 1992: 248): wholeness and negativity coincide. The greatness of film noir is that, to use a psychoanalytic slogan popularized by Žižek, *it enjoys its symptoms*: It represents a type of cinema defined by its proclivity to set up a perfectly round and compelling narrative, which, however, at the same time constantly derails, threatening to implode through sheer enjoyment of its symptomatic excesses, so many embodiments of contradiction and thus negativity. In Lacanian terms, this 'negative enjoyment' takes the name of *jouissance*, and manifests itself chiefly through the self-destructive drive of the noir hero/heroine vis-à-vis a symbolic universe whose reliability has suddenly disintegrated. To speak of noir is to speak of a parallactic object situated along the overlap of wholeness and negativity.

The previous investigation of Fleischer's *The Narrow Margin*, for instance, unravels speculative identity as a dialectical coincidence of consciousness (the hero's subjectivity) and the object of consciousness (substance, the distorted microcosm the hero struggles to understand). This coincidence does not ratify the triumph of subjectivity over the object, or vice versa. Rather, it accounts for the overlapping inconsistencies of both. First, I have noted how the inherently 'ideological' conclusiveness of the film narrative – emotionally and psychologically captivating through its fast-paced action – is substantially undermined by an underlying narrative incongruity formally vehicled by stylistic expedients such as the peculiar use of mirror shots. Such incongruity constitutes the film's other side, no less representative of its noir status. Furthermore, one can appreciate this coincidence of opposites (positive ideological outcome and negative underside) by relating it directly to the main character's vicissitudes: Though eventually his mission is accomplished and objective reality 'conquered' (all false identities are revealed to him), retrospectively his consciousness remains mired in self-deception, a feature the film captures via the hero's fraught relationship with the Lady qua double – his suspended rapport with the 'dark Lady', as well as his hazardous link with the 'fair Lady'. The ideological wholeness of the film is thus correlative to its fragility, narrative and formal, objective and subjective.

As far as ideology is concerned, let us recall that what Adorno and other critical theorists saw in cultural products was the replication of the deadly instrumental conditions conducive to the reification of thought. Mass-produced popular culture, and film especially, were recognized as reproducing the very atrophy of reason that marked the progressive affirmation of instrumental rationality within modernity. In one among the many passages against cinema written by Adorno during his American exile, films are regarded as 'fairy-tale dreams, appealing so eagerly to the child in the man', thus epitomizing the 'regression organized by total enlightenment', betraying the onlooker and making reification imperceptible:

> Immediacy, the popular community concocted by films, amounts to mediation without residue, reducing men and everything human so perfectly to things, that their contrast to things, indeed the spell of reification, becomes imperceptible. The film has succeeded in transforming subjects

> so indistinguishably into social functions, that those wholly encompassed, no longer aware of any conflict, enjoy their own dehumanization as something human, as the joy of warmth. (Adorno 2005a: 206)

In a nutshell, instrumental thought's lethal compulsion to identify is deemed by Adorno to be embodied in such cultural commodities as Richard Fleischer's previously discussed 'cheap' film.

As we have seen, in order to counteract the compulsion to identify, Adorno developed a concept later ratified with the expression 'negative dialectics', stressing the necessity for non-identitarian thinking, a type of rationality that would defy the intellectual misery of cultural commodities by driving critical thought to reject the numbing identificatory processes made available by mass culture. Thus, negative dialectics advocated the short-circuiting of reason as the only properly rational moment, aprioristically rejecting all mass culture as ideological inasmuch as its function would be to mollify people's alienation. If, as I believe, there is something deeply problematic in this intellectual stance, it has nothing to do with the emphasis on the negative and the attendant critique of the culture industry per se. Rather, it has to do with the deliberate choice, especially on Adorno's part, not to apply its dialectical method to those cultural products it deemed regressive. I argue that the desperate, even hopeless endorsement of the negative moment as the only moment of salvation from the 'ever-same sold as ever-new' of the late-capitalist condition, should be vindicated by a truly dialectical analysis of cultural commodities such as those churned out by Hollywood. Critical Theory's attitude of intellectual revulsion towards mass culture and its artefacts misses the crucial Hegelian point about dialectics: The negative is nothing but the other side of totality. Where a cultural product appears ideologically pregnant in its unity of narrative purpose and formal consistency, there one should look for its immanent contradictions, which, when locatable, speak against the language of the commodity and thus threaten to subvert its ideological closure.

It is telling and somewhat ironic that Adorno himself upheld the view that logical consistency was a necessary feature of all great art, one that makes the artworks' internal organization 'analogous to the logic of experience' (Adorno 1999: 136), regardless of the artistic distance from empirical reality achieved through technique. To put it in Adorno's dialectical terms, in artworks 'a feeling of coercive logical consistency is bound up with an element of contingency'. Only by defending such unity of opposites (logical consistency and contingency) can Adorno assert the negative power of art, here defined summarily, yet accurately, as 'a shadowy quality of being at once binding and slack' (p. 137).[58] In fact, Adorno refers to Schopenhauer's *principia individuationis* – space, time and causality – to bolster his compelling argument that art reflects (is an image of) the elementary structure of external existence, though it becomes art precisely when it divests space, time and causality of their compulsiveness and empirical purpose (see 137–8). Art, Adorno tells us 'is not synthesis, as convention holds; rather, it shreds synthesis by the same force that affects synthesis' (p. 139). However, he also tells us, in unmistakably dialectical terms, that the negative, disruptive quality of art cannot be severed from art's discursive logic and internal consistency:

> If art had absolutely nothing to do with logicality and causality, it would forfeit any relation to its other and would be an a priori empty activity; if art took them literally, it would succumb to the spell; only by its double character, which provokes permanent conflict, does art succeed at escaping the spell by even the slightest degree. (Adorno 1999: 138)

This 'slightest degree' which sums up the dialectical nature of art in so far as it reflects reality by incorporating what reality itself constantly represses, that is, its vertiginous openness, is the 'narrow margin' that gives the title to Fleischer's film. It is the very thin, almost invisible margin between the gripping synthetic force of film noir and its gaping inconsistency. As I see it, then, film noir offers itself as an ideal contender for the type of critical analysis that seeks to trace and untangle the symptomatic kernel of negativity at the heart of cultural commodities. The very fact that it emerged retroactively in France suggests that it articulates its specificity upon a paradoxical mixture of sameness and unruly, explosive fragmentation. Though it was invented after its most intense period of production (the second part of the 1940s), its organic resonance and coherence is as undisputable as its inherent distortion, which can never be adequately captured in language.

Let us exemplify this idea through a brief reference to a film noir that presents itself as explicitly ideological. Anthony Mann's gritty *Border Incident* (1949), the fourth of his collaborations with legendary cinematographer John Alton,[59] openly promotes the notion of lawful and selective immigration against the exploitation of clandestine migrant workers – a theme, incidentally, whose topicality for today's geopolitical universe is self-evident. Set in the Imperial Valley (United States) and Mexico, and relentlessly plunged in quintessentially noir darkness, the film recounts the joint effort of a US federal agent and his Mexican counterpart as they try to infiltrate a gang running an illegal smuggling racket of immigrant workers. The film's ideological strength relies on the subtle gentrification of the term 'border'. On the one hand, as we are shown at the start, the border between the United States and Mexico is the place where the criminal organization arrange for illegal

Mexican workforce (*braceros*) to enter the United States, earn a few dollars working the land of 'agri-Mafioso' Owen Parkson (Howard Da Silva), only to be ruthlessly killed and robbed by the members of the same organization once they make their way back to Mexico. On the other hand, as we are reminded by the burdensome voice-overs at the beginning and at the end of the film, border is also the place indicating the 'good and fair' route of legal migrant workers under the concerted approval and monitoring of the US and Mexican laws. By indicting the evil exploitation of clandestine workers – an indictment peppered with strong sadistic undertones (see especially the opening scene where the Mexican workers returning home are ambushed in a canyon, slain, robbed and their bodies thrown into a swamp of quicksand) – the film effectively promotes the 'legal exploitation' of Mexicans. The border it obfuscates by focusing on legal and illegal migration, then, is none other than class division. In doing so, it also suggests, *against* its driving ideological line, that the good old American values of nationhood and hard work are strictly dependent on the arbitrary importation of starving workforce from a poor neighbouring country – hardly something to be proud of. The point to highlight, then, is not simply that the film is ideological, as emphatically confirmed by the voice-over. Much more subversive is to unravel how, despite its explicit intention, *Border Incident* constantly 'stumbles against' the very lack of foundations of its dominant rhetoric. This short circuit between explicit ideological intention and concealed significance is perhaps nowhere more evident than in Mann's recurrent reference to what Jonathan Auerbach, in a brilliant analysis of the film and its historical context, calls 'the elemental muck and chaos that underlies civilization' (Auerbach 2011: 142). The typically noir intrusion of negativity qua elemental, untamable force is particularly obvious in two scenes that appear disturbing even today: The previously mentioned passage where dead bodies of Mexican workers disappear in a bog of quicksand, and especially the famous scene depicting the murder of the American federal agent, who dies as if in a nightmare, squashed into the muddy soil by a huge tractor with rotating blades. The ambiguity of the scene is radical: If it is true that his death, which takes place in US territory, lends itself to be read as that of 'the American hero who is fatally sacrificed in yet another reenactment of blood and soil nationalism', perhaps it is more fruitful to consider that the scene is actually staged for the horrified gazes of two Mexicans (the federal agent and an immigrant), who are therefore forced to witness the spectacle of the 'American dream turned nightmare'. As Auerbach aptly puts it, this death reveals 'the terrifying underbelly of the U.S. farm industry itself' (p. 142). *Border Incident*, then, manages to surreptitiously uncover this dark, brutal, elemental side as *the truth-content* of its ideological message.

This secret, unwitting self-subversion of film noir's ideological thrust is perhaps nowhere more evident than in the documentary-style noirs of the immediate post-war years. The more they try to peddle a moralistic message, the more these films risk uncovering their real concerns, which are at the heart of the noir universe and have little to do with morality. To mention one case in point, let us recall Henry Hathaway's *Call Northside 777* (1948), where the blend of realism (on-location shooting in Chicago) and unambiguous message (the American individual's 'innate' propensity towards justice) do not manage to entirely conceal traces of another, less conscious dimension. James Stewart plays a Chicago newspaper reporter who is slowly but inexorably drawn into believing in the innocence of a Polish convict named Frank Woicek (Richard Conte), to the extent that, through sheer bravery and determination, he eventually manages to prove his innocence. The film ends with reassuringly patriotic words, as the American journalist tells the Polish convict, now free, that 'not many governments in the world' would 'admit an error'. Immediately after, the stentorian voice-over reminds the audience that, however mistaken a sentence can be, the honest citizens' sense of duty, courage and perseverance eventually are bound to restore justice. If we stopped at this succinct summary, however, we would miss the best part of the film, which has to do with the passage when the journalist decides to venture into the netherworld of the city (the Polish community) in search of the witness (another Pole) who had framed the convict. As he conjures up the courage to intrude into the witness's apartment, as a result of which he almost gets killed, we realize that what the film is promoting as the individual's heroic sense of duty has to do with something else, namely a category of the human psyche that Freud had a few decades earlier captured with the name of 'death-drive'. The James Stewart character is here definitely driven, yet not by a noble desire to reinstate justice; he is simply *driven*, in an entirely self-referential way – precisely as he will be, a few years later, in Hitchcock's *Rear Window* (1954) or in Otto Preminger's *Anatomy of a Murder* (1959). What he gets entangled with is the formal loop of drive, which feeds on desire's self-propelling logic: The more the object is missing (here, the piece of evidence that would exonerate the Polish convict), the more he desires to find it, until this desire turns into drive, that is to say into a form of potentially lethal enjoyment (Lacan's *jouissance*) which has no other object apart from lack itself.

Drive is, of course, also the defining feature of countless femmes fatales à la Phyllis Dietrichson (*Double Indemnity*). Let us take the Lizabeth Scott character in *Too Late for Tears* (Byron Haskin, 1949): Like few other femmes, she appears unstoppable, ready to do anything to achieve her object (including killing her feeble husband and her similarly puny lover). This object is a suitcase full of money that she accidentally comes in possession of, and which would open for her the doors to the high life. What should be retained in women like her is the *form* of their drive, in itself the very index of revolutionary subjectivity. For this reason, we should read the noir reference to drive against the various films' ideological agenda. In fact, going back to *Call Northside 777*, we can single out two more issues that contribute to undermine such agenda there. First, we should notice how the insight into the corruption of the police, key to the narrative, remains undeveloped and eventually is altogether dropped, leaving the story oddly incomplete, to the point that the identity of the killer remains elusive (as a consequence of which the other Polish convict, accused of teaming up with Woicek, stays in prison). Secondly, there is the fascinating detail of the blown-up photograph revealing the piece of evidence (a date on a newspaper) which allows the journalist to win his case *in extremis*. The fact that truth is restored thanks to a fictional element (the photo that furthermore needs to be enlarged, like in Antonioni's *Blow-up*, to work as concrete evidence) secretly destabilizes the film's dependence on realism.[60]

The theme of the enlarged photograph revealing a crucial detail is also used in Joseph H. Lewis's last and most accomplished of his noirs, *The Big Combo* (1955). Aside from being a formally outstanding film,[61] to the extent that narrative continuity is constantly at risk of being overwhelmed by stylization, which inevitably fragments the story, it nevertheless gives us narrative situations that capture very precisely the status of the noir subject as driven, well beyond his fictional identity. Here Det. Diamond (Cornel Wilde) is fixated on arresting mafia hoodlum Mr Brown (Richard Conte) not because of his sense of justice, but, explicitly, because of his attraction to Brown's girlfriend Susan Lowell (Jean Wallace). The latter is presented as a sublimated Lady: blonde, fragile, and yet strangely active in enjoying the criminal's wealth and power (see for instance the famous scene of the suggested 'cunnilingus', where she gives in to sex after trying to resist the hoodlum). Det. Diamond, on his part, is morally ambiguous, as can be gauged from his relationship with Rita (Helene Stanton), a poor dancer he uses for emotional and sexual comfort when trying to forget the blonde (eventually, Rita gets killed in place of Susan, thus forcing Det. Diamond to fully confront his fascination with the latter). In fact, the film suggests that the antagonism between Diamond and Brown, the detective and the gangster, should be read as an internal battle between the subject and its double: The two characters are not only physically similar, but especially resemble each other in the way they are constantly beside themselves. In this film, it seems, ideology is a very thin veil, as what emerges is not so much the traditional fight of good versus evil which earlier noirs tended to affirm, but a more complex reflection on how good itself is intrinsically evil, that is, supplemented by a libidinal charge that simply bypasses morality.

Another way of putting the coincidence of ideology and subversion in a filmic text is through the specific declension of speculative identity as the coincidence of necessity and contingency. When, in Hegelian terms, we say that the emergence of film noir was an utterly contingent event, we also state, simultaneously, that it was necessary. In Hegel, such coincidence of necessity (film noir is embedded in the dialectical development of film) and contingency (it was an accident, unrelated to any causal determination) is postulated on two movements. First, the fact that in dialectics necessity exerts its control over any contingent formation – turning anything contingent into the expression of inner necessity. Secondly, the equally crucial insight into how necessity itself is strictly dependent on (or even more explicitly: *it is made of*) a series of contingent formations. The difference between necessity and contingency is thus purely formal, the effect of a slight parallax shift. In relation to our general argument, we can therefore conclude that the genus 'film' encounters itself in the contingent species 'film noir', while the *trait d'union* between them is the negative. The contingent emergence of noir gives form to the inherently split, antagonized notion 'film'. Let us recall the ideological dimension of a 'middle class' noir like the rarely discussed *Pitfall* (Andrè de Toth, 1948), which is played on the standard opposition of domestic security and its transgression via marital infidelity and, collaterally, crime. Johnny Forbes (Dick Powell) is portrayed in a fairly safe but dull routine: He is married, lives in a middle-class suburb of Los Angeles, works for an insurance company (like Walter Neff in *Double Indemnity*) and craves excitement beyond his repetitive existence. Temptation comes when, upon investigating a case of embezzlement, he meets model Mona Stevens (Lizabeth Scott). In his pursuit of Mona, Johnny of course gets entangled with something much bigger than he had anticipated (in other words, his desire for an extramarital relationship turns into *real enjoyment*, something to do with crime and thus potentially lethal). Eventually, however, the film reveals its ideological aim to reaffirm those middle-class domestic values that the male protagonist had been tempted to subvert. After his perilous adventure, the insurance salesman returns to the mediocrity of his everyday life, safe in the knowledge that, as his wife had pointed out to him, he is 'like fifty million other Americans', and as such 'the backbone of the country'. It seems to me that the danger of interpretations that insist on the ideological dimension of films like *Pitfall* is, in a nutshell, that they miss the paradox of the coincidence of the ideological framework with its inherent contradiction. In connection with the above narrative, what I would highlight is therefore the strict correlation between ideology (bourgeois routine, etc.) and its excess: It is not simply that Johnny is a weak noir hero because eventually he accepts the necessity of self-sacrifice, of loss of enjoyment, of an intrinsically castrating symbolic framework (here, middle-class domesticity)[62]; much more productive is to draw attention to the fact that the fantasy of transgression is a constitutive element of the very articulation of the orderly framework. Balance and transgression are thus coincidental, just like necessity and contingency in Hegel, to the extent that the ultimate form of transgression is always the establishment of a new disciplinary order. That Johnny appears castrated hardly turns him into a weak character, for, in Lacanian terms, symbolic castration is the defining feature of subjectivity (either we accept our constitutive alienation in the symbolic order, or we simply fail to form our identity). If there is an ideological dimension to the film, then, it should be located in the very notion of transgression it evokes: The thrilling fantasy of breaking out of the monotonous symbolic order by endorsing a contingent encounter (with the Lisabeth Scott character) is internal to that order, fully taken into account by it.

A very similar situation is developed in Anthony Mann's vastly underrated *Side Street* (1949),[63] which begins with an aerial shot of Manhattan providing an architectural metaphor for the sense of entrapment experienced by the film's young and newly married protagonist Joe Norson (Farley Granger). Here, temptation comes not in the (voluptuous) form(s) of a femme fatale, but as a hefty sum which the Granger character steals from a corrupt attorney, which in turn plunges him into a violent noir microcosm. Although the aim is not to transgress a boring middle-class life, but of providing a better life for his family, the overall narrative mechanism is the same as that of *Pitfall*, inasmuch as the film pits a situation of seeming normality against its transgression. This binary logic, again, should be read as part of the same ideological construct: The young man's temptation to improve his life illegitimately does not mark a potentially self-destructive flight from his social conditions but it is the very fantasy scenario that sustains those conditions. Nothing keeps us within our symbolic boundaries (within ideology) like fantasizing about transgression! The fact that in both films the hero enacts the fantasy only to end up exactly where he started, confirms that the fantasy and its enactment were always included in the ideological framework within which he operated. Transgression is thus revealed to stem from the very ideological matrix which it aims to antagonize.

To conclude with another variation on the link between order and lethal transgression in noir, let us recall Ida Lupino's suspenseful and claustrophobic *The Hitch-Hiker* (1953), mostly shot in the Mexican desert. Before being kidnapped by the psychotic killer, the two middle-aged male protagonists are shown leaving for a short fishing holiday, away from their families. Crucially, as they drive through a Mexican village they are tempted to stop 'for some fun', even reminiscing about the good old days when they were unmarried and could freely chase after women. It is clear that what we are dealing with here is the usual repressed (male) fantasy that seeks an outlet: Enjoyment tempts these two self-satisfied men away from their drab and ordinary lives, if only for a short while. While the Edmund O'Brien character would like to stop, his more conscientious pal pretends he is asleep so that his friend cannot decide on his own to indulge in a detour (while some Mexicans approach the car to offer 'fun'). Later, however, they give a ride to a man who turns out to be a dangerous kidnapper wanted for the murder. The question to ask is a simple one: What is the status of this third character, the kidnapper, in relation to the two men's fantasy of transgression? In a classic case of what Hegel would call 'reflexive determination', he embodies the real stakes of the two men's (repressed) desire, in other words, the objectivized kernel of their subjectivities. In psychoanalytic terms, he stands for their unconscious *jouissance*. In this film, entirely populated by men, made by one of the first women to have achieved success in Hollywood both as an actress and as a director, what is staged with remarkable precision is the dialectical relationship between necessity and contingency, order and transgression – or, in Lacanese, the symbolic order (ideology) and the traumatic Real of *jouissance*.[64]

Notes

1 Slavoj Žižek has commented on the intrinsic transhistorical and trans-cinematic richness of noir as a canon that cannot be confined to the 1940s, but should instead be thought of in conjunction with other genres such as, for instance, science fiction (see Žižek 1993: 9–10).

2 This is exactly what Jacques Lacan had in mind when he defined the gaze as the object-cause of visual desire (see Lacan 1998a: 67–119). For Lacan, the gaze can be found in the visual field precisely as a traumatic instance of self-reflexivity: The subject encounters itself in its radically decentred mode, as its other qua *jouissance*. The elusive thing that causes the subject's scopic desire is revealed to coincide with nothing other than the fully objectivized subject of drive, 'the thing in me more than myself', which in my ordinary existence I never encounter. 'Gaze' is thus a tautological notion asserting the subject's coincidence with its own disavowed substance. At the same time, the encounter with the gaze signals a traumatic event, a short circuit that radically undermines the allegiance between desire and the visual field: 'Is it not precisely because desire is established here in the domain of seeing that we can make it vanish?' (Lacan 1998a: 44–5). This vanishing of desire, correlative to the showing of the gaze, implies *aphanisis* (see Lacan 1998a: 216–29), the collapse of the subject's symbolic efficiency.

3 James Morrison puts the terms of this opposition very clearly: 'Drawing upon traditional rhetorics of stability and ideologies of coherence, the Hollywood cinema fulfills its self-appointed function to mass-produce mass fantasies and, in doing so, gains worldwide dominance in international film culture as early as the 1910s. The European cinema, meanwhile, is in these narratives a united front [. . .] in its opposition to Hollywood's domination, valuing character over plot, expressive subjectivity over genre formulae, exploratory style over codified procedure, sceptical inquiry over populist faith, critique over affirmation' (Morrison 1998: 7). The point with regard to this sharp opposition between the two filmic traditions is not merely to highlight how in reality things are much more fluid and hybrid, but rather to try and develop a critique of cinematic ideology (Hollywood) which focuses on the gaps and inconsistencies within the explicit ideological text.

4 See for instance Paul Schrader's well-known essay on the subject, which highlights precisely the modernist self-consciousness of film noir as a specific cinematic style (Schrader 1986).

5 Among others, Bordwell, Staiger and Thompson (1985: 77), in *The Classical Hollywood Cinema*, rightly emphasize how, despite undermining from within the Hollywood canon, 'formally and technically these noir films remain codified'.

6 Cornelius Schnauber (1997) claims that between 1933 and 1952, over 1,500 German and Austrian exiles found work in Hollywood.

7 The correlation between dialectics and excrements is often deployed by Žižek. See for example his chapter 'Hegel and Shitting: the Idea's Constipation', in Žižek et al. (2011: 221–32).

8 Critics have articulated different opinions when debating whether film noir should be regarded as a genre or not (see Conard 2007: 9–14). This is not simply an idle philological question though, since it brings to light the inherently divisive nature of noir. If the word 'genre' implies the definition of film as a fixed category in terms of its essential narrative and stylistic conventions, then perhaps the only way to apply the word genre to noir would by defining it solely in terms of its negative features, that is, those features – both narrative and stylistic – that dramatize the inherent antagonism embodied by the noir canon. The essential noir element, if there is one, is the negativity it manages to give form to, and which, strictly speaking, works as a kind of attractor for a number of narrative patterns that are both transnational and transhistorical.

9 In a survey of the critical reception of film noir, James Naremore has dissected the overarching tendency to think of noir as a deeply fraught concept (see Naremore 1998: 9–39). The French critics who first analysed the noir phenomenon in the immediate post-war period, and later those writing for the *Cahiers du cinéma*, as a whole tended to praise 'its dynamism, its cruelty, and its irrationality' (p. 17), considering film noir as a category of existentialism. They saw its pervasive sense of dissonance in unison with the modernist sensibility, and as such implicitly subversive (inevitably, the *Cahiers* critics structured their analyses around issues of *auteurism*, privileging personal visions to

general themes). The Anglo-Saxon critical literature by and large endorsed the fascination with noir as an implicitly fractious type of film-making. British critic Raymond Durgnat, particularly, emphasized the surrealist penchant of noir and went as far as to identify it with a transhistorical dimension coextensive with psychoanalysis. On the other side of the Atlantic, bar a few exceptions like auteurist critic Andrew Sarris, most of the commentators acknowledged the French view of noir, though those of more recent generations began to treat the canon 'nostalgically, as a phenomenon linked to classic Hollywood in the 1940s' (p. 30).

10 Discussing the opening scene of *Double Indemnity*, for instance, Aaron writes: 'I am not arguing simply for the instatement of masochism in the text but in the audience's approach to the text, an approach that is directed by the film but also exists outside of it' (Aaron 2007: 70).

11 As low-budget commercial films, B-noirs became particularly popular when they started being incorporated into film theatres as part of the double-feature screenings. This 'two for the price of one' strategy became common practice during the Depression era. B-noirs were produced not only by the so-called Poverty Row studios (Grand National, Republic, Monogram) but also by the big studios (the 'Big Five', as they were then known: MGM, Paramount, 20th Century Fox, Warner Bros and RKO Radio Pictures) and the intermediate ones (United Artists, Columbia, Universal). Their essential features were a tight production schedule (which could be as short as four working days) and a short running time (around an hour), though the distinction between A- and B-movie has always been more ambiguous than is often thought (see Jacobs 1992). The film often considered the first noir ever made, *Stranger on the Third Floor* (Boris Ingster, 1940), was a low-budget noir released by RKO Radio Pictures, the financially weakest of the big studios.

12 Apropos the unlikelihood of this couple, Claussen argues: 'The current belief that Adorno's elitist preference for high culture implied a contempt for the film as an art form is contradicted not only by the value he placed on Chaplin but also by the esteem in which he held Lang. Film had been a prominent feature in the Adorno household from the 1920s on. He went regularly to the cinema with his aunt Agathe and was able to discuss films on equal terms with the much older Siegfried Kracauer. [. . .] Adorno also introduced one of his most talented pupils, Alexander Kluge, to Fritz Lang, his old friend from his Hollywood days' (Claussen 2008: 172). A similar argument is developed, with plenty of documentation, by David Jenemann in chapter 3 of his *Adorno in America* (see Jenemann 2007: 105–47). While Adorno's interest for the cinema as a form of art is undoubtedly well documented, my overall argument questions his decision not to submit to dialectical analysis films that were not considered art but cheap entertainment. And if it is true that he held Lang in high esteem, one wonders why his cinema never entered his critical radar.

13 Incidentally, Dieterle directed some successful noirs like *The Accused* (1948), *Rope of Sand* (1949), *Dark City* (1950) and *The Turning Point* (1952).

14 I am referring to Lang's so-called Expressionist period (1918–1933), when he made such masterpieces as *Metropolis* (1927) and *M* (1931), the latter being his first sound film.

15 Detlev Claussen argues the following: 'Although there is no documentary evidence on the matter, it is inconceivable that their [Adorno and Horkheimer's] close friend the "Badger" would not have had access to the Culture Industry chapter as it was being written. It is replete with references to films and well-known actors and directors. The underlying ironic tone that can be understood only as a result of familiarity with the objects of its criticism has mostly passed academic posterity by unnoticed: "For centuries society has prepared for Victor Mature and Mickey Rooney"' (Claussen 2008: 165). Let us also recall that although the *Dialectic of Enlightenment* was published in 1947, its original version came out in 1944 with the title of *Philosophische Fragmente* (on the revision of the original see van Reijen and Bransen 2002).

16 *Man Hunt* (1940), *Hangmen Also Die!* (1942), *The Ministry of Fear* (1944) and *Cloak and Dagger* (1946).

17 Lang's 'Freudian tetralogy' in the United States was completed by *Secret Beyond the Door* (1947) and *House by the River* (1949).

18 On this issue, and the related one of Adorno's relationship with American society, see particularly Jenemann's *Adorno in America* (2007).

19 See also Adorno's essay on Chaplin (Adorno 1964).

20 Adorno (2001: 178–9) defends a 'comparatively awkward and unprofessional cinema, uncertain of its effects' since there 'is inscribed the hope that the so-called mass media might eventually become something qualitatively different'. He adds that 'works which have not completely mastered their technique, conveying as a result something consolingly uncontrolled and accidental, have a liberating quality.' And again, liquidating realism: 'Film [. . .] must search for other means of conveying immediacy: improvization which systematically surrenders itself to unguided chance should rank high among possible alternatives'.

21 'Irrespective of the technological origins of the cinema, the aesthetics of film will do better to base itself on a subjective mode of experience which film resembles and which constitutes its artistic character' (Adorno 2001: 180). Adorno then draws a parallel between film and 'dream or daydream': 'As the objectifying recreation of this type of experience, film may become art. The technological medium par excellence is thus intimately related to the beauty of nature' (p. 180).

22 We read in the same essay: 'That which is irreducible about the objects in film is itself a mark of society, prior to the aesthetic realization of an intention. By virtue of this relationship to the object, the aesthetics of film is thus inherently concerned with society. There can be no aesthetics of cinema, not even a purely technological one, which would not include the sociology of the cinema' (Adorno 2001: 182).

23 Kluge has recalled how he became a film-maker thanks to Adorno, who introduced him to Fritz Lang in 1958 after dissuading him from becoming a writer (see Kluge 1988: 36).

24 In 'Transparencies on Film', Adorno first praises the un-cinematic aspects of Antonioni's *La notte* (1962) and then, returning to the central concern of his book with Hanns Eisler (*Composing for the Films*, first published in 1947), suggests how 'film's most promising potential lies in its interaction with other media, themselves merging into film, such as certain kinds of music. One of the most powerful examples of such interaction is the television film *Antithese* by composer Mauricio Kagel' (Adorno 2001: 183).

25 See for instance Adorno's considerations on the treatment of tragedy within the culture industry (Adorno and Horkheimer 1997: 151–6).

26 'There is no one who will agree with you more than I when you defend *kitsch* cinema against the quality film; but *l'art pour l'art* needs just as much defending, and the united front which now exists against it and extends, I know, from Brecht right through to the Youth Movement, is itself encouragement enough to undertake a rescue attempt' (Adorno and Benjamin 1999: 129).

27 I am referring here to one of the overarching points made by Jameson in his classic text *Late Marxism: Adorno or the Persistence of the Dialectic*. For an incisive defence of Adorno's negative use of the dialectic, see for instance the conclusive part of the book, the chapter titled 'Adorno in the Postmodern' (Jameson 2007: 227–52).

28 As he put it at the beginning of *Negative Dialectics*, 'the appearance of identity is inherent in thought itself, in its pure form. To think is to identify' (Adorno 2000: 5).

29 In *Mimina Moralia*, Adorno's sentence is translated as 'the whole is the false' (Adorno 2005a: 50), which does not quite render Adorno's original intention to reverse Hegel's claim from the preface to the *Phenomenology of Spirit* that 'das Wahre ist das Ganze' (the true is the whole).

30 As demonstrated by Buck-Morss (1977: 63–5), these two early definitions were by and large analogous to that of negative dialectics, which Adorno first used, though rather loosely, in his seminars on Hegel of the 1950s.

31 Adorno's ambivalent position towards Chaplin is well known. On the one hand, as we have seen, he never shared Benjamin's endorsement of 'the [audience's] progressive reaction toward a Chaplin movie' (Benjamin 1992: 227); on the other hand, especially in the 1960s, he ascribed to Chaplin's restless playfulness a utopian value defined, typically, as an impossible condition of detachment from the self, that is, a kind of 'extinguishment into the object': 'he plays with the countless balls of pure possibility, and fixes their restless circling into a fabric that has barely more in common with the causal world than Cloud Cuckoo Land has with the gravity of Newtonian physics. Incessant and spontaneous change: in Chaplin, this is the Utopia of an existence that would be free of the burden of being one's self' (quoted in Leslie 2002: 179). Incidentally, it is precisely for this recourse to nonsense that Adorno and Horkheimer had criticized Chaplin in *Dialectic of Enlightenment* (see Adorno and Horkheimer 1997: 137).

32 This is Buck-Morss's conclusion (see Buck-Morss 1977: 185–90). More recently, Žižek has commented that although Adorno was *the* great critic of cultural fetishization, ironically 'traces of this same fetishizing procedure can be found in Adorno's own writings.' Adorno, in other words, often 'gets caught up in his own game, infatuated with his own ability to produce dazzlingly "effective" paradoxical aphorisms at the expense of theoretical substance' (Žižek 2010: 227).

33 'Those who produce important artworks are not demigods but fallible, often neurotic and damaged, individuals. An aesthetic mentality, however, that wholly swept away the idea of genius would degenerate into a desolate, pedantic arts-and-crafts mentality devoted to tracing out stencils. The element of truth in the concept of genius is to be sought in the object, in what is open, not in the repetition of the imprisoned' (Adorno 1999: 171). And again: 'Without the ever present possibility of failure there is nothing genial in artworks' (p. 172). It is with these quotations in mind that we should go back to our previous discussion of Lang's *Scarlet Street*, and especially of his protagonist Chris Cross.

34 On this level, I fully endorse Adorno's thesis that the formal specificity of an artwork is dialectically linked with its content, inasmuch as it gives body to its repressed or sedimented core.

35 The opposite is true for postmodern thought: The more one affirms difference and fragmentation, the more one risks endorsing a specific totality.

36 Lang himself recalled a riot he saw, which began with someone shouting 'Let's have some fun!' (in Bogdanovich 1967: 31).

37 Incidentally, in *Out of the Past*, one should underline the role played by the deaf–mute boy (Dickie Moore), the one who knows the Mitchum character better than anybody else. In the final scene, for instance, he nods to Ann Miller (Virginia Huston), Jeff's girlfriend from the village, confirming that Jeff was really leaving with Kathie, in the hope that Ann can finally forget the man she was besotted by – after which he winks at Jeff's neon-lit name at the gas station, suggesting that he knew what Jeff wanted. The whole point of this character, the only positive one in the entire film, would seem that of emphasizing the degree of alienation implicit in the subject's entrance into language: As psychoanalysis tells us, the moment we accept language, we inevitably contract a debt of guilt towards anything we do. By being spared at least the canonical ways of communication, the boy embodies an innocence which is lost to all other characters.

38 This self-destructive act should perhaps be read alongside the ending of *Out of the Past*: In the latter, however, the Jane Greer character is faithful to her cynical role until the very end, first shooting Jeff and then coming under the fire from the police.

39 A variation on the theme of the partially redeemed femme fatale vis-à-vis the man who is (wants to be) deceived can be found in one of William Dieterle best-known films, the noirish exotic thriller *Rope of Sand* (1949), set in North Africa. French actress Corinne Calvet here plays Suzanne, a prostitute hired to seduce and betray the male hero (Mike Davis, played by Burt Lancaster);

eventually, however, she chooses to help him. A similar situation is presented in Jules Dassin's *Thieves Highway* (1949), where it is prostitute Rica (Valentina Cortese) who gets Nick (Richard Conte) out of trouble.

40 Again, one must add that the sense of utmost displacement, here brought to its extreme, is one of the classic traits of noir. Suffice it to think of some of the best adaptations from Dashiell Hammett and Raymond Chandler such as, respectively, the highly influential *The Maltese Falcon* (John Huston, 1941), one of the first noirs, and *Murder, My Sweet* (Edward Dmytryk, 1944), also known as *Farewell My Lovely* (the original title of Chandler's novel). In these films, private detectives Sam Spade and Philip Marlowe are literally overwhelmed by events they have absolutely no control over, nor are they fully aware of – and yet these events secretly exert an irresistible fascination on them.

41 The noir fascination with hypnosis (within the wider fascination with psychoanalysis) is interesting precisely because it yields results that clearly go beyond mere narrative intentions. The notion of total submission to somebody's willpower recalls the Lacanian fundamental fantasy, in so far as the latter is a traumatic subjective scenario of total submission and passivity. In this respect, the main character in *Fear in the Night* is the ultimate 'noir puppet', completely at the mercy of someone else's will. The only act he seems able to perform is suicide: He is first saved by his brother-in-low (the detective) as he is about to jump off his hotel window, and he is saved again at the end after the second hypnosis, when he is about to drown. For most of the film, he looks and acts more like a ghost than a human being. In Preminger's *Whirlpool*, on the other hand, it is the kleptomaniac heroine, played by Gene Tierney, who is hypnotized by an evil psychoanalyst and involved in a series of murders. The remarkable thing here is that the heroine's hypnosis works as a symptom of her unhappy marriage with another psychoanalyst (played by Richard Conte), who treats her as a kind of ornamental wife. It is therefore the corrupt psychoanalyst who manages to encroach upon the heroine's unconscious *jouissance*, thus effectively leading her, as well as her husband, to confront the deadlock in their relationship. The heroine's utter passivity when under hypnosis, in other words, corresponds to the symptomatic kernel of her being (her fundamental fantasy), which manifests itself in kleptomania as an unconscious rebellion against her unhappy marriage (and, earlier, against a troubled relation with her father). In noirs like *Whirlpool*, the apparently simplistic use of psychoanalysis as an in-vogue narrative trope leads to surprisingly interesting (partly unconscious) results.

42 As Žižek puts it, 'the noir narrative reduces the hero to a passive observer transfixed by the succession of fantasy scenes, to a gaze powerlessly gaping at them: even when the hero seems "active", one cannot avoid the impression that he simultaneously occupies the position of a disengaged observer, witnessing with incredulity the strange, almost submarine, succession of events in which he remains trapped' (Žižek 1993: 223).

43 Adorno was perfectly aware of the psychoanalytic axiom whereby any act of communication, including film, is disturbed or 'derailed' by the excess of unintended meaning it conveys. In his view, this excess was what cinema needed to attempt to capture. Arguing against the possibility of deriving norms of criticism from cinematographic technique alone, for instance, he defended what he regarded as the strictly speaking non-cinematic character of films like Antonioni's *La notte* (The Night, 1961): 'Whatever is "uncinematic" in this film gives it the power to express, as if with hollow eyes, the emptiness of time' (Adorno 2001: 180). However, one should stress also the opposite, less obvious strategy: Precisely because highly organized, narrative symbolization in film always produces a surplus of sense that needs to be located.

44 Lacan defines separation as the overlapping of two lacks: The subject's and the symbolic order's lack (see Lacan 1998a: 204–5). In Bruce Fink's concise definition, separation '*involves the alienated subject's confrontation with the Other, not as language this time, but as desire*' (Fink 1995: 50). In other words, in separation, Lacan's 'big Other' – the invisible network of symbolic relations the subject needs to presuppose in order to function – suddenly appears to the subject as lacking, as deeply inconsistent, thereby producing the subject's exclusion from it: 'Separation implies a situation in which both the subject and the Other are excluded' (p. 53).

45 In relation to the pervasively antagonistic logic of the film, the ending is also revealing. Bill and Jane finally have a chance to escape. Surprisingly, however, they decide to stop running away and instead they consign themselves to justice. While the couple's decision is edifying, at the same time one cannot resist the temptation to conjecture that such decision might be caused by the couple's unconscious fear to confront the freedom of their relationship. Perhaps what this finale truly signals is the impossibility of a sexual relationship that is not held together by the reference to a common fantasy that sets a limit to what can and cannot be done. A similar logic is presented at the end of Claude Chabrol's underrated *Les noces rouges* (Weddings of Blood, 1973), where a man and a woman fall in love, kill their respective partners, but eventually do not seem to have the desire to escape. Particularly poignant is the final shot of the two lovers as they are taken away by the police. When the inspector asks them why they hesitated so much, Pierre (Michel Piccoli) grasps the hand of his lover Lucienne (Stéphane Audran) and eerily replies: 'we have never dreamed of leaving'.

46 The sentence is taken from the well-known passage from the Preface to the *Phenomenology of Spirit* where Hegel praises the 'tremendous power of the negative' as 'the energy of thought': 'Spirit is this power only by looking the negative in the face, and tarrying with it. This tarrying with the negative is the magical power that converts it into being. This power is identical to what we earlier called the Subject [. . .]'. Here Hegel proceeds to reassert the identity of subject and substance on the grounds of its correlation with the power of tarrying with the negative which ultimately is nothing but 'mediation itself'. Dialectical mediation between subject and object is therefore the 'magical power' of 'tarrying with the negative'.

47 As argued by Žižek, who links the 'noir effect' with the paintings of Edward Hopper, 'The intersubjective, "public" symbolic space has lost its innocence [. . .]. What one should bear in mind here is that this *neutrality* of the symbolic order functions as the ultimate guarantee for the so-called "sense of reality":

as soon as this neutrality is smeared, "external reality" itself loses the self-evident character of something present "out there" and begins to vacillate, i.e., is experienced as delimited by an invisible frame: The paranoia of the *noir* universe is primarily visual, based upon the suspicion that our vision of reality is always already distorted by some invisible frame behind our backs' (Žižek 2001a: 152).

48 Another character whose identity is highly deceptive for much of the film is overweight railroad agent Sam Jennings (Paul Maxey). From the start, he is visually linked with the two mobsters on the train, to the extent that Det. Brown also believes he belongs to the gang. Despite also contributing a sense of comic relief, the sheer size of his body adds to the feeling of entrapment and claustrophobia in the scenes where he literally blocks the narrow corridors of the train.

49 For instance, in Robert Siodmak's first noir (the B-noir *Phantom Lady*, 1944), the mysterious vanishing of a woman with an eccentric hat at the beginning of the film is used as a pretext to develop a complex crime story. In *The Narrow Margin*, on the other hand, the woman's disappearance breaks all causal links.

50 In *L'avventura* Antonioni cleverly stages what Pascal Bonitzer (1985: 148) has aptly called 'the disappearance of the disappearance of Anna', the implication being that the film erases the very assumption that the female character has gone missing, thus creating the odd feeling that her motivations were utterly insignificant and dispensable. This enigma of feminine superficiality is paradoxically what gives most of Antonioni's heroines the status of true subjects. As I have argued elsewhere (see Vighi 2006), in many of his films, Antonioni construes a representation of femininity where the failure to resolve the mystery of feminine desire ('what does she want?') bears witness to the ontological lack that defines the subject as such. For this reason, as well as for the treatment of other themes, it would not be improper to establish a direct connection between the tradition of film noir and Antonioni's filmography. Early works such as *Cronaca di un amore* (Chronicle of a Love, 1950), *I vinti* (The Vanquished, 1952) and *La signora senza camelie* (Camille without Camelias, 1953), as well as more mature ones such as *Il grido* (The Cry, 1957) and *L'avventura* (1960), or even more explicitly *Blow-up* (1966), *The Passenger* (Professione: reporter, 1975) and *Identificazione di una donna* (Identification of a Woman, 1982), all exhibit strong commonalities with the noir universe. Naremore includes *Blow-up*, as well as Bernardo Bertolucci's *Il conformista* (The Conformist, 1971) in what he calls 'the Italian tradition of philosophical noir' (Naremore 1998: 203).

51 This shift takes place the very moment Frankie meets Lynn when visiting Vicky at the two sisters' apartment. As Lynn opens the door, Frankie is immediately enthralled by the appearance of Vicky's double, his sexually charged gaze becoming enigmatically suspended between the two sisters.

52 For a number of insightful references to the film's artistic and intellectual complexity, highlighting the influence of the German cultural tradition on Siodmak, see Lazaroff Alpi (1998).

53 Something similar can be argued apropos Robert Siodmak's already mentioned *The File on Thelma Jordon* (1950), where assistant district attorney Cleve Marshall (Wendell Corey) is entrusted with leading the prosecution against Thelma Jordon (Barbara Stanwyck), whom he is having an affair with. Though the charge of murder against the woman is supported by plenty of evidence, the lover/prosecutor sabotages the prosecution in order to let his beloved off the hook.

54 See for instance the various uses of mirrors in the films he made with RKO, especially *Bodyguard* (1948) and *The Clay Pigeon* (1949), but also in later noirs such as *Compulsion* (1959).

55 An example above all is the final showdown in Orson Welles's *The Lady from Shanghai* (1948), where the characters are surrounded by a myriad of mirrors and cannot fathom whether they are shooting at real people or their reflected images.

56 Here we have, then, the opposite situation to the one previously described apropos the ending of Welles's *The Lady from Shanghai*: the reflection does not make killing problematic but actually aids it.

57 In an essay that focuses on the negativity of film noir from a philosophical angle, Steven M. Sanders writes: 'The thread running through the design of film noir is the sense that life is meaningless per se, not that one life just *happens* to be going wrong for the time being and in one particular respect. The philosophically most prominent feature of film noir, then, is the portrayal of the problematic fabric of life as such. In this respect, every noir film thrusts its protagonist into crisis because of the very character of life itself' (Sanders 2007: 93). While I endorse such reading, which by and large transposes on a philosophical ground the film studies analyses of noir as an inherently subversive canon, I also claim that to fully capture the defiant essence of noir, one should evaluate it in terms of its speculatively identical relationship with the objectively conclusive narrative framework in which it is embedded.

58 Or, even more pointedly: 'All aesthetic categories must be defined both in terms of their relation to the world and in terms of art's repudiation of that world' (Adorno 1999: 138).

59 The three earlier collaborations between Mann and Alton were *T-Men* (1947), *Raw Deal* (1948) and *He Walked by Night* (1948).

60 In Jean-Pierre Telotte's words, the photograph 'is a trope for the film itself [. . .]. In privileging the film apparatus and its techniques [. . .] *Call Northside 777* testifies to film's ability to transmit reality and to the documentary *noir*'s special power to provide a normally unavailable and telling vantage on our world. Through such technical prowess, we are assured, films can provide the images we *need* to see, those that might hold a key to our own truth' (Telotte 1989: 148–9). This reading (film's generic ability to provide 'fictional truths') should be radicalized, and in the case of Hathaway's film the ultimate reliance of the 'jigsaw narrative' on a fictional piece of truth should be pinned against the film's documentary realism as well as his ideological content.

61 Above all, one should focus on the scene of the execution of Brown's older accomplice with the hearing aid: Before the gangsters open fire with their machine guns, Brown takes off the hearing aid of the old man and all of a sudden the sound disappears diegetically, as if we were forced to experience the scene from the old man's perspective. Brown's act thus implies a sudden shift to a subjective perspective which is enhanced by the flashes of light from the machine guns, acquiring an almost surreal formal value. What strikes us is the rapid, seamless passage from objectivity to a subjective shot, as if there was no difference between them.

62 See for instance Frank Krutnik's and Steven Cohan's otherwise compelling readings of the film (Krutnik 1991: 147–54; Cohan 1997: 39–49).

63 I agree with Jeanine Basinger (2007: 60) that *Side Street* should be re-evaluated in respect of some of Mann's more acclaimed works such as, especially, the stylish *T-Men* (1947) and *Raw Deal* (1948), both made with cinematographer John Alton.

64 With regard to the psychoanalytic tension of the film, it is worth noting that the most tense and indeed imaginative part is the one where the kidnapper sleeps with one eye open in the desert, in order to deter his two prisoners from running away at night. In the wonderful ambiguity thus created (is he asleep or awake? shall they attempt to run away?) resides the mystery of the Lacanian gaze: It exists as a potential look, an empty gaze that looks back at us all the time.

2

Critical Theory's dialectical dilemma

Horkheimer's method

The term 'speculation' is at the heart of early Critical Theory's anti-empiricist and anti-dogmatic stance. It is through the speculative and therefore dialectical emphasis on cognition that Max Horkheimer and the first generation of critical theorists attempted to connect philosophy with the social sciences, challenging positivism as the 'religion of facts' as well as any doctrine asserting metaphysical closure. It is worth reminding ourselves that the term speculation comes from the Latin word *speculum*, meaning mirror, that is, reflection. It is a word, therefore, that one would not be mistaken to associate directly with the art of cinema, since the latter constitutes the most blatant form of artistic reflection. The idea that all reality, whether subject or object, reason or matter, is caught in a mirroring or reflective relationship is constitutive of the very nature of cinema as well as of Critical Theory. In both, to exist something must be mediated, caught in a web-like network of connections, which ultimately dethrones any presumption of autonomy. On the contrary, the acceptance of the 'givenness' of things, 'reality as it is', has always been a distinctly conservative axiom. Dialectics is first and foremost the 'art' of understanding the intricately mediated nature of the relation between subjectivity and objectivity, thought and the object of thought. Dialectical reasoning implies learning to appreciate historically bound social relations and their products by going back and forth between the knowing subject and the object of knowledge, in a movement that deeply affects any pre-constituted understanding of either. In dialectics, then, the identity of a given element is always given in connection with that of another that opposes it, and it is only through such opposition that the notion of reality comes into being. The progressive, emancipatory dimension of this understanding of dialectics was concisely conjured up by Herbert Marcuse in his 1940 book *Reason and Revolution*: 'the real field of knowledge is not the given facts about things as they are, but the critical evaluation of them as a prelude to passing beyond their given form' (Marcuse 1973: 145). Of course, the centrality of the Hegelian notion of mediation (*Vermittlung*) in Critical Theory is always counterbalanced by a strong warning against the hypostatization of mediation itself into instrumental rationality. Reason as medium can easily forsake its dialectical task and rigidify into mere instrument of tyranny, as Adorno and Horkheimer tell us so purposefully in *Dialectic of Enlightenment*. From their point of view, one must therefore distinguish between dialectics as a means of domination and dialectics as a critique of such domination. In this first case, reason turns irrational, while in the second it fulfils its potential.

Horkheimer was the thinker who moulded the Institute of Social Research in Frankfurt according to an original intellectual venture that was later captured by the name Critical Theory.[1] Theodor Adorno, a friend of Horkheimer since the 1920s and a fellow-Marxist, joined the institute only in 1938, having opted first for a career as a composer and then, with more success, as an academic. The innovative pledge carried by Horkheimer's project resided in the attempt to bring both Marxist and idealist traditions into dialogue with the social sciences so as to transform the former's metaphysical leanings into a set of propositions to be tested morally and empirically. The social sciences, however, were never particularly attractive to Adorno, who, under the influence of Walter Benjamin since the late 1920s, started using Marxism more as a tool to investigate philosophical and aesthetic matters than to directly analyse society (see Buck-Morss 1977: 20–3).

In his inaugural address as director of the Institute for Social Research in 1931, Horkheimer presented his method as a 'continuous, dialectical penetration of philosophical theory and specialized scientific praxis' (Horkheimer 1995: 9). The emphasis on critical theoretical analysis already signalled a considerable methodological shift within the institute which – having gained independence in 1923 under Felix Weil (a student of Karl Korsch) and then developed through the 1920s under the directorship of Carl Grünberg – had until that moment engaged solely in empirical sociopolitical research, pushing for the socialist agenda. Against the background of the orthodox Marxist belief in the objectivity of historical development, then, Horkheimer brought in a new concern with subjectivity and consequently a new method of enquiry:

> This conception – according to which the individual researcher must view philosophy as a perhaps pleasant but scientifically fruitless enterprise (because not subject to experimental control), while philosophers, by

> contrasts, are emancipated from the individual researcher because they think they cannot wait for the latter before announcing their wide-ranging conclusions – is currently being supplanted by the idea of a continuous, dialectical penetration and development of philosophical theory and specialized scientific praxis. (Horkheimer 1995: 9)

Horkheimer was keen to marry the existing strands of empirical work carried out by the various members of the institute with a materialist account of the critique of reason which would involve the study of its limits and conditions of existence. In short, he was hoping to found an interdisciplinary social science, 'critical' instead of merely 'descriptive' or 'contemplative', aimed at emancipation and informed by a non-dogmatic dialectical analysis of social relations. While renouncing metaphysics and economic reductionism, in his work of the 1930s Horkheimer nevertheless asserted the gap between true and false consciousness, placing thought firmly within finitude, its role defined by its dependence on changing historical conditions:

> Having confidence in rigorous, conscientious thinking on the one hand, and being aware of the conditionedness of the content and structure of cognition on the other – far from being mutually exclusive, both attitudes are necessarily of a piece. The fact that reason can never be certain of its perpetuity; or that knowledge is secure within a given time frame, yet is never so for all time; or even the fact that the stipulation of temporal contingency applies to the very body of knowledge from which it is derived – this paradox does not annul the truth of the claim itself. Rather, it is of the very essence of authentic knowledge never to be settled once and for all. This is perhaps the most profound insight of all dialectical philosophy. (Horkheimer 1995: 362)

What we should retain in Horkheimer's early account of Critical Theory is precisely its dialectical imprimatur. As the dominant social sciences were increasingly modelling themselves after the natural sciences, thus embracing a positivistic method that allegedly gave them the right to monitor and manage social as well as economic variables, Horkheimer attempted to fashion a theory whose primary task was to challenge these purportedly neutral perspectives. While keeping faith with the Marxian framework of political–economic critique of society, his project placed itself fully *within* the dynamic process of sociocultural synthesis it aimed to comprehend and criticize. Against classical philosophy, Horkheimer argued that it would be impossible to comprehend the dynamic structures of thought without forcing thought through socio-historical enquiries. Against the dominant trends in social science (the 'long, boring, individual studies that split up into a thousand partial questions, culminating in a chaos of countless enclaves of specialists' (Horkheimer 1995: 9)), he called for a dialectical approach centred on the materialist critique of reason. The immediate aim was to unmask the abstractions of traditional theory, which in his view were closely connected with social injustice and suffering.[2]

The Kantian subtext

If Marxism undoubtedly represented the main philosophical concern for early Critical Theory, to the extent that a number of commentators have debated whether the institute was insufficiently or excessively Marxist,[3] the other key influence was German idealism, and specifically Kant's epistemological thought. Although less interested in philosophical problems per se than Adorno, Horkheimer's insistence on the necessity of a speculative method of investigation is central to his thought. As such, it derives from Hegelian dialectics as well as from Kant's theory of knowledge as developed in the first *Critique* (the *Critique of Pure Reason*), in so far as Kant's explicit project was that of delimiting the epistemic application of reason to knowledge. Kant was indeed a significant influence on Horkheimer's formation since his philosophical apprenticeship, which took place under the supervision of neo-Kantian philosopher Hans Cornelius. It is no surprise that he opened his first address as Director of the Institute with a reference to Kant as the first thinker to have tried to link *reason* as autonomous and eternal subjective property with *knowledge* as empirical socializing tool. Following from this, for Horkheimer, the importance of Hegel lied in rendering explicit the social dimension of Kant's thought by liberating the subject from 'the fetters of introspection' (Horkheimer 1995: 2) and inserting it fully within the overarching dialectical logic of history. Indeed, the resonance of Hegel's thought on Horkheimer has to do first and foremost with Horkheimer's own attempt to historicize and socialize philosophy ('idealism thus became social philosophy with Hegel' (p. 3)). What Horkheimer laments when discussing his contemporary philosophical scene (in 1931) is the abandonment of that project of mediation between free consciousness and empirical life that he sees as reaching its apex with Hegel's philosophy of history. His view of social philosophy, however, is ultimately divorced from Hegel's in that it affirms not an ontology or a metaphysics but the ever-shifting character of theoretical knowledge under the stimuli of 'the most precise scientific methods' (p. 9). The emphasis is clearly laid on a constant revision and refinement of philosophical questions, which must 'become integrated into the empirical research process' (p. 10).

Although Horkheimer's texts from the 1930s never forsake independent philosophical work, what emerges as central there is the recommendation to engage in relentless empirical research. At the end of his opening address, in fact, Horkheimer refers explicitly to the need for acquiring material of study such as statistics and reports, while using survey questionnaires as methods of enquiry.

Undoubtedly, all this concern with the primacy of material reality and empirical research seems at odds with Kant's postulation of the transcendental constitution of knowledge, that is, the conviction that any empirical knowledge of reality is ultimately a mere form of representation rooted in ahistorical consciousness intended as the domain of transcendental, absolute and 'pure' ideas. In Horkheimer's essay 'On the Problem of Truth', Kant's dualistic concern with empirical existence and metaphysics is identified as a mark of his greatness but also of the unresolved idealistic contradiction carried by his thought (see Horkheimer 1995: 179–80). Hegel, on the other hand, is seen as making a step forward from Kant's relativistic formalism. The image Horkheimer conjures up in this respect is a rather suggestive one: With Hegel, he tells us, the conditional nature of any concrete knowledge does not 'simply fall through the sieve in the sifting out of pure knowledge' (p. 184). In other words, Hegel retains the basic dualism (the systemic contradiction) of Kant's philosophy but shifts the emphasis away from any relativizing scepticism; he does so by transforming the unknowable character of Kant's realm of pure ideas into an instance of negativity that inheres in every limited and transitory conception of reality, without making the latter less concrete. It is on account of this move away from the transcendental source of Kant's philosophy that 'Hegel does not need to make a fetish out of an isolated concept like duty' (pp. .184–5). As far as Kant's concept of morality is concerned, Horkheimer consistently discards it as nothing other than a pious illusion, rejecting altogether any 'metaphysically grounded morality' (Horkheimer 1992: 44).

What I want to argue, however, is that in spite of its materialist criticism of Kant's philosophy, Horkheimer's advocated blend of theory and empirical research, which captures the very essence of Critical Theory, retains the formal structure and implicit limitations of Kant's transcendental theory of knowledge. This is already perceivable in the distance Horkheimer assumes towards Hegel immediately after praising him against Kant. What he rejects in Hegel – voicing, *in nuce*, the same line of criticism that Adorno will develop later – is the 'indifference to particular perceptions, ideas, and goals', originating in the 'hypostatization of conceptual structures', in the dogmatic reassurance that knowledge achieves its goal in grasping the unity of subject and object (Horkheimer 1995: 185). We should therefore keep in mind that, as underlined by Martin Jay (1996: 41), '[a]t the heart of Critical Theory was an aversion to closed philosophical systems', which in Horkheimer arguably originated both in his disillusionment with what he perceived as the dogmatic turn of Marxism, and in the early influence from thinkers like Kant and, on a different level, Schopenhauer. Horkheimer sees Hegel as setting up an innovative dialectical method which, however, is eventually beset by a dogmatism derived from the idealistic legacy of his thought. It is revealing that in the previously mentioned essay, he refers twice, very critically, to the passage of the *Phenomenology of Spirit* where Hegel asserts the perfect correspondence between notion and object, claiming that 'knowledge no longer needs to go beyond itself' (Horkheimer 1995: 185 and 187). To contrast the Hegelian thesis of the identity of thought and object, which he liquidates as a metaphysical legend highly representative of bourgeois ideology (in the same manner as, a few years later, he will repeat with Adorno),[4] Horkheimer presents an open-ended materialistic account of the dialectic which he specifies as follows:

> Materialism, on the other hand, insists that objective reality is not identical with man's thought and can never be merged into it. As much as thought in its own element seeks to copy the life of the object and adapt itself to it, thought is never simultaneously the object thought about, unless in self-observation and reflection – and not even there. To conceptualize a defect is therefore not to transcend it; concepts and theories constitute one moment of its reification, a prerequisite to the proper procedure, which as it progresses is constantly redefined, adapted, and improved. (Horkheimer 1995: 189)

Similarly, in his 1932 piece 'Hegel and Metaphysics', he had expressed his repudiation of Hegel's ontological claims on the ground that Spirit 'may not recognize itself either in nature or in history, because even if the spirit is not a questionable abstraction, it would not be identical with reality' (in Jay 1996: 47). To the expert critical eye, the above excerpts will have sounded strikingly reminiscent of Adorno's oft-rehearsed passages on the 'preponderance of the object', which is *the* crucial notion for his entire theoretical edifice – and, indeed, for Critical Theory, in so far as it advocates the principle of a negative (i.e. non-identitarian) brand of dialectical materialism. Like Adorno later, Horkheimer here defends the non-subsumable and non-identifiable quality of the object of thought, of matter as such, against the tendencies of 'an era which in its hopelessness tries to make everything into a fetish, even the abstract business of understanding' (Horkheimer 1995: 193).

It is here that we should locate the Kantian reference that (more or less secretly) sustains Adorno's thought and, more generally, all Critical Theory.[5]

The elementary principle of the negative dialectic already clearly anticipated in Horkheimer's writings of the 1930s emerges rather seamlessly, at least in its form, from the Kantian 'regulative idea', the original insight that any empirical knowledge of the structure of the world is based on the awareness of the limitation of thought. Such limitation, as is well known, is guaranteed in Kant by the reference to the unknowable *Ding as Sich* (the Thing in Itself). The logic of the 'preponderance of the object' and that of the *Ding as Sich* are thus closely related, in view of the fact that, in both, the cognitive process is safeguarded and supported by the reference to what defies it radically. Consider for example the following passage from Adorno's *Negative Dialectics*, where the dialectic is defined precisely in non-identitarian terms: 'The analysis of the object is tangential to the rules of thinking. Thought need not be content with its own legality; without abandoning it, we can think against our thought, and if it were possible to define dialectics, this would be a definition worth suggesting' (Adorno 2000: 141). This 'thinking against thought' – against the identitarian/ideological penchant of instrumental reason – is of course the central dialectical problem at stake. How is it possible to think against thought without abandoning thought? Adorno's answer is: Only by positing the existence of an object that constantly defies thought, that is, that forces thought to think against its own tendency to identify, to appropriate the object itself. In other words, we are back to Kant's fundamental principle of cognition, though here the non-identifiable object allegedly produces a (not better specified) 'liberation of thought'.

Although Critical Theory chides any transcendental illusion in the same manner as Kant chided the chimera of the constitutive and dogmatic existence of God, similarly to Kant the critical theorists unwittingly (and often purporting to do the opposite) hold on to the transcendental dimension as one that, in Kant's own words (referring to the *idea* of God), 'completes and crowns the whole of human knowledge' (Kant 1933: 531). For Kant, transcendental ideas have a regulative use which is good and proper, in so far as they establish the unity of knowledge and systematic nature of thinking. For critical theorists such as Horkheimer and Adorno, real knowledge and truth, given their changing historical conditions, depend on the reference to an objective, material limit to knowledge and truth. In one of Horkheimer's most significant essays of the 1930s, 'Materialism and Metaphysics', we find the following passage, which, again, could easily be mistaken for a passage from Adorno's *Negative Dialectics*: 'Materialism, on the contrary [against metaphysics], maintains the irreducible tension between concept and object and thus has a critical weapon of defense against belief in the infinity of the mind' (Horkheimer 1992: 28). In both Adorno and Horkheimer, materialism essentially 'challenges every claim to the autonomy of thought' (Horkheimer 1992: 32).

Already with Horkheimer's founding work of the 1930s, then, it is clear that the attempted synthesis of Marxism and German idealism was going to be based on the Kantian endorsement, though from a materialistic angle, of the fundamental discrepancy between knowledge and its object, which in turn was to lead to embracing a non-dogmatic Marxist stance. As succinctly put by Fred Rush:

> Critical Theory dissents from some specific core elements of this Kantian picture, but it remains allied to the self-reflective critical model according to which there is never equivalence between thought and its object – that is, the concept of experience still plays a central philosophical role in Critical Theory. (Rush 2004: 10)

Although Horkheimer repeatedly criticized Kant for overstating the function of subjectivity and thereby remaining stuck within the boundaries of bourgeois philosophy, his own (Horkheimer's) materialist theory of society profoundly relied on that basic incongruity between reason and its object which was at the heart of Kant's epistemological enquiry, and was to become the theoretical catalyst of Adorno's critique of instrumental reason. Horkheimer's rejection of 'vulgar Marxist' materialism (which included his rejection of the a priori, objective primacy of the economy), coupled with his dismissal of materialist relativism (positivism), lead him to embrace a dialectical materialism which was essentially *critical*. Unwilling and unable to provide ontological platforms for emancipation, this early, dialectical and materialist Critical Theory has often been depicted as a 'by-product of the theoretical innovations undertaken by Georg Lukács and Karl Korsch in the early twenties' (Brommer 1994: 77) – in so far as they also had promoted a dialectical and materialist critique of economic reductionism and theoretical teleology – though different from theirs in endorsing the principle of non-identity between subject and object. As early as 1933, in the essay 'Materialism and Morality', Horkheimer wrote that the new theory should be 'not a metaphysics of history but rather a changing image of the world, evolving in relation to the practical efforts toward its improvement', while offering 'no clear prognosis of historical development' (Horkheimer 1995: 44).

Hegel: Contradiction (not) resolved

As anticipated, Horkheimer's specific recipe for leaving Western metaphysics behind was the amalgamation of philosophy and socio-scientific research. This effectively implied a return to the main concern of the Left Hegelian of the 1840s, despite the awareness of a number of crucial events such as, especially, the (by then already perceived as) failed outcome of the proletarian revolution. In respect of the above parallel, Martin Jay tends to elucidate the transcendental dimension of Critical Theory precisely in terms of the changed historical situation:

> Thus, it might be said of the first generation of critical theorists in the 1840s that theirs was an 'immanent' critique of society based on the existence of a real historical 'subject'. By the time of its renaissance in the twentieth century, Critical Theory was being increasingly forced into a position of 'transcendence' by the withering away of the revolutionary working class. (Jay 1996: 43)

Although perfectly reasonable, Jay's argument risks losing sight of the key theoretical stakes involved in Critical Theory's 'transcendental (re)turn'. This is because the rejection of Hegel's 'identity thesis' as characteristic of a somewhat monstrous panlogicism – a closed metaphysical system where the dialectic eventually erases itself by setting up a monolithic conceptual totality – should be read in the first instance as a return to Kant's dualistic impasse and, in the second (crucial) instance, as a failure to fully comprehend the measure of Hegel's own dialectical recasting of such impasse as always-already constitutive of reality itself. Placing Hegel's Spirit or Logic on the same essentialist level as Plato's Ideas or Kant's universal moral command, in so far as these figures were supposedly guilty of purging human existence of its ineliminable contingency, Horkheimer and Critical Theory effectively missed the paradox embodied by Hegel's notion of totality. What we find in the latter is nothing but the endorsement of contingency, that is to say of the radical, foundational presence of negativity within both substance (the self-deployment of the dialectic) and subject (qua 'empty signifier', to say it with Lacan). In fact, all major leftist criticisms of Hegel, at least in the twentieth century, have as a rule insisted on the supposed closure of his system, missing Hegel's elementary dialectical insight into how every external opposition is rooted in *immanent self-contradiction*.

When, for instance, at the beginning of the 'Doctrine of Essence' in the *Science of Logic* Hegel claims that knowledge finds itself as *essence* by way of a recollection [*Erinnerung*], that is to say an inward movement that looks back towards the background of being, trying to penetrate the immediacy in which being is enveloped, he is beginning to assert the basic retroactive mechanism of his dialectic. The whole point is that the essence of being is not outside being, but the self-mediation of being which at the end of the dialectical process arrives at its identity with an utterly ephemeral appearance. As such, reflection embodies the paradox of a 'movement of becoming and transition that remains internal to it [to essence]' (Hegel 1969: 399), ultimately revealing nothing but the self-difference of essence itself. Essence is unravelled via the notion of *reflection*, which is asserted as the power of mediation pure and simple. However, if there is a presupposed immediacy of essence, then there must be reflection qua other of immediacy, external to it. The externalizing movement of reflection – which, as anticipated, ends up being an inward, self-related movement – is explained by Hegel through the well-known figures of *positing reflection*, *external reflection* and *determining reflection*, whereby essence has to go through the illusion of its detached, transcendent externality in order to fall back upon itself as a decentred, self-split entity. Particularly important is the passage from *external* to *determining* reflection, where Hegel dismantles the primacy of the given over reflection – how? By showing that reflection's relation to an other is always-already reflection's own self-relation. Put differently, essence qua other is revealed to be the kernel of reflection. The distance between reflection and the externally given essence collapses into reflection's determinations, thus uncovering how the problem of the 'true meaning' of essence is strictly speaking a false problem, inasmuch as it coincides with the problem incarnated by determinate reflection itself, that is, with the problem of how reflection attempts to impose a determinate meaning over essence. Herein resides the crucial difference between Adorno's Hegelianism and Hegel. Adorno understands the overcoming of external reflection as a somewhat simplified return to positing reflection, thus 'denouncing' the subjective gesture of positing substance, and consequently theorizing the preponderance of the object over subjective positing. With Hegel's determining reflection, however, we become aware of the fact that the presupposed independence of essence was posited by reflection itself *in a thoroughly contingent gesture*.

The same triadic movement is repeated in the subsequent determination of the properties of essence (essentialities) as identity, difference and contradiction: 'Essence is at first, simple self-relation, pure *identity*'; secondly, however, it discovers *difference* in the form of an external opposition; then, crucially, this external opposition is reflected back into the very ground of essence, as the self-fracture within essence ('Thirdly, as *contradiction*, the opposition is reflected into itself and withdraws into its *ground*', p. 409). Essence, then, discovers itself to be constitutively traversed by contradiction, which means that external opposition (conflict, antagonism with another object) was always-already *essential*, inward-looking, 'bending back', that is, immanent to essence itself. It is because of this return of difference within identity that for Hegel it is impossible to distinguish between the inner developmental potential of a given identity and the oppositional pressure exerted by external circumstances: Rather than being opposed to each other, the two forces are dialectically indistinguishable; they would not exist without strict correlation to the other. For instance, the birth and development of a given political movement that seizes power in a given country is correlative to, and ultimately overlaps with, the historical conditions qua external antagonism. What is perceived as a gap, a border, or more explicitly an obstacle that thwarts the self-development of the political movement, falls back upon itself as the very dynamic 'engine' of the movement itself, the self-division of identity on account of which, paradoxically, we have a certain identity. And since the inner potential of the political movement, ultimately, can only 'posit itself' – that is, measure itself by its own standards, tautologically – at the cost of endorsing its founding negativity ('the movement X is the movement X'), this means that it cannot be thoroughly explained through context alone (external pressure). As we shall see, it is precisely at this radically contingent conjuncture where the essence of a thing is, as it were, both inside and outside itself (both its inner potential and its external impediment), that the Hegelian subject comes in, accomplishing its purely formal act which retroactively converts the contingency of the situation into necessity – in our example, it retroactively frames the historical context as necessarily overdetermined by the victorious political movement. In fact, we should specify that there is no such thing as a historical context without a founding act or decision (implicitly political) that sustains the specific configuration of that context. Every context is the result of the drawing of a line that establishes the presence of a boundary, thus deciding what is to be included and excluded from that context. Put differently, every reference to context is ideological.

The redoubling, and at the same time subjectless movement of the dialectic, is asserted again and again throughout the first two books of the 'objective' *Logic* (the 'Doctrine of Being' and the 'Doctrine of Essence'). Its mechanism suggests the usual 'odd' coincidence of movement and inertia, for the effort to build, advance and establish the dialectical self-deployment of substance is always-already matched by the inherence of an ontological deadlock which stalls the impetus to move forward, producing a situation reminiscent of the standard angst-ridden nightmare scene where we see ourselves running *surplace* – attempting to run away while remaining stuck to the same spot.[6] From this angle, we should insist that the hindrance posed by external reflection – whereby essence can only be grasped as a warped external reflection and not directly for what it is – is not merely resolved, subsumed through the mediating activity. Rather, Hegel's solution is that of unveiling the inconsistency pertaining to the logic of external reflection itself. The posited essence qua unattainable externality of the thing is revealed to consist of the necessarily distorted determinations of reflection and nothing else. Essence does not possess itself fully, it does not have an external consistency of its own, detached from reflection; on the contrary, it is ontologically inconsistent, that is, it exists only in relation to its determinate reflections. Thus, what takes place in the passage from external reflection to determining reflection is a redoubling move which reveals the immanent reflexive determination of essence, the fact that essence can only be conceived as an entity embodying self-relating negativity. As Hegel puts it (before giving a long series of examples):

> for external reflection, it is a simple consideration that, in the first place, the positive is not an immediately identical, but on the one hand it is an opposite to a negative, having meaning only in this relation, so that the negative itself is contained *in its* notion; on the other hand, that it is in its own self the self-related negation of mere positedness or the negative, is therefore itself *absolute negation* within itself. (Hegel 1969: 436)

It is for this reason that Hegel can claim that '[r]eflection is *the showing of the illusory being of essence within essence itself*' (p. 409). This illusory showing, or evanescent appearance, is ultimately what essence is, namely a phenomenon through which the essential negativity or inconsistency of substance shines.

The overarching Hegelian point is that the force of the negative (contradiction) that allows for the self-development of the given potential of a particular situation is always-already inscribed in the totality of the relations between that particular situation and the external conditions in which it finds itself. In the chapter on 'Ground', in the 'Logic of Essence', Hegel applies the usual dialectical insight according to which the difference between two opposites is reflected back into the inherent 'self-difference' of one of the two terms. In this case, the difference between ground (a given foundational element) and its conditions (whatever it is that this ground 'grounds', i.e. contains and supports) is inherent to ground, inasmuch as the latter, in its grounding function, coincides with its relation to its grounded conditions. This is exactly what 'complete ground' (the final stage of the dialectical development of ground into 'formal' and 'real' ground) stands for: Not a higher and more complete synthesis of ground and conditions, but the identity between ground and a part of the grounded content, *in so far as only through such identity can ground exercise its grounding function*. Thus, far from representing an all-comprehensive, pacifying synthetic unit, the notion of ground can only be given as both grounding and inherently contradictory, for in order to exercise its grounding function, it has to apply itself as a distortion of the very notion of ground qua substrate.[7] Because of this definition of ground, the thing or fact that emerges from it is both *unconditioned* and *groundless*, as Hegel tells us at the end of the chapter:

> Ground, therefore, does not remain behind as something distinct from the grounded, but the truth of grounding is that in it ground is united with itself, so that its reflection into another is its reflection into itself. Consequently, the fact is not only the *unconditioned* but also the *groundless*, and it emerges from ground only in so far as ground has '*fallen to the ground*' and ceased to be ground: it emerges from the groundless, that is, from its own essential negativity or pure form. (Hegel 1969: 478)

Through the vanishing of the dialectical process of mediation, the fact emerges as unconditioned, that is to say, as something seemingly immediate and self-identical. But it also emerges as groundless, since the ground has sublated itself, 'fallen to the ground'; that is to say, it has imploded into its inherent distortion or groundlessness. Simply put, then, the emergence of reality in its essential immediacy is strictly correlative to the vanishing of ground qua external support. This paradox has to be taken literally: Ground 'does its job' of grounding reality, thus allowing it to emerge in the guise of a consistent entity, by vanishing (or morphing) into a particular relation with its conditions. Ground and conditions mediate themselves to the extent that, as Hegel puts it concisely, '[t]he emergence into Existence is therefore immediate in such a manner that it is mediated only by the vanishing of mediation' (p. 477). What confers consistency upon life is precisely an invisible, tautological gesture of grounding whereby ground grounds itself in a specific relation with its conditions.

A nice exemplification of this logic of ground comes from cinema: Is not editing, the splicing together of different shots, precisely the epitome of the invisible, vanishing function of ground which presents us with a consistent, self-sufficient narrative construct? Like Hegel's complete ground, editing can only manifest itself in a unique conjuncture with what it supports, namely the various shots which make up a particular film. In itself, editing is nothing but self-relating negativity. However, to fulfil its grounding or bonding function, editing must appear and then vanish, in other words, it must appear for what it always was, namely a concretion of the negative itself. Editing is nothing but the self-fracture of film qua fiction, and as such *it is essential*, the site of an infinite virtuality that is glued to the making of cinematic meaning. The fact that for meaning to emerge, this virtual kernel has to be compressed within the imperceptible interstitial breaks between shots, only attests to editing's fundamental role, while the force of its presence can be measured through the specific 'determination' taken by the narrative. Editing thus discloses the binary logic of film-making. Cinema is not just a field antagonized by a multitude of contents relating to a transcendental and constitutively lost Truth. It is, first and foremost, a field antagonized by its own self-generated impediment, the structuring fracture separating its fictional status from the negative underside concealed by the editing process. Editing is thus a Hegelian concept through and through; its speculative significance has to do with the fact that the ultimate truth about film has to be looked for in film's relation with the negativity from which its meaning springs forth, a negativity that is inscribed in the cinematic field as its intrinsic self-division.

And, *mutatis mutandi*, the same holds for Hegel's conceptualization of the logic through which reality itself comes into existence. Hegel's speculative idealism, as we have seen, undermines the supposition (which Adorno's brand of critical theory, despite its dialectical imprimatur, avows) that the object, reality in its material evidence, exists before the intervention of reflection, and consequently retains a certain priority over thought. It asserts that the constitution of reality is *consubstantial* with the dialectical self-development of knowledge. Another way of putting this is that the forms of thought cannot be understood as separate from their contents, since they provide the necessary relational frameworks within which contents can be grasped. Hegel's central thesis is that subject and object, thought and reality, cannot be conceived as detached, for each constitutes itself through the other, to the extent that, at a fundamental level, they coincide as embodiments of negativity (the epistemological limit *is* the ontological deadlock; that is to say, the constitutive inadequacy of thought vis-à-vis reality *is, embodies*, reality's own fundamental meaninglessness, its utterly contingent status). The impasse of knowledge is therefore constitutive of the object of knowledge too. Far from affirming the ultimate freedom and autonomy of thought as the mediating agent who 'creates the world' (far from concluding that the dialectical process implies the triumph of the Notion, or Absolute Spirit, over the object), Hegelian speculative idealism asserts that every meaningful concretion of reality is erected upon a negative foundation which is at the same time subjective and objective. We should not forget that at the end of the dialectical process, when the contingent openness of reality is fully mediated into necessity, we are always thrown back against the essential inconsistency that characterizes the edifice of reality itself.

The logic behind the constitutive amalgamation of reflection and substance can be further clarified by considering the speculative coincidence of the Hegelian couple 'in itself' and 'for itself'. The passage from 'in itself' (inner essence qua potential) to 'for itself' (actualized potential) does not account for a linear progression and final actualization of, say, a given identity (becoming aware of the potential, then testing it against the external circumstances, planning its actualization, and executing it when the external conditions 'are right') but hinges on the recognition that the two overlap, that they are the same thing (as Hegel often puts it, something is 'in and for itself'). As anticipated, the inner potential or true nature of a thing ultimately coincides with the nature of its actualization in the external circumstances, and vice versa (the circumstances are always-already the result of a certain potential). Again, the radical dimension of this claim cannot be ignored, as it implies that a given potentiality (for political change, for instance) either expresses itself *where it always-already belongs*, that is, in the social arena, or it simply does not exist, it is a mere chimera. The illusion dispelled by dialectical reflection concerns the assumption of the presence of an external obstacle thwarting a given potential, hindering its self-realization; contrary to the logic sustaining this illusion, the Hegelian lesson is that a given potential exists only as consubstantial, or speculatively identical with, the external obstacle/condition itself. From this, it follows that the coincidence between 'in- and for-itself' can only be predicated upon the primacy of negativity.

Notwithstanding such primacy, it would of course be wrong to infer that the Hegelian system corresponds in the final analysis, to the simple endorsement of the negative. The crucial issue rests on how we understand the coincidence of negativity and totality (or contingency and necessity). This seemingly oxymoronic coincidence is explicitly put forward, for instance, when Hegel discusses the 'law of contradiction' (see Hegel 1969: 439–43). There he begins by claiming that contradiction should be grasped as a law, in so far as 'the truth and the essential nature of things' is best expressed by the law that '*everything is inherently contradictory*'. He then proceeds to assert that contradiction, against what is assumed by ordinary thinking, which tends to regard it as a contingency or abnormality, is a more essential, a more profound determination than identity, for it is 'the root of all movement and vitality', or 'the principle of all self-movement'. Here Hegel specifies that this self-movement 'consists solely in an exhibition of it [of the negative]'. The subtlety of this reasoning, which is at the heart of Hegel's understanding of the self-determining character of knowledge as presented in the *Science of Logic*, is evidenced as follows: 'Something moves, not because at one moment it is here and at another there, but because at one moment it is here and not here, because in this "here", it at once is and is not'. Self-movement, in other words, is an '*instinctive urge*' originating in the self-contained deficiency of a finite being – a finite being, in other words, is always self-split, not whole. Having restated the foundational role of negativity and contradiction, Hegel then embarks on a sophisticated analysis of the latter's role in speculative thinking. What he now underlines is the inevitability for reflection to contain both contradictions and their resolution, which he repeatedly defines as a 'negative unity':

> Now the thing, the subject, the Notion, is just this negative unity itself; it is inherently self-contradictory, but it is no less the *contradiction resolved*: it is the *ground* that contains and supports its determinations. The thing, subject, or Notion, as reflected into itself in its sphere, is its resolved contradiction, but its entire sphere is again also *determinate, different*; it is thus a finite sphere and this means a *contradictory* one. It is not itself the resolution of this higher contradiction but has a higher sphere for its negative unity, for its ground. Finite things, therefore, in their indifferent multiplicity are simply this, to be contradictory and *disrupted within themselves and to return into their ground*. (Hegel 1969: 442–3)

To say that a finite being is 'inherently self-contradictory, but it is no less the *contradiction resolved*', does not mean, of course, that the contradiction disappears, but rather implies the recasting of contradiction as the paradoxical *ground* of that finite being. The substrate of our finitude is not a solid ground but the infinitely fragile moment where contradiction becomes aware of its grounding role, of the fact that there is no other ground apart from itself. The key to understanding Hegel's dialectic lies in this acknowledgement that the very moment the contradiction seems to be dissolved, it reappears as the very constitutive element of this resolution: 'The resolved contradiction is therefore ground, essence as unity of the positive and negative. [. . .] Opposition and its contradiction is, therefore, in ground as much abolished as preserved' (p. 435). Hegel continues from there by introducing the issue of the relation between finite being and absolute, or contingency and necessity. The passage from contingent being to absolutely necessary being, he claims, is substantiated by the fact that being 'is only in a state of collapse and is inherently self-contradictory'. It is impossible, Hegel tells us, merely *to infer* the absolute from consistent, finite things. Instead, 'the truth is that the absolute is, because the finite is the inherently self-contradictory opposition, because it is *not*. [. . .] the non-being of the finite is the being of the absolute'. This conclusion confirms the Hegelian thesis of the coincidence of finite and infinite: As anticipated, the infinite for Hegel is not to be found in an endless series of events constantly overcoming each other (the quantitative dimension of infinity, which he calls 'bad' or 'spurious') but in the qualitative event that structures a potentially infinite series, the intervention that puts a limit to the spuriously infinite, futile complexity of finite reality in order to allow it to thrive in its properly infinite complexity.[8] Again, the thesis advanced by Hegel's speculative idealism is this: The object of our knowledge, reality itself, is not something detached from our knowledge, from our perception of it, but dialectically interconnected with it, to such an extent that it is the finite imperfection of our knowledge that grounds, that is, sets up, reality in its infinite richness.

Katrin Pahl (2011) has recently highlighted this paradoxical logic apropos the role of despair in Hegel's *Phenomenology of Spirit*, claiming that the laborious journey of the Hegelian consciousness is at once the cheerful construction of a teleological narrative and the crushing realization that every aspect of such *Bildung* is torture, the collapse of consciousness itself, its failure. The difficulty lies precisely in grasping the dialectical correlation between these two opposite dimensions of contingency and necessity, which in Hegel are truly inseparable, two sides of the same coin. While ultimately there is nothing but contingency and contradiction, that is to say nothing but an ontological 'crack' that affects everything and overlaps with the limitation of our knowledge, at the same time we are always embedded within a fixed constellation, an ideological context, a seemingly unbreakable chain of causality, a teleological narrative whose symbolic consistency threatens to deprive us of an authentically free choice. This concurrence of openness and closure, contingency and necessity, is the central paradox endorsed by Hegel – but how can such concurrence take place? It is precisely at this point that the Hegelian subject comes in (a subject, of course, to be intended not as a self-transparent, empirical individual, but as a self-contradictory, deeply inconsistent entity ultimately defined by its potential to endorse its own constitutive negativity). The actual closure of the context in which we operate, as already suggested in the discussion on ground, is nothing but the result of an act – *not* a conscious act, and for this reason a *free* act – through which the subject has delimited such context *in advance*, a decision where the presuppositions of our activity, of our being in the world, were posited. By 'positing the presuppositions' of its activity, the subject effectively steps into an uncharted territory where the emergence of meaning coincides with the *tautological* act of 'naming reality' – an act that retroactively impresses upon reality the mark of necessity.

To put it in terms of Lacan's 'logic of the signifier', this corresponds to the original moment of symbolization, the moment the signifier 'falls to the rank of the signified' (Lacan 2006: 594). What this means is that for reality to be 'sutured', and appear as a consistent symbolic whole, the signifier must, as it were, both name reality and range among the objects it names, like in tautological expressions such as 'God is God'. It is this tautological coincidence of signifier and signified – whereby the series of attributes of God (merciful, gracious, long-suffering, etc.) is supplemented *by the signifier itself* – that sutures the signifying chain. How? By generating an ineffable surplus of sense that cannot be fully captured by language, but is instead approached through fantasy, and represented by what Lacan calls *objet a*, the object-cause of desire.[9]

For Lacan, it is *objet a* qua 'embodiment of void', a supreme fascinating/fantasmatic lure, that 'holds up' reality for us, conferring upon it a semblance of consistency. And the emergence of *objet a* is the inevitable consequence of the intervention of the signifier in its symbolizing function.[10]

As for Lacan, then, for Hegel the subject's intervention amounts to a thoroughly *formal* act in which, as it were, the subject confronts the radical contingency of substance and consequently assumes responsibility (again, *formally* speaking) for the modality of its closure and signification. But despite such closure, the fracture at the core of reality cannot be eliminated, or sutured; rather, it remains inextricably enmeshed within our universe of sense in the form of those gaps where an act once inscribed itself, determining our context by 'drawing a line' between in and out, between the whole and its inherent exception, thereby transforming chaos into symbolic order, or into ideology. It is for this reason that every mediated whole in Hegel is not a return to homeostatic balance but is erected upon the volatile force of the negative – or, to put it differently, of an excluded exception. Consequently, the Hegelian freedom consists not in trying to directly or actively change the context, but in identifying the gaps where a formal decision or empty gesture to retroactively assume external reality *as our own making* can be re-inscribed. This freedom testifies to the always unfinished, indeed infinite dimension of Hegel's logic of relation. It is a logic that, to put in Kimberly Hutchings' concise definition, 'simultaneously speaks to the necessity and the inadequacy of the determinations of thought' (Hutchings 2006: 106).

From mimesis to utopia

In respect of what is argued above apropos Hegel, Horkheimer's endorsing of dialectics can be seen as inherently ambiguous and, for want of a better word, contradictory. While reclaiming the unity of the dialectical method that informed both German idealism and Marxism, he also retained traditional theory's axiom of the autonomous, self-standing moment in the object of thought, albeit not as a 'mere given'. On this aspect, Adorno will of course wholeheartedly radicalize Horkheimer's position, emphasizing the negative aspect of the subject–object dialectic, thereby inevitably attracting charges of relativism. By the 1940s, Horkheimer's driving, if half-hearted, defence of dialectical unity was replaced by the opposite emphasis on disunity and fragmentation (championed by Adorno) in the name of a recalcitrant rejection of any notion of harmony or spurious reconciliation. If it is true that initially Horkheimer pressed for a dialectical critique of empiricism, he did so while safeguarding the primacy of the object. More to the point, he argued that any object of social-scientific investigation retains a theoretical hubris derived from previous, historically situated interpretations of its meaning.[11] This insight, however, was not strong enough to lead to the assertion of the theoretical nature of the object, since in Horkheimer's view thought itself, in its specific historical contexts, depends on non-discursive stimuli. Conceptual mediation of the object is always-already mediated, conditioned by its relative historical forms; at the same time, and crucially, it is also deeply connected with non-discursive experience. The early Horkheimer effectively hesitates between a theory-laden understanding of dialectical cognition and a materialistic defence of the irreducible independence of the object, in so far as the latter is not only a predominant aspect of thought itself in its various historical concretions, but also rooted in the *hic et nunc* of experience. It is no surprise, then, that at the very beginning of *Dialectic of Enlightenment* we find the defence of the 'holiness of the *hic et nunc*' (Adorno and Horkheimer 1997: 10) qua inalienable somatic dimension of existence which has a chance to contrast the alienation brought about by the hypostatization of instrumental reason.

In the famous section 'Elements of Anti-Semitism' of the same book, the authors refer to one of the central and more ambiguous themes of their work, that of the mimesis between subject and object, human beings and nature; they do so by connecting it with the sense of smell, with the aim of demonstrating that '[i]n the bourgeois mode of production, the indelible mimetic heritage of all practical experience is consigned to oblivion' (p. 181). As the embodiment of a mimetic impulse which runs counter to civilization's alienating pressure, smell embodies

> the archetypal longing for the lower forms of existence, for direct unification with circumambient nature, with the earth and mud. Of all the senses, that of smell – which is attracted without objectifying – bears clearest witness to the urge to lose oneself in and become the 'other'. When we see we remain what we are; but when we smell we are taken over by otherness. Hence the sense of smell is considered a disgrace in civilization, the sign of lower social strata, lesser races and base animals. (p. 184)

Of course, Adorno and Horkheimer were perfectly aware that mimesis *per se* carries no direct emancipatory value. However, they criticized the Enlightenment for having progressively erased the individual's potential for authentic mimetic experience, which in turn has not merely eliminated mimesis, but reintroduced it through the backdoor (as in Freud's 'return of the repressed') in the guise of Fascism:

> The purpose of the Fascist formula, the ritual discipline, the uniforms, and the whole apparatus, which is at first sight irrational, is to allow mimetic

> behaviour. The carefully thought out symbols [. . .], the skulls and disguises, the barbaric drum beats [. . .] are simply the organized imitation of magic practices, the mimesis of mimesis. (pp. 184–5)

Or, as they put it in a well-known maxim: 'Civilization is the victory of society over nature which changes everything into pure nature' (p. 186). In *Eclipse of Reason*, published in 1947, Horkheimer confirms, in a more nuanced way, that 'the mimetic impulse is never really overcome. Men revert to it in a regressive and distorted form. Like the prudish censors of pornography, they abandon themselves to tabooed urges with hatred and contempt' (Horkheimer 2004: 79). In Adorno and Horkheimer's vision, then, anti-Semitism is nothing but the logical consequence of the progressive instrumentalization of reason which accompanies Western civilization since its dawn, and has its origin in the repression of authentic mimetic impulses. To put it as directly as possible, it is the result of man's renunciation of the (somewhat mythical) possibility of experiencing the inalienable otherness of the object, a tragic mistake that Adorno and Horkheimer detect already in Homer's *Odyssey* (see their famous analysis of the Sirens episode). This is to say that the defence of individual somatic experience qua mimetic 'loss of the self into the other' is strictly correlative to Critical Theory's avowal of the primacy of the object qua object of experience: The self should not merely incorporate the object into its (falsely) rational compass, but be given the opportunity of 'losing itself', throwing itself into the object *à fond perdu*, as Adorno put it in *Negative Dialectics*. The keystone of Critical Theory's theoretical framework is the ultimate belief in the inalienable, non-subsumable quality of the object of human knowledge.

The influence exerted by Freud's theory of libido on Adorno and Horkheimer's, but also Marcuse's, dialectical concept of the object, is all too evident, and yet the issue of mimesis ought to be explored precisely in relation to dialectics and not necessarily as a matter of libido and/or utopian happiness alone. In *Eclipse of Reason*, Horkheimer discussed how the mimetic strategies adopted by the child vis-à-vis the object of cognition, that is, the way in which the child learns through imitation rather than through the cold exercise of reason, are repressed by the process of socialization, only to threaten to return with a vengeance (see Horkheimer 2004: 78). No doubt, the general aim of Horkheimer, Adorno and Marcuse, as well as of other members of Frankfurt School, in relation to mimesis, is to unmask the deleterious features of instrumental rationality. As such, mimesis functions in Critical Theory as an element of resistance, at least in utopian terms (e.g. in art), against the universalization of the modern *ratio* – even when mentioned in its perverted guise, i.e. as a case of the 'return of the repressed'. In dialectical terms, mimesis embodies nothing less than the very impasse that allows

Adorno to put forward his notion of *negative* dialectics, the theory of the non-identity of subject and object. Mimesis is thus functional to the affirmation of the primacy of the object over instrumental reason, and as such it is regarded as closely connected with the faint yet ever-present hope in a liberated rationality, a reason that would no longer be *ratio*, no longer obliged to identify.

It is here that I propose another reading of mimesis, one that relinquishes the link with utopia and instead prompts for its identification with the very project of civilization it was supposed to criticize. If we return to Horkheimer's mention of the mimetic strategies of the child, which are later supposedly foregone by the instrumental use of reason, could we not argue, instead, that mimesis is *consubstantial* with every civilization, yet not in the sense that civilization imposes a perverted version of it, but because without the one we would not have the other? Is not the child's *imitative tactic* in dealing with the object not the very substance of any social order, the basic and fundamental ingredient of any rationally organized society? In this respect, the mimetic impulse is a properly dialectical notion, for it does not merely antagonize reason as its other, but speculatively coincides with it, exactly in the same way as subject coincides with object in Hegel. The alleged 'loss' of subject in the object, captured by mimesis, is at the very heart of subjectivity, and therefore represents the central feature of reason itself, its condition of possibility. The mistake is to conceive it as something external to, or preceding, the subjectivizing and socializing intervention of rationality, as something that can save reason from its atrophy.

We can now better understand Adorno and Horkheimer's rejection of the Hegelian dialectic on the ground that it sets up a system dominated by a teleological principle that eventually does away with the particular autonomy of the object, and thus with what they perceive as the dynamic core of the dialectic itself. According to Horkheimer, in Hegel consciousness eventually achieves an unwavering control over the relation between thought and object, thus dissolving any potential for dialectical historicism. Although, as Horkheimer writes in his 1937 essay 'Traditional and Critical Theory', Hegel escaped the 'embarrassment' of Kant's contradictory dualisms ('between activity and passivity, *a priori* and sense data, philosophy and psychology') 'the Hegelian solution' nonetheless 'seems a purely private assertion, a personal peace treaty between the philosopher and an inhuman world' (Horkheimer 1992: 204). This view will be endorsed by Adorno, who, despite a much more acute, nuanced and altogether profound analysis of Hegel's dialectic, commented:

> The debate between Kant and Hegel, in which Hegel's devastating argument has the last word, is not over; perhaps because what was decisive, the superior power of logical stringency, *is untrue in the face of the Kantian discontinuities*. Through his critique of Kant, Hegel achieved

> a magnificent extension of the practice of critical philosophy beyond the formal sphere; at the same time, in doing so he evaded the supreme critical moment, the critique of totality, of something infinite and conclusively given. Then he highhandedly did away with the barrier after all, with the experience of something that cannot be dissolved in consciousness, which was the innermost experience of Kant's transcendental philosophy, and he stipulated a unanimity of knowledge that becomes seamless through its discontinuities and that has something of a mythical illusory quality to it. (Adorno 1993: 86; my emphasis)

It is undoubtedly true that in his lectures on Hegel, dating back to the late 1950s and early 1960s, Adorno defends Hegel against the various attacks he was subjected to from different quarters (positivism, Soviet Marxism, Gestalt psychology, etc.). However, this defence, which was by and large replicated in the later *Negative Dialectics*, was based on an expressly anti-Hegelian conception of the dialectic which Adorno himself was refining at the time and that, as we have seen, was already part of Horkheimer's critical thought. Adorno believed that in Hegel the dichotomy subject–object eventually dissolves, obfuscated by a tyrannical subjectivism. He claimed that abstract subjectivity in Hegel triumphs, particularly in the passage from the *Phenomenology of Spirit* to the *Science of Logic*. If in the *Phenomenology of Spirit* the principle of the negative still qualifies thought, in the *Science of Logic* every enemy of the concept is eliminated, vanishes and '[t]he spirit wins its fight against a non-existent foe' (Adorno 2000: 39).[12] Adorno was clearly aware of the centrality of contradiction and negativity in Hegel's dialectics, and yet he never tired of lamenting how ultimately Hegel relapsed into subjectivism by dissolving the concrete, material presence of the object. Hegel's mistake was not to have preserved the dimension of objective materiality as heteronomous to the subject (that is to say, whose concrete experience is denied to subjective experience): 'The idealist will not see that, however devoid of qualities "something" may be, this is no reason yet to call it "nothing"' (Adorno 2000: 173).

From Hegel, then, Adorno intends to wrest a 'truth-content' that he sees paradoxically hidden where Hegel's thought is more blatantly untrue. At the end of his essay 'The Experiential Content of Hegel's Philosophy', he indeed comes very close to grasping the dialectical core of Hegel's system:

> This is the truth in Hegel's untruth. The force of the whole, which it mobilizes, is not a mere fantasy on the part of spirit; it is the force of the real web of illusion in which all individual existence remains trapped. By specifying, in opposition to Hegel, the negativity of the whole, philosophy

> satisfies, for the last time, the postulate of determinate negation, which is a positing. (Adorno 1993: 87–8)

While I would argue that the coincidence of the whole and the negative (or of reason and mimesis) is what marks the originality of Hegel's thought, and is therefore not 'in opposition' to it, Adorno's conclusion discloses an intention that clearly cannot be ascribed to Hegel: 'The ray of light that reveals the whole to be untrue in all its moments is none other than utopia, the utopia of the whole truth, which is still to be realized' (p. 88). Typically, in Adorno, the negative acquires a utopian function in so far as it embodies the impossible 'plenitude to come' which, precisely because utopian, can only be experienced via a reference to the negative. In a more radical reading of Hegel, on the other hand, the negative qua determinate negation, being nothing other than the whole itself in a different modality, cannot stand for a reminder of a messianic 'whole truth' whose realization is forever postponed. This would amount to 'bad infinity' for Hegel. Likewise, the function of the negative is dialectical not because it provides a negative image of plenitude, but because it offers itself as an inherently traumatic 'crack' through which the whole qua 'real web of illusion' is resignified, reloaded with a radically different content. There is no room for any links with utopia in Hegel's notion of negativity, only for dialectical resignification. In its minimal but crucial difference from Hegel's, then, Adorno's and by extension Critical Theory's concept of the dialectic can be seen as characterized by a messianic longing that inevitably acquires melancholic undertones, and as such effectively abandons the original aim of the struggle against capitalism.

Critical Theory's fetishistic disavowal

The novelty of Critical Theory's method can be summed up in its rejection of all kinds of philosophical dualisms which isolate intellectual substance from external reality: It implies the rejection of what Horkheimer defined as the contemplative realm of traditional theory, whether embraced by Descartes or Hegel. At the same time, however, despite discarding Kant's dualism between a transcendental subject and an empirical dimension in the object, Horkheimer first, and later Adorno, retained the antinomical form of Kant's thought, transposing it (at least in principle) onto an immanent plane. Thus, Kant's antinomies became, for Critical Theory, the insoluble contradictions affecting the search for truths, inasmuch as such operation can be detected in the social arena. The emphasis on the negativity of dialectics was aimed at endorsing the inherently contradictory character of consciousness vis-à-vis the object. As Kant had demonstrated, any doctrine that tries to achieve the correspondence of reason to truth inevitably ends up entangled in irresolvable contradictions. Although, departing from traditional theory, these critical theorists claimed that any knowledge of the world is by definition sustained by a series of dialectical mediations between subject and object, the fact that for them the object remains, in its ultimate configuration, irreducible to thought, implies that dialectical mediation is predicated upon its own failure. Since its dawn, Critical Theory was caught between Kant's principle of the regulative idea, whereby the ontological limitations of the cognitive power of the subject is the condition of possibility of thought, and Hegel's dialectical method. Ultimately, it claimed to reject both positions in the name of *negative* dialectics.

The key substantive implication of this philosophical legacy is that Critical Theory is by definition radically self-reflexive: Critique is never mere criticism of external reality but it always implies, dialectically, self-critique. There is no domain of knowledge that does not include the context from which reason is applied. Critique must be wholly immanent, since it must include its own presuppositions; one cannot apply it from a neutral standpoint, for one is always positioned within the epistemological boundaries of the object of critical analysis. But how can this dialectical critique be applied? How can thought be at once a critical agent and the object of criticism without constantly 'falling off its ground'? In psychoanalytic terms, the only way out of this conundrum lies in positing the split nature of thought itself. In other words, the only way the very same thought can be both critically conscious and an object of criticism (beyond the relativistic clichés of postmodernism) is by conceding that the dialectical link between itself and the object of knowledge takes place, paradoxically, at the level of what we might call regimes of unconscious enjoyment. This is why Horkheimer's project sounds more appealing in theory than in practice. As a compromise between universalism and relativism, and with at least one foot firmly placed in the social sciences, it sounds ideal. I argue, however, that Critical Theory misses the truly dialectical insight into how the substance of thought is at the same time nothing but the substance of the object of thought. In other words, Critical Theory's important dialectical premise is not carried through to its final, decisive consequence. The theme of the reflexivity of critical thought in relation to social research, so dear to the critical theorists and at the heart of their concept of dialectics, remains an abstract injunction if it is not completed by the affirmation of the speculative identity of subject and object. The claim that any critical investigation into social dynamics is a moment of the very social process it aims to understand or unmask risks sounding either hollow or relativistic, or both (which would justify the postmodern variation of critical thought), if not supplemented by a more consistent application of the dialectic itself, one that endorses the moment of overlap of knowing subject and object of cognition. As we have seen, this fold marks the identity of subject and object in so far as the two terms of the dialectic are self-fractured, traversed by a foundational inconsistency.

With this in mind, we could argue that Horkheimer's original project was open to, and tempted by, two alternatives, as it transpires if we consider its noble attempt to salvage the critical consciousness of the world while denying such consciousness any ontological ground. It could either fall back on the Marxist 'grand narrative', where the ontological ground is rebuilt into the critical framework through the assertion that the aim remains the rational organization of society and the harmonization of individual and social labour (hence Habermas's criticism of the residue of 'philosophy of consciousness' within original Critical Theory); or it could give in to relativism in the vein, for example, of contemporary 'cultural studies'. Adorno will choose to stick with the middle term between these two alternatives, remaining faithful to Horkheimer's initial compromise. The rejection of transcendental reason and grand narratives was to be accompanied by either bouts of empirical social research, or, especially in Adorno's case, the return of transcendence, albeit in the shape of a non-representational, utterly evanescent utopian dimension which only 'true art' had the privilege of capturing.

It seems to me that the impasse faced by Critical Theory from its very inception, and which became tangible with Adorno's symptomatic swerve towards aesthetic theory, has to do with the obstinate defence of that negative dialectics which in fact, if submitted to proper scrutiny, misses the real paradox of dialectics itself, namely that the non-identitarian dimension of thought (negativity) is always-already operative within thought. Put differently, what Horkheimer and Adorno, despite their partially different approaches, never fully considered is that, no matter how negative and anti-transcendental, how wary of extramundane standpoints, reason by definition works through the displacement of its own excessive, unacknowledged core. This means that reason needs to achieve identity with an object, though it coincides with it only at the level of their respective inconsistencies (Hegel's 'Spirit is a bone'). On this account, any explicit and programmatic endorsement of the negative moment within rationality should be taken with the proverbial pinch of salt, as it relies on a degree of disavowal; conversely, identification is achieved at the level of what psychoanalysis defines as the real core of consciousness, namely practices of unconscious identification.

Here Lacan meets Hegel: In both, knowledge of the object matters supremely because sooner or later knowledge stumbles against those nodal points at which *it fails*, thus producing *truth effects*. Thought is thereby conceived as a topographical construction traversed by generative cuts rather than as an instrument to systematize phenomena and consolidate meaning. The only certainty about thought is that it fails. Far from implying a retreat into relativism, however, this stance is qualified by Hegel's infamous notion of 'determinate negation': It suggests that the failures of thought are connected with truth, seeing that *they enable thought to regenerate itself by moving into a different direction*, that is, by attempting a new systematization of reality. In *Negative Dialectics*, Adorno endorsed the basic Hegelian premise: 'The antithesis of thought to whatever is heterogeneous to thought is reproduced in thought itself, as its immanent contradiction' (Adorno 2000: 146). And yet he missed the decisive reflexive move, for example when he claimed: 'To be an object also is part of the meaning of subjectivity; but it is not equally part of the meaning of objectivity to be a subject' (Adorno 2000: 183). What is missing here, in Adorno's defence of the primacy of the object, is the awareness that 'the meaning of objectivity' is always-already decided by the subject *in its radically decentred mode*. In fact, to speak of the preponderance of the object is homologous to speaking of the preponderance of the subject, for reality emerges for us as an object of cognition *only on condition that a part of thought is radically disavowed and projected onto external reality itself*, in the guise of that 'intrinsically elusive, unknowable object' that triggers our desire for knowledge. Differently put, the 'immanent contradiction' of thought rightly denounced by Adorno, in Hegelian fashion, as a 'reflexive determination' of the gap between thought and its object, simultaneously works as the very *condition of possibility of knowledge*. The inerasable inconsistency of thought vis-à-vis the object is at the same time precisely what allows thought to exercise its cognitive function over the object. The crucial paradox, which is absent in Adorno, is that signification (qua identification) emerges only because thought never coincides with itself – because thought is intrinsically inconsistent. This reflexive twist missing from Adorno's strenuous defence of the object is, on the other hand, intrinsic to psychoanalysis. It was Lacan especially who developed the dialectic subject–object to its utmost reflexive (Hegelian) consequences, in such a way that it would seem to find an ideal application in the study of cinema. Adorno indeed stops a step short of the Hegelo-Lacanian twist connecting subject and object in their reciprocal and overlapping inconsistencies. When, for instance, he claims that 'the solid, lasting, impenetrable side of the I mimics the outside world's impenetrability for conscious experience' (Adorno 2000: 179), he nevertheless refrains from adding that the fundamental impenetrability of the object (the outside world) is speculatively identical with the subject's self-division, that is, it is dialectically interconnected with the latter. Precisely because he does not assert this final twist, his method is not fully dialectical: The non-identity of thought and object is connected only one way, from thought to object, but not the other way around. In other words, Adorno tells us that thought's inconsistency is caused by the preponderance of the object, but he omits the proper dialectical insight that the non-identity of the object is itself always-already coincidental with the subject's own non-identity, or inconsistency.

When Adorno claims that, on account of the preponderance of the object, one can write a primeval history of the subject but not a primeval history of the object, because the latter 'would be dealing with specific objects' (Adorno 2000: 185), it is clear once again the extent to which he misses the final dialectical link between the two terms. A history of the object is impossible to write not merely because of the non-identity of the object, its ultimate autonomy from thought, but because the object cannot be wrenched away from the subjective mechanism through which the very notion of objectivity arises. In 2010, the British Museum hosted an exhibition titled 'The History of the World in 100 Objects', which is meant to tell the story of humanity from 2,000,000 BC to the present (from the first spear tips to the credit card). This exhibition provides interesting material to reflect on what a dialectical analysis of objectivity should do. The dialectical question to ask is: To what extent can these objects be isolated in a progressive sequence as examples of the development of civilization? The answer cannot be simply confined to a description of human progress over nature through the centuries, but should take into account the dialectical wisdom that every such object ultimately reflects the same attempt to deal with the subjective deadlock that connects man with the external world. From the Egyptian Sphinx to the Hebrew astrolabe or the Russian revolutionary plate, what is at stake in these fascinating objects is, in the final analysis, the enigma of the birth of man's subjectivity out of the foreclosure of its own *objective* surplus of sense or inconsistency (in psychoanalytic terms, *jouissance*) – the same surplus which was 'put to work' in the creation of these objects, whose function is precisely to mask this enigmatic 'excess' of the human condition through their material presence.

Critical Theory's desperate attempt at safeguarding the primacy of the object against the deadly voracity of instrumental reason by 'denouncing' the finite and contradictory nature of reason itself, then, effectively ignores its own presupposition. It ignores how *only* a fundamentally contradictory, self-divided reason can try to establish a link with the object of knowledge. It is therefore not enough to claim that reason gets back from the object the truth about its own contradictory nature, or that 'the I mimics the outside world's impenetrability'; what Hegelian dialectics makes us aware of is that this reflexive mechanism is inbuilt in what we call knowledge, in so far as it works as its condition of possibility. While Adorno's subject can only be conceived as striving indefinitely to attain the object, that is, to extinguish itself in the other, the Hegelo-Lacanian subject is always-already the object, in that it embodies its own otherness, and for the simple reason that *it is only by being in excess of itself that the subject is able to relate to the external world qua object*. Only by displacing its own objective excess outside of itself can the subject establish a relationship with the world, perceiving itself as part of a given social framework.

The difference might seem minimal and yet it is decisive, since it highlights the distance between Adorno's negative dialectics (a 'melancholic' dialectics in which thought effectively renounces its inbuilt ambition to systematize reality, denouncing it as ideology) and Hegel's dialectical method, which asserts the *inseparability* of thought's inconsistent, contradictory nature from its 'ideological' appropriation of the object. Politically, the distinction between the two conceptions of the dialectic is breathtaking: In Adorno's and Critical Theory's view, ideology emerges when thought illicitly claims to correspond exactly to reality, ignoring the surplus in the object that escapes thought while reflexively making it radically inconsistent; in Hegelian dialectics, on the other hand, ideology is consubstantial with the exercise of thought, and yet the coincidence of thought with its object takes place at the level of their overlapping inconsistencies.

Only via the latter understanding of the dialectic can we grasp how ideology works: Not just by demanding from us identification with it, but by 'hooking' us through radically disavowed (unconscious) stimuli. Ideology therefore always relies upon a degree of what Slavoj Žižek has aptly named 'fetishistic disavowal': We believe not by fully identifying with the official ideological text, but by disavowing or displacing our attachment to its injunctions. We are truly caught in ideology when we believe by proxy, that is, when we believe that someone else is the idiot who believes, and not us. When Adorno criticizes the idiocy of modern moviegoers, he does not simply forget to include himself in the equation – thus, incidentally, betraying the original self-reflexive and historicist mandate of Critical Theory (social subjects are caught in the same dynamics that shape their objects of knowledge); most importantly, he fails to radicalize such a view so as to reflect upon the identity between his disavowed participation in the ideological game and ideology's own idiotic, senseless core. The importance of Lacanian psychoanalysis, and simultaneously the place where it meets Hegel's speculative idealism, can be summed up in the following dialectical axiom: Every ideology, every social substance, is erected upon a founding inconsistency, a nonsensical injunction which constitutes its *rational* core;

and, crucially, this crack in the social substance is precisely the place where the subject emerges.

Interestingly enough, the notion of 'fetishistic disavowal' is also pertinent to describe Adorno's own critical method. Let me indulge here in a brief personal recollection. When I first came across Adorno's work, a long time ago, I became so obsessed with his theories that, as it is often the case in these situations, the German philosopher started appearing in my dreams. In a recurrent dream of the time, I was sitting at home with Adorno watching a football game on TV, one that involved my favourite team. The incredible kernel of the dream, which regularly provoked my sudden awakening, had to do with my realization that Adorno was much more excited about the game than I was, jumping on the sofa while vehemently shouting at the TV set in the manner of a proper fan. Needless to say, I found the dream particularly disturbing, especially as I tended to fully share Adorno's damning views on mass culture. In his *Living in the End Times* (2010), Žižek comments on Adorno's well-known dislike of Wagner, based on the alleged fetishizing elements in Wagner's leitmotifs (see Adorno's *In Search of Wagner* (2005b), as well as Žižek's forward in the same book). Žižek begins by arguing that Adorno was *the* critic of fetishization in mass culture. Then he adds: 'It is with supreme irony that traces of this same fetishizing procedure can be found in Adorno's own writings' (p. 227). Incidentally, the Lacanian point of this counter-intuitive insight is that a degree of fetishization cannot be eliminated from communication, of whatever kind it is. Žižek continues:

> Adorno gets caught up in his own game, infatuated with his own ability to produce dazzlingly 'effective' paradoxical aphorisms at the expense of theoretical substance (recall the famous line from *Dialectic of Enlightenment* on how Hollywood's ideological manipulation of social reality realizes Kant's idea of the transcendental constitution of reality).

The latter is a statement that 'effectively overshadows the theoretical line of argumentation' (p. 227). Paradoxically, one can therefore establish a parallel between Adorno's writing and Wagner's leitmotifs:

> instead of serving as a nodal point in the complex network of structural mediations, it [Adorno's statement] generates idiotic pleasure by focusing attention on itself. This unintended self-reflexivity is something of which Adorno undoubtedly was not aware: his critique of the Wagnerian leitmotif was an allegorical critique of his own writing. Is this not an exemplary case of the unconscious reflexivity of thinking? When criticizing his opponent

> Wagner, Adorno effectively deploys a critical allegory of his own writing – in Hegelese, the truth of the relation to the Other is a self-relation. (p. 227)

We should therefore reflect on what perhaps is the central compromise formation utilized by Critical Theory in its bid not to completely relinquish universals, namely the appealing utopian dimension of a transcendentally given beyond which works as a reminder that we should not give up looking for a way out of ideological mystification. This dimension is perceivable in all the main critical theorists: Horkheimer, Adorno, Benjamin and Marcuse. If we take Adorno, it functions as a formal remainder of Kantian transcendentalism, in so far as Adorno's critical thought (for example, of the culture industry) is legitimated by the secret reference to an *other* (strictly unknowable, i.e. negative) dimension which speaks for a utopian condition where human beings would be relieved of their social alienation and, in short, would live in harmony with nature (as also the young Marx believed). In Hegel's speculative idealism, as well as in Lacan's psychoanalysis, on the other hand, alienation cannot be transcended but only, as it were, made to implode immanently. What lies within (and not beyond) the smokescreen of ideological and symbolic fictions or illusions is, for Lacan, the viscous 'stuff' of the Real, whose function is not to provide a negative template for utopian reconciliation, but to bind us to the explicit ideological text by making itself available as a secret mode of enjoyment. Similarly, Hegel radicalizes Kant by transposing the latter's regulative transcendental vision of the gap between intelligible objects and the unknowable 'thing-in-itself' into an immanent universal disjunction affecting substance as well as subject. The difference between the latter view and that of Critical Theory is perhaps best exemplified by the evolution of Horkheimer's thought vis-à-vis utopia. In the 1930s, he still retained some of his 1920s' belief in a philosophy of universal history moving towards progress and liberation; then, starting from his collaboration with Adorno (*Dialectic of Enlightenment*), history's teleology was inverted,[13] while utopia was not altogether jettisoned but became an evanescent image of salvation. Humanity's blind faith in instrumental reason now ratifies the collapse into barbarism, so that the aims of the enlightenment are reversed. Yet the notion of a positive enlightenment in a utopian future is never wholly abandoned.

In the light of this briefly sketched philosophical critique of Critical Theory, the study of narrative cinema, and especially *film noir*, provides a vivid cultural exemplification of the speculative identity of subject and object. My view is that, if submitted to an investigation which rethinks the purpose of Critical Theory, films which are often viewed as implicitly ideological because of their narrative structures and stylistic conventions can actually be shown to comprise recipes against their alleged performative ideological function. In the case of film noir, I show that, while providing palpable identificatory patterns, they also, more often than not, fail to conceal the fact that these patterns are in fact *inseparable* from the negativity, or inconsistencies, at the heart of their narrative configurations and formal standards. To only highlight the negativity of film noir, its fractious nature, is to ignore its ideological character, thus forsaking the possibility of dialecticizing it. On the contrary, what a critical theory of film should do, is unravel the paradoxical logic which tells us how the cinematic production of meaning is strictly coincidental with the production of gaps and contradictions within the filmic body. The aim of this exercise is, however, not merely to deconstruct the spurious ideological closure of the filmic text, but, quite differently, to illustrate how such closure is by necessity interlocked with instances of contingent openness. It is only by locating this level of inseparability between film as an implicitly ideological construct and film as a field beleaguered by negativity, that a critical theory of film can begin its course.

Notes

1 The term was first used by Horkheimer in his 1937 seminal essay 'Traditional and Critical Theory' (see Horkheimer 1992: 188–243).

2 We should add that before this Critical Theory turn, Horkheimer, unlike Adorno, still relied on rational and scientific discourse to assert materialism against abstract idealism. In the 1920s, he was attuned to the idea that a scientifically planned economy was the way forward to overcome capitalism, a view that was always alien to Adorno. In the early 1930s, however, he grew increasingly suspicious of the claim, made especially by Lukács in his 1922 *History and Class Consciousness*, that the superiority of Marxism to all bourgeois theory was based on its trust in the concept of totality – in Lukács's terms, on the idea that the proletariat is both the subject and the object of history.

3 See Anderson (1976); Slater (1977); Bottomore (1984); Held (1980); Kellner (1989); Jay (1996).

4 As regards the attitude towards Hegel, the *Dialectic of Enlightenment* confirms Horkheimer's stance of the 1930s, for instance, in the following passage: 'With the notion of determinate negativity, Hegel revealed an element that distinguishes the Enlightenment from the positivist degeneracy to which he attributes it. By ultimately making the conscious result of the whole process of negation – totality in system and in history – into an absolute, he of course contravened the prohibition and himself lapsed into mythology' (Adorno and Horkheimer 1997: 24).

5 Incidentally, in an essay of 1964, Adorno himself remembers how it was his friend and film historian Siegfried Kracauer who introduced him to Kant, for years reading with him the *Critique of Pure Reason* on Saturday afternoons (see Adorno 1992: 58–9). What was to remain impressed in Adorno's mind was particularly how Kant's theory of the antinomies did not result in the liquidation of contradiction and the consequent claim of the concordance of thought and external reality, but instead preserved contradiction's dialectical function.

6 As Žižek observes, 'the innermost "motor" of the dialectical process is the interplay between epistemological obstacle and ontological deadlock' (Žižek 1999: 55).

7 Incidentally, this is what Hegel has in mind when he refers to 'concrete universality': The universal is not a neutral frame within which different particular entities struggle with each other, but the very antagonism that cuts across the field and decides which of these entities is to prevail over the others.

8 To explain the 'hollow exaltation' arising from the notion of spurious infinite Hegel mentions, for instance, Kant's sublime, those terrifying natural representations that make imagination fail and thought succumb. This infinite 'is nothing else but the wearisome repetition which makes a limit vanish, reappear, and vanish again', that is, it yields no result. Immediately after, he quotes from a poem by Albrecht von Haller where, again, the infinite is described as an endless piling up of things, of reaching beyond. However, Hegel stresses how the poet eventually 'declares this so-called terrifying journey into the beyond to be futile and empty, and that he closes by saying that only by giving up this empty, infinite progression can the genuine infinite itself become present to him'. The final lines of the poem read as follows: 'All the might of number increased a thousandfold / Is still not a fragment of thee. / *I remove them and thou liest wholly before me*' (Hegel 1969: 229–30).

9 When I say 'God is God', instead of merely enumerating his attributes, I generate that sense of sublimity ('there is in God something more than what the word God can say') which is precisely what makes him God. In this respect, it is the signifier, by 'falling into the signified', that structures reality as a meaningful whole (for those who believe in God, of course).

10 Departing from Saussure's theory of signification, Lacan claims that the signifier enjoys precedence over the signified. As he puts it in *Seminar III*, the signifier plays a crucial performative role, it acts: 'The signifier doesn't just provide an envelope, a receptacle for signification. It polarizes it, it structures it, and brings it into existence' (Lacan 1993: 260). And again later: 'The signifier polarizes. It's the signifier that creates the field of meanings' (p. 292). The reason why it is able to assume such a role is that '[t]he signifier is a sign that doesn't refer to any object' (p. 167); in other words, 'every real signifier is, as such, a signifier that signifies nothing' (p. 185). Owing precisely to this tautological function, the signifier sets up the symbolic framework of reality.

11 At the same time, he accused logical empiricism (the Vienna Circle) of a degree of disavowed Kantianism, since in his view it retained the a priori of 'formal invariance' (see his essay 'The Latest Attack on Metaphysics', in Horkheimer 1992: 132–87).

12 In connection with this, it is revealing to note that while Adorno rightly criticizes the dialectical procedure according to which the Hegelian formula of the 'negation of the negative' is turned into positivity, at the same time he attributes this procedure to Hegel himself, thus missing the subtlety of the Hegelian double negation (see Adorno 2000: 158–61).

13 As he famously put it in *Negative Dialectics*: 'No universal history leads from savagery to humanitarianism, but there is one leading from the slingshot to the megaton bomb. It ends in the total menace which organized mankind poses to organized men, in the epitome of discontinuity. It is the horror that verifies Hegel and stands him on the head' (Adorno 2000: 320).

3

A configuration pregnant with tension: Fritz Lang for Critical Theory

In an influential article published in 1969 in the *Cahiers du Cinéma*, and translated for *Screen* 2 years later, Jean-Louis Comolli and Paul Narboni introduced the 'category e' film to define a special type of ideologically driven cinema. This category included those films which appeared to ostensibly voice a given ideological stance but actually managed to surreptitiously subvert it:

> An internal criticism is taking place which cracks the film apart at the seams. If one reads the film obliquely, looking for symptoms; if one looks beyond its apparent formal coherence, one can see that it is riddled with cracks: it is splitting under an internal tension, which is simply not there under an ideologically innocuous film. (Comolli and Narboni 2004: 817)

As shown in the previous chapter, this critical position is crucial for a dialectical analysis of film. I begin this third and final part of the book with the analysis of Fritz Lang's *Beyond a Reasonable Doubt* (1956), a work that could be defined with the oxymoron 'modernist Hollywood masterpiece' for the way in which it manages to convey its complex self-reflexivity by embracing the standard Hollywood format. Particularly with this film, Lang manages to express his genius through strategies of self-limitation. A film explicitly about framing, both literally and metaphorically, this last of Lang's American works will be read dialectically as a powerful if at least partly unconscious endorsement of the ontological status of fictions, and consequently as a demonstration of the fallacious nature of any alleged subject/object or appearance/truth split. Construed as a theorem, it strives to lay bare not so much the non-representable status of truth (as most commentators have read it), but instead the *very representable* coincidence of truth and fiction. Read against the grain, then, *Beyond a Reasonable Doubt* offers us a chance to locate the fundamental theoretical problem with Critical Theory, namely, its allegiance with a Kantian perspective that, while opening up the space for a dialectical understanding of the connection between subject and object (or appearance and truth), nevertheless does not manage to bring that connection full circle. Lang's cinema, on the other hand, lends itself to a type of analysis that shows how the gap between subjective fictions and objective truth is internal to 'objective truth' itself. Whether in its modernist (Adorno) or postmodernist (from Foucault to Derrida and Baudrillard) guise, Critical Theory postulates the limit or deadlock of any representation of reality, which consists in the failure of such representation to give us an 'objective depiction of a stable other' (Lindlof and Taylor 2002: 53). This is and has always been the basis for any critical theory–type enquiry, whether sociological, political, literary or philosophical. As my analysis of some of Lang's most accomplished American films attempts to show, such view misses the reflexive twist of its own theoretical presupposition: The awareness of how the cognitive deficit distorting any representation of reality is the very deficit that qualifies the 'stable other' as such.

Beyond the doubt of appearances

As a film deprived of psychological depth, stylistically neutral, and drenched in almost geometrical conceptual abstraction, *Beyond a Reasonable Doubt* has often been regarded as a work that brings to new heights Lang's proverbial pessimism about the human race. At the same time, it is generally read as a work whose despondent attitude introduces classical cinema into modernity and thus crisis. That is to say, it supposedly signals the exhaustion of classical narrative film style as well as the coming to an end of the ideology represented by the Hollywood studio system. The reason for this is often found in the way it abruptly disrupts spectators' identification with the main character (thus signalling the beginning of Hollywood's search for alternative narrative styles). Moreover, together with its predecessor *While the City*

Sleeps (1956), the film is taken to mark the bitter conclusion of Lang's love-affaire with Hollywood. As summed up by Joe McElhaney (2006: 65),

> in *While the City Sleeps* and *Beyond a Reasonable Doubt*, Lang presents a world that often seems to be drained of organic life, so much so that the films have been read almost exclusively in relation to the supposed contempt Lang has for the characters, for the world being depicted and, finally, for the Hollywood environment out of which they were produced.

Indeed, the general critical view is that towards the end of his Hollywood career, Lang increased the dosage of pessimism that already ran through his cinema, turning such pessimism into contempt towards the ideologically harnessed context in which he had been working. *Beyond a Reasonable Doubt* has often been seen as representing the apex of Lang's bleak *Weltanschauung*, expressing a particularly damning assessment of the American society. Most critics and fellow directors have commented that this work, together with the previous one, is the product of someone who, to put it in Martin Scorsese's words, 'had finally had it with America' (in Haller 2000: 31). It allegedly reflects the attitude of a bitter cynic who by then only cared to express his utter contempt for the characters and their world, as well as the Hollywood system. As is well known, the emphasis on human and moral corruptibility is a central feature of Lang's cinema as a whole. Hopelessness in light of the human tendency towards self-destruction is perhaps the single most recurrent theme in his work, which would explain his friendship and spiritual affinity with Adorno during and beyond their 'California years'. While the director himself always played down the value of his last Hollywood contribution,[1] critics like Walter Metz (2006), Tom Gunning (2000) and Catherine Russell (1995) have argued that, as well as being concerned with the great modernist theme of art's ultimate powerlessness vis-à-vis reality, this is a landmark film about mortification and death.

While on first impression *Beyond a Reasonable Doubt* confirms and indeed increases the pessimistic and implicitly critical tone of Lang's film-making as a whole, I argue that it nevertheless demands to be read as one of the most effective claims ever made *not* on the tragic crisis of truth in modernity, but in defence of the truthfulness of cinematic illusions – so, in a profound and perhaps unwitting way, it actually works as a homage to Hollywood. Despite all the obvious signals, one cannot overlook the precision of Lang's gaze in defending the ontological primacy of the filmic illusion.[2] In his 1957 review of the film for the *Cahiers du Cinéma*, Jacques Rivette wrote:

> We are plunged into a world of necessity, all the more apparent in that it coexists so harmoniously with the arbitrariness of the premises; Lang, as is well known, always seeks the truth beyond the reasonable, and here seeks it from the threshold of the unreasonable. (Rivette 1957: 140)

Later in this review, Rivette claims that in his last American film Lang destroys the scene, in so far as 'no scene is treated for its own sake' but simply retains a 'mediatory aspect', a 'condition of pure spatio-temporal reference, devoid of embodiment' (p. 141). He then adds that characters are also utterly dehumanized, reduced to nothing more than ideas, because ultimately what interests Lang is the dialectical progression of the concept. Asking himself whether the film reaches the *beyond* of representations (in relation to its theme of the ambiguity of guilt) thus touching upon a truth, Rivette concludes with a rhetorical and subtly provocative question: 'Beyond appearances, what are guilt and innocence?' (p. 142). Without developing the insight, the French critic/director captures in a nutshell the film's ontological regard for appearances. Before tackling this issue, which also provides us with an angle from which to explore the theoretical tension within Critical Theory, let us first remind ourselves of the plot.

Beyond a Reasonable Doubt presents its main storyline as a *self-confessed* fiction, a story explicitly manufactured to belie the law and especially capital punishment. As often in noir, and generally in detective stories, the reliable part of the narrative is unmasked for what it really is, thanks to a twist conveniently placed towards the end of the story, a twist which forces us to reconsider the whole narrative. Here, however, such trope reaches beyond its standard narrative function. As a fiction within the fiction, it is clear from its inception that *Beyond a Reasonable Doubt* is also meant to be a self-reflexive commentary on the nature of film-making. The blatant lie we are presented with is made up by the (officially) morally virtuous journalist and writer Tom Garrett (Dana Andrews), together with powerful liberal publisher and future father-in-law Austin Spencer (Sydney Blackmer), a fervent campaigner against the death penalty. The two men agree that Garrett should incriminate himself for the killing of a young dancer named Patty Gray in order to demonstrate, later, his innocence, thus indicting the public with regard to the dangers of capital punishment. With the help of Spencer, Garrett plants a number of clues against himself while documenting every move with photographs showing how it is all staged. It works. Garrett is accused of the killing and eventually condemned to death. In his cell, he calmly awaits Spencer's intervention, safe in the knowledge that the photos his friend possesses are going to uncover the fake self-incrimination and true reasons behind it, namely the exposure of the fallibility of human judgement and the absurdity of capital punishment. However, while heading for the courtroom to exonerate his friend, Spencer dies in a car crush and the photographs are burnt beyond recognition. Eventually, shortly before Garrett's execution, new evidence is produced (Spencer had also written about their plan in a letter), and Garrett is now assured that he will be pardoned. The truth about his innocence is about to be restored. However, in a wonderful twist, the writer accidentally betrays himself to his ex-fiancée Susan (Joan Fontaine) by naming the assassinated woman by her real name (Emma), which he could not have known had he never met her. He is thus left with no choice but to confess to Susan that he killed the dancer. He explains how he had married Emma (Patty) Gray but she had become a burden from the moment he had decided to re-marry. The plan concocted by Spencer had offered him the perfect opportunity to eliminate her. Susan, however, decides against protecting him, and Garrett finally walks to the electric chair.

Clearly a far cry from anti death-penalty films like Richard Fleischer's *Compulsion* (1959), which features Orson Welles's famous tear-jerking speech, Lang's film nevertheless demands that we look beyond its immediate concern with capital punishment, which works as a pretext for other kinds of investigations. Judging this film by its bleak finale (which disproves the initial case against the death penalty), or by the fact that all characters are presented in a negative light, means overlooking its implicit preoccupation with the status of fiction. This is indeed a complex work that does not hide its concern with images: They are scattered everywhere along its narrative, precisely to call attention upon their fictional dimension. There are innumerable shots of mirror reflections, of frames of all kinds (photography, television), of audiences, of characters dressing up, pretending to be someone else. Without being at all spectacular – in a way in which, for example, Max Ophüls's 'reflexive' cinema is –[3] and, simultaneously, avoiding the cumbersome self-referential weight of many an 'art film', Lang's last American effort stubbornly demands to be read as a meditation on reflexivity. It is enough to consider the fact that the evidence Spencer and Garrett intend to use against Garrett's fake incrimination consists of a series of Polaroid pictures, photos on which Lang's camera often lingers by way of extended close-ups. The film's denouement eventually reveals that this substantial amount of photographic evidence was nothing but the work of a cynical manipulator, whose interest was, in fact, to conceal his crime. However, as we shall see below, it would be a mistake to conclude with the worn-out argument that opposes unsatisfactory, frustratingly incomplete fictions (film, photography etc.) to a real that eludes filmic representation (many critics have remarked that the only real act is the killing of the girl – a 'truth' that is radically excluded from representation).

On photos and truth

Let us recall Roland Barthes's groundbreaking argument against the truthfulness of the photographic image. According to Barthes, images are both denotative and connotative, that is, they possess a literal meaning (denotation) and a contextual meaning (ideological, emotional etc.). Ultimately, however, denotation (*what* is photographed) is for Barthes nothing but a powerful illusion simply hiding the fact that everything in the image is connotation.[4] In semiotics, of course, every signifier is coded. As semioticians never tire of emphasizing, the interpretation of a given sign depends on the social, cultural, ideological, historical context in which that sign is embedded. Nothing has a 'literal' meaning. In Barthes's terms, when a sign acquires a literal meaning, it obeys 'the very principle of myth: it transforms history into nature' (Barthes 1973: 140). And myth

> abolishes the complexity of human acts, it gives them the simplicity of essences, it does away with all dialectics, with any going back beyond what is immediately visible, it organizes a world which is without contradictions because it is without depth, a world wide open and wallowing in the evident. It establishes a blissful clarity: things appear to mean something by themselves. (Barthes 1973: 156)

In so far as it *naturalizes* what is cultural, that is, it *objectivizes* a sign that is by definition subjective, unstable and ambiguous, myth according to Barthes serves bourgeois ideology. The obvious consequence of this line of thought is known to everyone: It involves the necessity of deconstructing or denaturalizing what appears as mythical, essential, self-evident, natural, whole (the list is endless). Although Adorno (unlike the majority of today's Cultural Studies critical theorists) was far from altogether dispensing with questions of 'truth-value', one should detect in his theoretical arguments against the culture industry that transcendental framework which later degenerated into an attitude of cognitive suspension, of 'ban' on ontological questions, as typified also by the historical relativism of most of today's Cultural Studies.[5] The dominant message of Critical Theory, including its branching off into post-structuralist Cultural Studies, might be said to conform to this injunction to denounce the false and ideologically pregnant 'claim to objective truth' that cultural products tend to embody in one way or other.[6]

Given this premise, we should immediately notice how Lang's film subtly sabotages the anti-essentialist agenda from within: Photographic images are from the start shown in their most explicit connotative status (they are *fabricated* as false evidence, they do not reflect what they denote) and yet they should be taken literally, since Garrett is objectively the killer. The procedure followed by Lang is thus the opposite one to Barthes's: It does not claim that denotation is always-already a form of connotation and that as such it should be unmasked, but rather it shows how connotation turns out to coincide with denotation. What seemed to be fictional, a 'cultural construct' even endowed with a precise and laudable moral intention, is revealed to be objectively true. It is this odd reversal of the standard critical procedure, according to which an objectively given text/narrative/stance is disclosed as a fabrication, that offers us the perfect angle for a critical approach to Critical Theory's 'anti-essentialist ontology'. My argument is concerned with the analysis of how, despite the proclaimed aim of denaturalizing cultural artefacts, Critical Theory's approach to culture has always tended to be supplemented by, as it were, a naturalized concept of nature.

From my dialectical viewpoint, problems arise when the critical approach grounds its theoretical, cultural and political claims in a division between the usurping mythical/ideological, non-reflective 'text' and a critical disposition which denounces and deconstructs (and thus supposedly helps us free ourselves of) such dogmatic positions. It is this line of thought that should set off alarm bells, for it can be said that the gap between essentialism and the anti-essentialist positions is already part of (any definition of) essence as its intrinsic other qua condition of possibility. By the same token, anti-essentialist Critical Theory needs to presuppose the myth of essence in order to exercise its critical power over it – essence is therefore its condition of possibility. To put it another way: The belief in the impossibility of a text to represent and thus grasp directly a given object bypassing its context – a belief that characterizes the anti-metaphysical relativism of much Critical Theory/Cultural Studies – can itself be regarded as an ideological/essentialist feature, in so far as it allows us critical theorists to participate in a specific universe of sense whose ideological coordinates remain fundamentally unquestioned. More to the point, if there is a dimension of social reality that has been progressively eroded and eventually altogether erased from Critical Theory's radar, it is that of political economy: Could we not maintain that the type of cultural criticism consonant with the tradition of Critical Theory (based on the castigation of instrumental reason, reification, fetishization, etc.) has as its common denominator (i.e. it is sustained by) its decision to ignore the dimension of political economy? And does this not imply that politics proper – politics concerned with universal struggles rather than 'identity struggles' – is also inevitably sidelined? With Cultural Studies having taken over and further diluted the political scope of Critical Theory, today we need a firm stance: All the accusations of essentialism in the name of plurality of discourses and tolerance of differences should be returned back to the sender, since it is today's hegemonic type of cultural criticism that is sustained by an essentialist platform, namely the silent prohibition to tackle substantial issues of universal concern. Trends change all the time within Cultural Studies, provided that they do not interfere with foundational issues and keep themselves within parameters of historical contextualization. And it goes without saying that this inherently essentialist relativism, or prohibition to ask basic questions related to truths, is functional to the unproblematic commodification of the Cultural Studies discourse itself. As I hope to be able to show with my incursion into Lang's Hollywood cinema, a dialectical conception of essence should prevent us from setting up such dichotomies, and instead shift the focus on grasping the coincidence of essence (truth) and fiction.

Framing the subject

In *Beyond a Reasonable Doubt*, Lang's genius emerges in the twist whereby the until then solid and reliable gap between truth and fiction suddenly gives way, and fiction comes to coincide with truth: However *artificially* planted, the clues against Garrett testify to the truth. Here, more than in any other previous Hollywood film, truth is blatantly, even outrageously placed on the side of fiction. We should not be afraid to take this conclusion to its full metaphorical value. Lang tells us that those who are 'in the know' are simply wrong, for they underestimate the foundational role of appearances. They are fools believing that appearances (the story fabricated by Spencer and Garrett) are meant to hide a deeper level of truth (the morally noble fight against the death penalty). The film, then, has more to do with Lang's endorsement of the truthfulness relative to the (cinematic) production of fictions, than with the director's pessimism about human nature.

The circular narrative opens with the scene of a man being sent to the electric chair, and ends with Tom Garrett preparing for the same fate. In the opening sequence, Garrett was depicted among the public, looking at the unknown man as he was escorted to his execution. By the end of the film, the distance between him and the unknown man has collapsed, as he turns into a dead man walking. This is indeed a film that collapses all comfortable distances, a film where the difference between subject and object (of the look) evaporates. *Beyond a Reasonable Doubt* shows that there is no comfortable external position from which we can look at another, safe in the assurance of our difference. This point is all the more evident in the way Lang organizes his ironic discourse on the presumed gap between being and pretending to be, facts and fictions.[7] Every character and situation is presented as ambiguously split between two sides, a fictitious and a real one. The remarkable conclusion, however, is that 'we are what we pretend to be', as epitomized of course by the wonderful idea embodied by the Dana Andrews character. This is to say that, contrary to standard strategies of dramatization, here we do not witness the unveiling of a pretence which reveals a deeper truth about a given character of situation. On the contrary, narrative construction reveals that where there was factual truth – a truth scientifically documented by plenty of evidence – there emerges, implacably, fiction. However, this emphasis on fiction is of course not meant to establish the plurality of discursive approaches to the real. Rather, Lang's film emphatically endorses the ontological primacy of the symbolic composition of reality. We are told about a writer who pretends to be a killer so that he can demonstrate the fallacious nature of capital punishment. He deliberately plants all sorts of evidence against himself. The distance between fact and fiction could not be more palpable. And yet, with his customary mordacity, Lang suddenly shows us that the writer was what he so blatantly pretended to be. Again, it would be wrong to conclude that, given the emphasis on deception, the core of reality is evoked as an ever-elusive truth – perhaps even pointing out its coincidence with what is by definition non-symbolizable, namely death. Against this commonplace, based on the spurious dualism of appearance and truth that has dominated Western thought since Plato, Lang affirms the absolute coincidence of essence and appearance – and therefore, metaphorically, the radical role of cinema in its openly embracing fictitiousness (since it is by lying, not by attempting to capture true facts, that cinema encroaches upon the real). Tom Garrett, the Dana Andrews character, is one cinema's most laconically successful incarnations of this overlapping of appearance and truth, which undermines our conceited conviction that our public face does not reflect what we truly are. *Beyond a Reasonable Doubt* is a parable on the non-existence of this gap between mask and true face, between manipulation and fact.

The revelation that no matter what we do we are operating within the symbolically construed horizon of reality, effectively oozes out of the film's every detail. Take for instance the few, seemingly secondary sequences of the trial where the 'silly dancers' are called to testify as witnesses. Lang's insistence on presenting these female characters in a comical way (see how the public at the trial laughs at their depositions) should not be taken as some kind of cruel misogynous form of entertainment in an otherwise bleak narrative. On the contrary, these scenes are fully justified if only we consider that the entire show which the trial turns into (TV broadcasting included) is representative of that fictional layer that eventually comes to overlap with factual truth. And this is nowhere more obvious than in the figure of the 'stupid' District Attorney (DA) who really believes that Tom Garrett is the assassin. At one point, he goes as far as to guess the motif of his murderous act (the killer had to get rid of the dancer/lover since he had decided to marry the daughter of his boss). Lang makes us look at the DA and his thesis as if we were looking at a fool who does not realize the extent to which he is being manipulated, and yet at the end *we* (spectators) – but also the other characters in the film – are the fools for believing that our gaze was somewhat immune to manipulation. Although he was being duped, then, the DA was absolutely right, fully 'connected' with reality.

As with many noirs, the key stylistic feature introducing elements of self-reflexivity within the Hollywood canon is the reference to mirrors, which are both literal and metaphorical instruments of reflexivity. The first observation to make here is that every character is presented as redoubled, as if in front of a distorting mirror. Not only Tom Garrett (the most obvious case), but also Austin Spencer, the newspaper owner, who is split between his public persona of heart-bleeding liberal businessman (as well as Garrett's caring future father-in-law), and, more subtly, the jealous father who wants to preserve a privileged relationship with his daughter. We should not forget that the very plan to get Garrett incriminated (to prove that the law cannot be absolutely certain about a man's culpability) was Spencer's idea, in what could be legitimately read as a case of unconscious paternal rage against the future son-in-law. Furthermore, Susan herself is more ambiguous than it seems. On the one hand, she is presented as a balanced young woman and devoted fiancée (if rather frigid looking); on the other, she is eventually connoted as cold and detached when she effectively sends Garrett to his death.

With regard to the personality split that affects each of the film's main characters, we ought to note that it does not impact on the implicit thesis that 'we are what we pretend to be'. Instead, it alludes to a dimension beyond the symbolic configuration of the subject which, precisely by remaining radically disavowed, is responsible for determining such configuration. Our identity is the result of a kind of gravitational pull exerted by a foreclosed (unconscious) desire. In Garrett's case, it is therefore crucial that we never see him scheming, preparing his evil plan. Still, it is not enough to deduce that (after we discover how under the veneer of a civilized writer and fashionable journalist, there lies the ugly personality of a killer) he is a cynical manipulator. Much more disturbing is to claim that he is a civilized human being (about to marry the rich daughter of his boss) precisely because he is a killer. The two affirmations do not clash, but rather sustain each other – they constitute two faces of the same coin. This is perhaps the key (implicitly disturbing) insight of Lang's film: Our being coincides with the symbolic role we play within our social horizon in so far as it is secretly sustained by a 'dark desire' which potentially derails us. One can see how troubling this insight is if compared to the standard claim about our identity's division between its superficial appearance and deeper truth. Is not the same point made in *While the City Sleeps*, the previous Lang film of the so-called newspaper trilogy? There Lang equates (one is tempted to add 'speculatively') the rather stereotypical figure of the psychotic killer with the whole entourage of people working in the newspaper offices. As Jacques Rancière has put it commenting on this film: 'Lang's pessimism consists in observing, and making us observe, that all these people hunting down the murderer are as unpleasant as he is, perhaps even more so' (Rancière 2006a: 45). Indeed, this equation between psychotic evil and the sordidly cynical yet ordinary behaviour of the journalists embodies to perfection what Hegel had in mind with the notion of speculative coincidence of opposites: The gap between the antisocial criminal and the journalists qua repositories of the common values (freedom of press) of an entire civilization is always-already internal to the latter. The measure of evil is thus reflected back into what is presented as something that has nothing to do with evil. In fact, the truly noir dimension and real focus of *While the City Sleeps* concerns the nature of the activities taking place inside the newspaper offices, and not the pathological figure of the criminal.

Going back to *Beyond a Reasonable Doubt*, we should re-emphasize the relevance of the twist whereby Garrett inadvertently frames himself. What condemns Garrett is nothing but a good old-fashioned slip of the tongue: As he is talking to Susan, by then certain that he will be pardoned, he fatally utters the name 'Emma', a name he could not have known had he not met the murdered girl before she changed her name into Patty. In psychoanalytic jargon, here it is the unconscious that speaks – the same unconscious which, at least in terms of textual dynamics, ultimately was responsible for the murderous act. What I mean is that within the film-text, Garrett never for a second appears as if he could be able to kill.[8] With regard to its representation of the killer, in other words, the film-text is firmly situated on the side of appearances, happily endorsing its fictional status, establishing a precise correspondence between Garrett's public persona and the film's own consistent narrative fabric. So the signifier 'Emma' that brings ruin to Garrett emerges from a netherworld which the text itself does not claim to have a privileged relationship with – it simply 'pops up' when least expected. This name epitomizes the excess of subjectivity which captures the core of the subject, as well as an ontological split. In dialectical terms, Emma qua remainder is nothing but the object within the subject, the excess of materiality which language carries within itself as a symptom of human beings' divided nature. What Lang's cinema 'knows', then, is that subjectivity is never realized, never accomplished, but always thrown out of joint by some excessive surplus of sense that is thoroughly internal to the subject. The Langian subject coincides with the Lacanian subject: An excess/lack responsible for the ontologically unbalanced status of subjectivity. When the unconscious is foreclosed, subjectivity flourishes as the appearance of a consistent identity; when (as a consequence of this foreclosure) it suddenly emerges, its appearance throws subjectivity out of kilter, revealing its many gaps and radical incompleteness.

A nice example of this dialectical logic can be found in another deservedly famous film of the noir cycle, John Huston's *The Asphalt Jungle* (1950). The unmissable Langian moment in this film of many double-crossings comes right at the end, when the remaining two members of the gang that carried out the heist escape in different directions. First there is Dix (Sterling Hayden), the typical Huston hero: Despite being wounded, he drives with his girlfriend Doll (Jean Hagen) all the way to his Kentucky horse farm only to collapse and die right in the midst of his long-dreamed-of homeland. Then there is Doc, the gang's criminal mastermind (Erwin 'Doc' Riedenschneider, played by Sam Jaffe). He also attempts to escape, and it looks as if of the entire gang he is the only one who will make it alive. When he stops for a bite to eat at a diner, however, his fate turns. His attention is caught by a pretty-looking girl; he gives her some money for the jukebox, and lingers to watch her dance. This slight delay proves fatal, as a police officer peers into the diner, catches a glimpse of Doc and eventually arrests him. The similar yet profoundly contrasting fates of Dix and Doc should be analysed side by side, as they provide two different routes to subjectivity. With Dix, we are of course drenched in Huston's bucolic idealism: His life and eventual death are redeemed, literally, by his pastoral dream of communion with nature, where we find the leitmotif of Huston's humanist cinema as a whole. With Doc, however, the wound of subjectivity is not healed through idealistic longing but rather remains a wound, inasmuch as it gives body to that recalcitrant, uncontrollable excess that, like Poe's famous 'imp of the perverse',[9] drives a human being against his 'pleasure principle', forcing him to do exactly *the wrong thing* in a given situation. Doc knew that he could not linger, that his life depended on his resolution to run away without turning back. And yet, in the diner, the demon takes over, the excess of *jouissance* is released as the disavowed (foreclosed) substance of the subject. If we are looking for a definition of subjectivity, then, we should stick with Doc and his symptomatic enjoyment beyond the pleasure principle: A totally self-referential nucleus of *jouissance* that has no time (literally) for the subject's desire of self-preservation. When it makes its arrival, the subject's conscious plans are suddenly ignored, bypassed, and the real subject takes over, driving at full speed towards a potentially lethal destination. By contrast, Dix's idealism cannot but sound fake and hollow, given that his desire, despite eventually leading him to his death, is sustained by a precise fantasmatic scenario. Doc's lethal lingering, as he is mesmerized by the girl's frantic dancing movements in the diner, is therefore the Langian moment I was referring to – a moment that marks Lang's cinema down to its very roots.[10]

Here we should also highlight how unique this passage is by comparing it to the standard cinematic reference to the intervention of a malignant fate that disrupts the subject's plans. To exemplify this difference, let us briefly consider a powerful neo-noir like Robert Aldrich's *Hustle* (1975), starring Burt Reynolds in the role of deeply distressed, existentially wounded Lieutenant Phil Gaines. When the complex investigation is over, and all the main actors in this story of perversion and abuse have met their fate, Lieutenant Gaines's scarred identity also seems destined to find some peace in the relationship with ex-prostitute and fiancée Nicole Britton (Catherine Deneuve). However, in the cruellest turn of fate, Gaines is accidentally involved in a drugstore armed robbery and ends up killed. The small but crucial difference between this type of narrative resolution and the passage detailed above in Huston's film should be clearly spelled out: Although Gaines's death no doubt stands, metaphorically speaking, for the radically antagonized inner nature of his subjectivity (his dream of finding happiness with Nicole had no real foundations),[11] at the same time it is presented as the intervention of a merciless fate, of a thoroughly external force that can derail our lives at any given moment without taking our conscious desires into account. This corresponds to the existentialist topos of the irrational, senseless, absurd condition of humanity, so often and perhaps too precipitously associated with film noir. For what is missing from this scenario is precisely the subjective surplus of sense represented by Doc's fate in *The Asphalt Jungle*. The difference between the two types of senselessness (objective: 'life is a bitch', it does not make sense; and subjective: 'there is something in me that threatens to derail my life') should be underscored again and again, for the simple reason that when the surplus of sense emerges at the subjective level, we are accountable for it, and have to respond as to the consequences of our acts. The 'life is a bitch' scenario is ultimately a comforting one: what can we do – what responsibilities can we endure – if life is absurd and everything depends on fate? And although this is true (fate can always strike, no matter how safely I lead my life), the resonance of this truth is only brought to full fruition by the shattering experience of my radical self-division, whereby the 'crack' in the universe of sense is something that defines what I am and for which I, in my modest, insignificant existence, am and should be responsible for. Fate does not merely strike at me from outside, but it dwells within me as the core of what I am, of my subjectivity.

Sublimation in *The Blue Gardenia*

This consideration brings us to the first film of Lang's 'newspaper trilogy', *The Blue Gardenia* (1953). Within the three films of the trilogy, we should sharply distinguish between the critical context (Lang's acerbic representation of the

American media)[12] and the deep-seated, 'unconscious' message the films carry. I will not analyse here *The Blue Gardenia* in connection with the difficult circumstances in which it was created, namely that it was the first film Lang made after being blacklisted during the McCarthy era of anti-communist witch-hunting (it has already been amply documented that the shooting conditions imposed on the director by the studio, Warner Bros., were extremely harsh).[13] Instead, I will concentrate entirely on the narrative, with a view to uncovering its dialectical structure. The first consideration to make is that the conceptual closure (in Adorno's term) implicit in Lang's representation of the media is 'only' the necessary background against which the film's focal interests lie. We should underscore the subtle disruption at work within this seemingly ideological film (again, in Adorno's terms) while also insisting on the dialectical relationship between explicit context and disavowed core. The obvious starting point, at least from our dialectical perspective, can only be the central representation of the heroine's black out. Depressed after being dumped by her fiancé, telephone operator Norah (Anne Baxter) accepts a date with commercial artist and notorious womanizer Harry Prebble (Raymond Burr). She gets drunk with him, goes to his apartment, and upon realizing that she has made a mistake, she attempts to resist his protracted, unchivalrous advances by hitting him with a fireplace poker; he drops down and she blacks out. The day after, Norah does not remember a thing about the incident but upon learning that Prebble has been murdered, she begins to panic as all the clues seem to be against her. Eventually, it is revealed that the murderer was actually another woman named Rose Miller (Ruth Storey), who had also gone to Prebble's apartment that night after a series of humiliations she had suffered from him. Rose had used the same poker against Prebble to 'finish the job' began by Norah. This narrative structure is embedded within the relationship that ensues between Norah and 'superstar' newspaper reporter Casey Mayo (Richard Conte), who cynically lures Norah into confessing, which in turn leads to her being apprehended by the police. Having fallen in love with her, Mayo is also the one who, joining Captain Haynes (George Reeves), eventually unmasks the real killer.

So, why is Norah's black out so important for our analysis? Not only, of course, because it is the key ingredient in creating the typically noirish sense of mystery and suspense. Or rather, while creating suspense as the film's central enigma, it also demands to be read as a symptom of the film's fascination with a radical act that seems to escape symbolic representation. Here the parallel with *Beyond a Reasonable Doubt* imposes itself: Apart from their stylistic similarities, both films are effectively about symbolic fictions which have no place, in terms of cinematic representation, for the pivotal event (the killing) around which these fictions are woven. The murderous act which propels the narrative forward is excluded from representation: Not only do we not see it, but we also have to trust Rose's confession, not having any other evidence apart from her words – the words of a deeply depressed, suicidal woman – to arrive at the truth. We should also add the far from insignificant detail that Norah never regains her memory of the night she spent at Prebble's flat, and that therefore she has to accept Rose's confession as truthful.

To use Adorno's and Critical Theory's central theoretical tenet, the truth qua Absolute by definition remains out of reach, non-identical, and immersed in negativity. The fascination with the interconnections between guilt and law, typical of Lang's American films, needs therefore to be situated in a dialectical context whereby the film-text resists the temptation to portray (what in narrative terms is presented as) the truth. And if truth is not available, then, guilt is everywhere (here is another ready-made modernist trope). Given this reading, Norah's black out works as a literal instance of *blinding* which takes place when the subject is confronted with the truth about herself as well as the objective truth of the concrete situation. Whether or not Lang was aware of this, the missing link in the narrative (which, as we have seen, deep down remains a missing link *tout court* despite the standard recourse to the procedure of detection), coupled with Norah's amnesia, from which she never recovers, provides a clear visualization of the tension between knowledge and truth (subject and object, appearance and substance) which qualifies German idealism from Kant to Hegel. In fact, one is tempted to risk the hypothesis that, especially when confronted with the wonderful Hegelian accomplishment of *Beyond a Reasonable Doubt*, Lang's *The Blue Gardenia* remains ensconced in the Kantian transcendental dualism between the fundamental powerlessness of knowledge and the unreachable Thing-in-itself (*Ding as Sich*). Essentially, it fails to go beyond the representation of the epistemological limit of reason. The blacking out of the main character when confronted with the event qua truth of the situation (not only in elementary narrative terms – the killing – but also, and more importantly, in so far as it stands for the disavowed kernel of the subjects involved) would seem to attest to the impossibility for reason to have direct access to truth.

Indeed, the narrative does nothing but affirm again and again that any connection between human knowledge and the elusive/unreachable event can only take place via the mediation of what Kant in his *Critique of Judgement* (1790) defined as the *dynamically sublime*, that is to say, a feeling of immense powerlessness vis-à-vis the immeasurable might of nature which challenges the synthetic faculty of imagination and triggers in the subject the recollection of the infinite power of Reason qua moral law. Norah's helplessness vis-à-vis the mysterious event represents the dominant subjective mood within the entire film, often turning into a proper nightmare. Kant, as anticipated, resolves the issue of the failure of the imagination vis-à-vis the sublime by bringing into contention the moral law, which putatively absorbs the shock of this failure,[14] and recoups it in the unbearable pressure of the injunction to do one's duty (precisely because the feeling of the sublime conjures up the impossibility of reaching the Thing, we must submit to the moral law). In the film under scrutiny, however, there is no moral law. Instead, the negativity of the event continues to call into question the inadequacy of reason. If the event is finally explained, this is thanks to the standard romantic solution (Casey Mayo's falls in love with Norah and consequently rescues her from her predicament). The point we are making, on the other hand, is that the gap between everyday reality and the Thing-in-itself is bridged, in the film, precisely by that blacking out which would seem to introduce us, albeit negatively, into a dimension where 'the Thing shines'. As claimed by Žižek (1989: 203):

> The Sublime is therefore the paradox of an object which, in the very field of representation, provides a view, in a negative way, of the dimension of what is unrepresentable. It is a unique point in Kant's system, a point at which the fissure, the gap between phenomenon and Thing-in-itself, is abolished in a negative way, because in it the phenomenon's very inability to represent the Thing adequately *is inscribed in the phenomenon itself.*

It is possible here to draw a parallel between Kant's sublime and Lacan's *objet a*, seeing that, for Lacan, *objet a* represents *the paradox of an object elevated to the dignity of the Thing.* Lang gets close to this paradox precisely in the scene where the brutish Prebble (a real force of nature – a recurrent type in Lang's filmography) forces himself onto Norah. And perhaps the measure of Lang's accomplishment in *Beyond a Reasonable Doubt* can be gauged from the fact that there, in his last American film, he does not need the Sublime to establish the connection between phenomena governed by the fallibility of human reason and the absolute Thing-in-itself, since ultimately there is no difference between them, they coincide. As we have seen, *Beyond a Reasonable Doubt* establishes, in a thoroughly original way, the perfect coincidence between fictions and facts, thereby showing how the frustrating relativity of knowledge and its categories is always-already included in the object of knowledge as its ultimate constitutive feature. In *The Blue Gardenia*, on the other hand, the transcendental aspect of sublimation qua epistemological obstacle is dominant, obfuscating the ontological magnitude of the impasse that the sublime embodies.

From paranoia to repetition

If the crucial Hegelian motif of the overlap between epistemological obstacle and ontological deadlock is at least partially missed in *The Blue Gardenia*, in earlier films such as *Man Hunt* (1940) and *The Ministry of Fear* (1944), part of the anti-Nazi tetralogy of the 1940s, it is already fully endorsed. *The Ministry of Fear*, a film overladen with paranoia and run through by the Hitchcockian theme of hunting, is a perfect case in point.[15] The general feature to highlight about this film is that it presents us with mutually inconsistent systems: the British Ministry of the Interior is clearly inconsistent, as a pro-Nazi spy ring has managed to infiltrate it and is smuggling out vital information about war strategies; at the same time, the spy ring itself is flawed, since it allows itself to be uncovered by a man named Stephen Neale (Ray Milland), who has just been released from a mental asylum after serving a 2-year sentence for allegedly murdering his wife. To put it in simplified Hegelian terms, everything here, whether subject of substance, is deeply fraught with inconsistencies. But the detail not to miss is that the actual equivalence subject–substance is put forward, from the film's very inception, as the *unconscious* core of its narrative. The story begins with the shot of a deeply disturbed man (the Milland character) who anxiously awaits his release after 2 years spent in reclusion. He longs for a normal, ordinary life in London – despite the fact that, as we soon discover, this is the time of the London blitz. The following scene ranges as one of the most memorable of the entire film, and in my opinion stands among the best of Lang's entire filmography. It is already dark when Stephen Neale reaches the small train station of the fictional location of Lembridge, where he buys a ticket for the English capital. Just opposite the station, he notices a fête hosted by a charitable organization called 'The Mothers of Free Nations'. Intrigued, and looking for some amusement after the time spent in isolation, he takes a stroll inside, not knowing that he is about to be drawn into someone else's criminal plan. After the answer he gives to a palm reader ('enough of my past, tell me about the future') is mistaken for a coded message, he is urged to play at guessing the exact weight of a cake, which he wins and, eventually, goes away with. Later, we discover that the cake contained a microfilm with war information from the Ministry of the Interior.[16]

This classic case of mistaken identity (the person to whom the cake should have been delivered turns up when Neale is about to leave the fête, thus kick-starting the game of hunting which occupies the rest of the film) provides the clue for our claim that the subject in question effectively coincides with substance in its deeply fraught configuration. We notice, first of all, that by entering the space of the fête Neale enters, literally, a somewhat illusory dimension, a microcosm structured around highly symbolic gestures (coded messages, innuendos, telling looks etc.). This confined space ruled by masquerade works as a perfect exemplification of the fictional/cinematic dimension that sustains reality. After such 'contagion', the rest of the film will never go back, it will remain steeped in an atmosphere of subterfuge where every identity, including that of the loved one, is enmeshed with a sense of precarious fictitiousness. But the speculative point to highlight concerns the overlap between the subject in its radically void framework and the inconsistency of the world around him. The all-important narrative detail is the portrayal of Neale as a man reduced to the empty set of his subjectivity – a deeply troubled individual who wants to start his life afresh, leaving his past behind. Crucially, the reference to a past to be erased is the exact narrative point where 'subject meets substance': The palm reader mistakes Neale's reference to his past for the coded message that would guarantee access to the spy ring. It is a wonderful case of overlapping lacks, a perfect cinematic rendition of what Hegel had in mind with his claim that the True appears not only as substance but also as subject, since the subject here is nothing but the name of the self-alienation of substance, its intrinsic deficit.

First, Neale's past (with the alleged killing of his wife) is what caused his psychic instability and the consequent desire to begin anew – in short, it caused the subject to emerge in its purest status, that of a split and therefore deeply inconsistent being. It is this very subject that, for the rest of the film, appears almost insanely driven to unmask the spy ring, to the extent of bypassing the law, as in the sequence that follows the suicide of the Dan Duryea character (and it is this obstinate, near-suicidal drive that almost gets Neale killed in the final sequence). The romantic ingredient spurring Neale's mad determination should not obfuscate the true origin of his drive, which ought to be connected with the character's original condition of instability. Then, if in this film the subject is a subject on account of his radically deracinated condition, the symbolic network around him (Lacan's 'big Other') is equally connoted as profoundly out of joint, lacking consistency – and this lack marks precisely the point of entrance of the subject (Neale). As anticipated, the 'crack' in the symbolic order of sense is redoubled, since the breach within the criminal organization is reproduced as a fault affecting the government, thus the law itself. In terms of their common negativity, then, not only subject and substance, but also law and crime are shown as speculatively identical.[17] Not surprisingly, police Inspector Prentice (Percy Waram) is portrayed as a thug constantly handling a cutter, and as a consequence he is mistaken for a Nazi by Neale.

This narrative structure is also detectable in Lang's first anti-Nazi film, *Man Hunt* (1941), and especially, once again, in its extraordinary opening scene, where the subject is shown as he stands alone against the Other in the usual guise of the Nazi threat (in fact, Adolf Hitler in person). In July 1939, before the beginning of the war, British Captain Alan Thorndike (Walter Pigeon), a formidable big game hunter, is hiding in the forest surrounding Hitler's residence. He brandishes a high-precision rifle, which he points at Hitler as the latter emerges from his mansion. As soon as he fires the shot, however, we realize it was only a blank. After briefly pondering the situation, he loads the rifle and prepares to shoot again. Before he has a chance to do so, however, his presence is spotted by a Nazi guard who jumps on him, making the shot go wild and subsequently capturing him. The rest of the film follows rather faithfully the tightly woven narrative action of *The Ministry of Fear*, in so far as it is characterized by a game of hunting, as the title explicitly suggests. From hunter, Thorndike becomes the hunted one: He miraculously escapes the Nazis' attempt to kill him and returns to London, where German agents are waiting to resume the hunting, until the final denouement.

Before commenting on the significance of the film's remarkable finale, let us return to the opening scene. More precisely, let us focus on what we might call, paraphrasing Lacan's notion of 'entre deux morts' (between two deaths), 'the space between the two shots', that is, between the blank one and the real one, which probably would have reached the führer had the guard not intervened. Interestingly, the film does not clarify whether Thorndike would have actually pulled the trigger a second time, when the rifle was actually loaded. Thorndike's hesitation, as well as his later protestations of innocence, rather suggest that he had not planned to kill Hitler. In fact, on an elementary level, the whole film can be read as a critical account of the failure of dealing with Hitler before things got very serious for Europe and the world. What is certain is that this gap between the two shots lends itself to a dialectical analysis of the relationship between subject and object. The central issue of the shooting can be abstracted from its context and discussed as a matter of representation of the subject's connection with the world. For it is clear that with the wonderfully suspended action of the initial scene, Lang attempts to portray the subject as prey to a strange 'call' beyond causal determinations: Thorndike is shown, for a few instants, as if he was *not* the master his own actions; he enters a shadowy zone where he acts as if acted – as if he was an automaton merely executing a desire whose cause he could not fathom. No wonder, then, that for the rest of the film we are unable to determine whether or not Thorndike wanted to kill Hitler: The truth is that he himself is unable to determine it. To borrow again from Lacan, for those few moments he was 'in him more than himself', in the precise sense that his act was performed unconsciously. In a similar vein to what takes place at the beginning of *The*

Ministry of Fear, the subject is introduced by Lang as a split entity – not as a furious, irrational 'beast' (as other, less interesting Langian characters are), but as a thoroughly rational being who, however, for a brief but crucial lapse of time reveals the pervasive absence of purpose of his actions, the defining lack of directionality of his existence.

This is therefore the subject in its true guise for it defies any knowledge or logical explanation he/we might want to assign to his actions. In dialectical terms, the only place human beings can find freedom is here, in the narrow margin, in the thin and often indistinguishable line that separates a conscious decision from its suspended meaning. Are we not back, here, to the Langian concern with the performative role of fictions? If the first shot can be categorized as fictional (Thorndike only *pretended* to shoot at Hitler), the second is not merely real in the common sense of the word (factual), but is instead enveloped in a radically fictional dimension, a zone of veritable undecidability (yes, the shot is eventually fired, but we and the bearer of the action remain fundamentally ignorant as to whether it was consciously meant to hit Hitler). The standard opposition fiction/fact (this most cherished principle of the tradition of our thought) should thus be supplemented by the couple fiction/Real, where the second term refers not to an objective fact but to what Hegel had in mind with the phrase 'appearance qua appearance' (Hegel 1977: 89) – the *distilled*, as it were, dimension of fiction itself, that is to say truth understood not as a positive entity but as *the appearance returning to itself after realising that it does not hide a truth*. And the lesson to be drawn from this second (dialectical) opposition is twofold: First, that symbolic fictions are constitutive of reality, in so far as reality is what we experience and plays a real/material role in our lives; secondly, that the only way out of the fiction that sustains our existence can only be defined and experienced as a radicalization of fiction itself, the suspension of the principle of sufficient reason through which, in normal conditions, we remain attached to reality. The second shot fired by Thorndike is therefore presented by Lang as Real precisely because its cause remains not merely hidden but thoroughly inaccessible. This effect of 'broken causation', as we shall see, is also at the heart of the film's conscious anti-Nazi message.

What about, then, the rest of the story (practically its entire duration) with its furiously paced, action-packed plot? Is it not clear that the amount of *action*, here, in its proper narrative meaning, is nothing but a 'poor substitute', a surrogate, for the initial act, whose crucial impact the film is built around? It is here that we should mention the film's coda, since it represents a *repetition* of its inception. In his final confrontation with the enemy, Thorndike emerges victorious but badly wounded. By the time he has fully recovered, the war has started. In the final scene, he has joined the British aviation (Royal Air Force) and goes on a mission to Germany; he parachutes into the Reich holding his high-precision rifle, determined to finish off where he had started a few months earlier. As anticipated, in the standard reading of the film this final declaration of intents works as a critique of the initial hesitation on the part of the lone sniper, which in turn sounds like a reproach made to the world powers' negligence in dealing with the Nazi threat. However, repetition here also retains a wider significance, one that involves the notion of temporality and allows us to perceive the dialectical tension between past and future. We could say that in a true act of repetition the agent's inscription within a given project literally rewrites the past. Repetition works retroactively. If the first act opens up the possibility of engagement (here, with anti-Nazism), it is only repetition that makes that possibility count.

Walter Benjamin's notion of repetition as the revolutionary realization of the repressed content of the past comes instantly to mind here. When, in 1940, he was writing the *Theses on the Philosophy of History*, Benjamin of course knew, like Lang, that the Nazi–Fascist threat needed to be confronted earlier. As he put it in Thesis VIII: 'One reason why Fascism has a chance is that in the name of progress its opponents treat it as historical norm' (Benjamin 1992: 249). Progress here included also the Social Democratic and 'vulgar Marxist' illusion that work itself, that is, faith alone in technologically conceived labour, would redeem the masses. In Thesis XI, Benjamin quotes Marx's critique of the Gotha Congress of 1875, which brought together the two German Socialist parties: 'Smelling a rat, Marx countered that ". . . the man who possesses no other property than his labour power" must of necessity become "the slave of other men who have made themselves the owners . . ."' (p. 250). A telling quotation from Nietzsche, used as an epigraph to Thesis XII, introduces us to Benjamin's critique of historicism: 'We need history, but not the way a spoiled loafer in the garden of knowledge needs it' (p. 251). Immediately after, he deploys his materialist notion of history against the naive historicist faith in the unbroken continuum of time: 'Historicism gives the "eternal" image of the past; historical materialism supplies a unique experience with the past. The historical materialist leaves it to others to be drained by the whore called "Once upon a time" in historicism's bordello' (p. 254). Finally, in Thesis XVII, comes the famous passage that connects with Lang's depiction of repetition in *Man Hunt*. Benjamin writes: 'Thinking involves not only the flow of thoughts, but their arrest as well. Where thinking suddenly stops in a configuration pregnant with tension, it gives that configuration a shock.' It is this 'configuration pregnant with tension' that, if my analysis is correct, Lang's cinema so distinctly manages to reclaim.

In specific relation to *Man Hunt*, Thorndike's initial hesitation corresponds to this configuration of, as Benjamin puts it, time crystallized into a monad. It is the encounter with this *crystal of time* (to borrow from Deleuze's film theory) that holds a crucial significance for the historical materialist, for there 'he recognizes the sign of a Messianic cessation of happening, or, put differently, a revolutionary chance in the fight for the oppressed past'. Here, then, we have an image of repetition resulting from the 'encounter'with a past event that suddenly yields a revolutionary chance. It is, therefore, a politically vital concept. In Benjamin's view such an encounter has the potential to 'blast a specific era out of the homogenous course of history'. The historical materialist's method of enquiry, based on the 'redemption' (qua repetition) of past events, is significantly characterized by Benjamin's use of the Hegelian verb *aufheben* in its threefold meaning (to preserve, to elevate and to cancel). In Hegelian terms, repetition can be understood as an operation involving the passage from an implicit assertion to an explicit one – or, more precisely, from In-itself (*an sich*) to For-itself (*für sich*), that is to say, from unreflective capacity (*potentia*) to fully developed actuality. As explained by Žižek: 'The passage from In-itself to For-itself thus involves the logic of repetition: when a thing becomes "for itself", nothing actually changes in it; it just repeatedly asserts ("re-marks") what it already was in itself.' Žižek then adds that this logic of repetition is at work, in a purified form, in Hegel's notion of 'negation of negation', which allows us to grasp the connection between repetition and negativity: '"Negation of negation" is thus nothing but repetition at its purest: in the first move, a certain gesture is accomplished and fails; then, in the second move, this same gesture is simply *repeated*' (Žižek 1999: 74).

Are we not dealing here with the ultimate wisdom of Lang's *Man Hunt*? What is at stake in this film is not just the simple repetition of a gesture, which goes from being implicit to being explicit; rather, we are discussing the repetition of a gesture embedded in negativity. The difference between the opening scene and the final one, then, is the difference between *abstract negation* and *negation of negation* (or *determinate negation*) in Hegel's dialectical sequence. What this means is that the first negation (Thorndike's blank followed by the skewed shot) failed because the agent was not yet able to fully comprehend and articulate his opposition to the enemy. Deep down, he knew that what he had to do was kill Hitler, and yet he could not bring himself to accomplish the act because of his belonging to that enervated European (British) opposition to Nazi-fascism discussed above and chastised by Benjamin. Although negation *per se* does qualify the subversive nature of his intention, it also captures the intrinsic impossibility to fully realize such intention the first time round, for it remains abstract, immediate, i.e. disconnected from a truly contrastive opposition to its context. In fact, what is negated in the film's coda is the very impediment (negation) involved in the character's ideological stance, his deep libidinal (unconscious) attachment to a weak opposition to Hitler. Contrary to what is often assumed in Hegelian critical literature, negation of negation, the third moment of the dialectical sequence, should be understood as a repetition of the first instance of opposition/negation which, however, is not aimed at the recuperation of a mythical positivity but at the redoubling/repetition of the first negation. This third moment is absolutely necessary if one is to accomplish the work of the negative, namely to gain a proper oppositional distance from what is perceived as the enemy.

One can see how Lang's film is not merely critical of the general attitude of the British (and the world) vis-à-vis the Nazis' rise to power before the war, but it also demonstrates that, as it were, 'one had to kill Hitler twice': The first strike could not be the killer blow as its real aim was to prepare the ground for the second strike, which, to go back to Benjamin's terminology, 'redeemed' the first. In light of this reading, we should perhaps reconsider the meaning of all the action that takes place in between the two negations. While in strict theoretical terms it remains a substitute of the act proper, the main character's involvement with a number of potentially fatal obstacles, within the typical Langian representation of the clash between hunter and hunted, suggests the necessity of a process whereby the subject becomes aware of the real potentiality of his intervention. As in *The Ministry of Fear*, the key factor in the character's decision to fully endorse his subversive drive is the woman he (eventually) falls in love with. Here, however, the characterization of the love affair is more complex and refined than in the later film, for the woman Thorndike becomes attached to, Jenny (Joan Bennett), is a humble working-class girl living in London. In fact, it is when she loses her life out of love for Thorndike, attempting to follow him in his escape from the German agents, that the hero becomes aware of his class-related arrogance and matures the decision to go back and fight the Nazis (almost kamikaze style).[18] In other words, it is the working-class girl's sacrifice that triggers the hero's resolve. More to the point, the sudden vanishing of the possibility of the relationship, the materialization of its lack, is translated by Thorndike into antagonistic drive against the Nazis. Although romanticized by the 'if only she had not died . . .' scenario, the impossibility of the sexual relationship is shown as strictly correlative to political antagonism, for we can safely assume that without the awareness of the girl's involvement and sacrifice, the hero would never have decided to go back to finish off his mission – he would never have negated the first negation. Far from standing merely as a romantic filler, the relationship between Thorndike and Jenny brings into relief the necessity for the hero to detach from his class to engage in a direct confrontation with the enemy.[19]

The gaze in the frame

The concern with the 'reality of fictions' is also evident in Lang's two overtly psychoanalytic films of the mid-1940s: *The Woman in the Window* (1944) and *Scarlet Street* (1945). It is immediately significant that both films are centred on the framing of the object-cause of desire which, as often in Lang, is represented by woman. With regard to these two films, it seems to me that, in line with the central preoccupation of Lang's cinema as a whole, the accent should be placed not on the masculine gaze framing woman, but instead on the ontological issue of the rapport between fiction and reality that overrides the question of sexual difference. It might help to recall that Lang's first three Hollywood films – the so-called 'social trilogy' composed of *Fury* (1936), *You Only Live Once* (1937) and *You and Me* (1938) – express a strong interest in the cinematic reference to framing. It is no coincidence that Lang's first Hollywood shot, in *Fury*, is that of a shop window portraying a couple staring through it as if watching a film: A tracking shot frames the stiffness of a mannequin in a wedding dress inside a bedroom, and then reveals the desiring gaze of Joe Wilson (Spencer Tracy) and Katherine Grant (Sylvia Sidney) from outside the shop. The first, crucial statement is made with this shot, for the question Lang asks concerns precisely the affinity of reality and appearance. In fact, as if to underscore this, the first line of the film is the following question that Joe poses to Katherine: 'What do you say kid, are we moving in?' When the next shot reveals the couple in their own bedroom, we understand that indeed they have moved in, in the sense that their life has become identical to the fiction displayed in the shop window.

Although critics have identified in this kind of scenes, and more generally in Lang's American cinema, a critical awareness of consumer society and its dangers (an awareness that would justify the parallel between Lang and Adorno), a different concern is also at work here, one that has to do with the definition of reality as such. It is as if Lang, newly arrived in the United States as a refugee from Nazi Germany, not only reflected in his cinema the deficiencies of the American model, but also, and more importantly, used this model (consumer society) as a way to continue his (implicitly philosophical) investigations into the status of reality as reflected by the cinematic eye.[20] Shop windows of course occupy a central position in consumerist societies, as they already did in 1930s America. While Lang undoubtedly understood the critical potential implicit in the cinematic image of a shop window, at the same time the dividing glass between consumers and commodities offered him the chance to explore the interconnections between 'being' and 'appearance'. What if appearances turn out to be constitutive of reality? And what if, even more interestingly, they turn out to be *more real* than the ordinary reality of our lives? These are the questions that Lang's cinema at its best encourages us to ask, whether consciously or unconsciously. One is tempted to emphasize the intrinsic Marxian breadth of these questions. Who does not remember Marx's dictum, from volume I of *Capital*, that commodities, once they emerge, acquire a *magical* aura through which they keep us under their spell (see Marx 1990: 167–8)? The paradox is that when we enjoy commodities (even simply by looking at them), we are in fact *enjoyed by them*, they control us – just like, for Lacan, when we speak, we are in fact spoken by language. More to the point: Commodities, the 'dead' objects we look at through shop windows, control us since they hold the key to our unconscious. Commodity *fetishism*, in other words, reaches right into the core of what we are, incarnating that surplus of disavowed, objectified enjoyment that lies at the core of subjectivity. In Lang's cinema, the relevance of the framing shot whereby characters look through a glass window has to do precisely with the dialectical rapport between the fictional object-image behind the glass and the reality in which these characters are immersed. The rapport is not naively oppositional, as many commentators seem to suggest (the fiction/lie of commodities risks turning us into alienated 'objects', etc.), but rather implies an overlap whereby the object-image is revealed as constitutive of reality itself, inasmuch as it is our fetishistic attachment to the object-commodity that allows us to set up a symbolically consistent world. As a matter of fact, images of shop windows cut across the entirety of Lang's production, retaining a value which goes beyond the specific concern with commodity fetishism and its effects on human beings. For instance, let us recall the centrality of these framed images in *M* (1931), with the film's perverse protagonist Hans Beckert (Peter Lorre) gazing enraptured at the little girl through a shop window.

Consider also the placid, monotonous existence in which the self-satisfied bourgeois professor Richard Wanley (Edward G. Robinson) is immersed in *The Woman in the Window*. As a couple of overlapping dissolves suggest, where his image is juxtaposed to an ornamental clock, his life is machine regulated. However, the day his family departs for a summer holiday, he comes across a striking painting of a beautiful woman exposed in a gallery window, just before joining some friends at an all-male club. Lang depicts this via a long shot of Wanley approaching the gallery redoubled by a shot of his figure reflected in the gallery window, as if to immediately suggest the overlap of reality and its reflection. Then, in the club with his friends (a Doctor and a Lawyer), he engages in a conversation about the exceptional beauty of the woman in the portrait, which then develops into a discussion on the advantages and disadvantages of routine, with Wanley complaining about the tedious security of his life and the 'stodginess' that he is beginning to feel. Here the explicit theme of the film is immediately pinned down as the typical noir opposition between a safe but boring routine and the excitement of an unforeseen, potentially dangerous encounter. If routine of necessity turns life into a pale copy of itself, the essence of life can be experienced via an exciting encounter that catches us off-guard.[21] Knowledge and wisdom (represented by the three professors conferring amiably while sitting on comfortable armchairs and drinking brandy) are contrasted with a reference to the unexpected and unknown, which in fact materializes later that very evening, when Wanley, after a few drinks, returns to marvel at the portrait of the woman in the window. Lang explores again the interconnections between fiction and reality when he shows us first the image of the painting without reflections, and then that of Wanley looking in, reflected on the windowpane, positioned in between a vase and a distorted image of another portrait. As the camera moves out to align with Wanley's gaze, we realize how startled he is to notice that the fictional image in the portrait has redoubled: A second image of the same woman has materialized alongside the picture, an image which is in fact the reflection on the gallery window of Alice Reed (Joan Bennett), the model who had posed for the painting and who now stands next to Wanley. The confused protagonist acknowledges this new appearance through a double take, which brings together the two fictional/reflected images and the real one.

The shot of the two images of Alice Reed next to each other (the painting and the reflection) provides the key to Lang's film as well as to the dialectical dimension of his cinema as a whole. Here we should be precise, for these images are positioned at a different distance from the onlooker. While the portrait remains in the background, the reflection of the Joan Bennett character is more superficial and thus closer to Wanley. The implication is that the more evanescent and intangible image (the reflection) is also the more vivid and concrete one. Once again, we should highlight how it is not a simple matter of reality versus fiction, but of fiction versus the Real of fiction, its distilled dimension: The portrait is, as it were, a copy not so much of the real flesh and blood woman, but of the stunning reflection that suddenly appears next to it. Another way of putting this is by saying that, although such reflection on the window originates in Alice Reed's flesh and blood person, it nevertheless captures to perfection what Alice becomes for Wanley, namely the evanescent, even hallucinatory object-cause of his desire.[22] Indeed, the real Alice remains a ghost, *more fictional than the image in the portrait* – and it is because of this ghost-like dimension that she is Real, that is, entangled with an unconscious desire.

We should therefore avoid the common critical remark as encapsulated in Tom Gunning's observation that 'from original reviewers down to contemporary student audiences, most viewers moan at the revelation that it was all a dream' (Gunning 2000: 292). The point is that such a revelation is absolutely necessary to confirm Lang's intuition that beyond fiction (the painting) there is not just merely factual reality, but rather the special, sublime materiality of a particular object that sustains our desires, fantasies and thus our universe of sense. This is why the film is Freudian to the bone. Freud's theory of dreams begins by posing the following question: How does an unconscious desire inscribe itself in a dream? His answer is that such a desire, precisely because unconscious, foreclosed and therefore illicit, cannot materialize in the dream-text directly, but it attaches itself to those fragments from the dreamer's recent waking experience that constitute part of the explicit dream-text. And the function of the latter is precisely to *disguise* the unconscious desire in order for it to elude the censorship of the ego. The unconscious kernel of the dream, then, cannot be located simply by deciphering the secret meaning of the dream-text. Rather, it is the desire that inscribes itself through the specific distortion embodied by the narrative content of the dream. In our film, the twists and turns of the narrative (Wanley's dream) are there, as it were, to smuggle the unconscious desire without it being recognized by the ego. The unconscious is therefore the *form* of the desire that by necessity attaches itself to a certain narrative, while the content of a dream is, as Freud famously put it, 'the guardian of sleep', a story whose main role is to allow us to continue sleeping, absorbing the shock potential of the forbidden desire. This is to say that the unconscious form in Lang's film – the unconscious kernel of Wanley's desire – can be identified in its first appearance as the initial reflection of Alice's figure on the window. A form, an illusion, an apparition that literally shapes the story that follows.

In relation to film, then, the unconscious of the Freudian tradition makes itself available as an utterly evanescent formal configuration, a sort of negative magnitude embodied by an image that exerts a gravitational pull on what we see and try to make sense of, conferring upon it its own specific distortion (its own narrative). With films, as well as dreams (and any other symbolic construct), the crucial psychoanalytic question to ask is not 'What is the meaning of this story?', but rather 'What act of repression, or foreclosure, allowed this narrative to emerge as it is?' The unconscious is precisely what needs to be foreclosed so that a certain narrative can emerge. What is at work in the unconscious is therefore the opposite of a synthetic function: The negative force of the imagination, the capacity of our mind to dismember what perception pieces together. The reflected image of Alice next to her portrait works as a perfect exemplification of that special thing that Lacan termed *objet a*: A formal configuration embodying the shattering force of negativity that an unconscious desire always is. It is the thing that, through the partial disavowal of its ultimate inconsistency, sustains our fantasy, and thus our sense of reality (without which there would be only madness, psychotic breakdown). When in the mid-1950s Lacan begins to propose his thesis that 'the unconscious is structured like a language' (see Lacan 1993: 167; 1998b: 48), he means to underscore the fact that there is a fundamental affinity between language and the unconscious, in so far as the unconscious too is, ultimately, fictional. In cinematic terms, it is an image – an image that embodies all that the subject (professor Wanley) had to forget (repress) to be able to live his placid, trouble-free, uneventful life.

We are therefore back to Lang's dialectical concern with fictions, which as we have seen, runs through the entirety of his 'American cinema' and comes to full fruition in his last Hollywood film. Lang's cinema 'knows' that, if on the one hand there is no substantial difference between its own fictional dimension and reality (in so far as reality is of necessity cinematic, i.e. it 'holds up' only if we fictionalize it), on the other hand reality, in its fictional configuration, hosts a real kernel which constantly threatens to derail it. As in *Man Hunt*, the finale of *The Woman in the Window* highlights precisely the narrow margin between fiction qua reality and fiction qua Real. After waking up, professor Wanley returns to the painting that caused his dream. As he is looking at it, a woman approaches him asking him to light her cigarette, at which point Wanley simply runs away – in other words, *he takes refuge in reality*, he escapes into the fictional fabric of his everyday existence so as not to 'get burnt' by the unconscious (or, more precisely, by what Lacan termed the Real of *jouissance*). This is what Žižek also alludes to in his commentary on the film:

> We must not, however, view the final turnaround as a compromise, an accommodation to the codes of Hollywood. The message of the film is not consoling, not 'it was only a dream, in reality I am a normal man like others and not a murderer!' but rather: *in our unconscious, in the real of our desire, we are all murderers*. Paraphrasing the Lacanian interpretation of the Freudian dream about the father to whom a dead son appears, reproaching him with the words 'Father, can't you see that I'm burning?', we could say that the professor awakes in order to continue his dream (about being a normal person like his fellow men), that is, to escape the real (the 'psychic reality') of his desire. [. . .] In other words, paraphrasing the parable of Zhuang-Zhi and the butterfly, which is also one of Lacan's points of reference: we do not have a quiet, kind, decent, bourgeois professor

> dreaming for a moment that he is a murderer; what we have is, on the contrary, a murderer dreaming, in his everyday life, that he is just a decent bourgeois professor. (Žižek 1992: 16–17)

This final observation brings us back to Lang's obsession with frames, which often takes up a metaphorical function as it is responsible for the pervasive sense of paranoia that, as widely acknowledged, Lang's cinema conveys. For is not Wanley's subjective position ultimately that of someone who is being framed – someone who passes from a position of external observer to that of being observed, subjected to others' gazes, which is exactly the position of the paranoiac? As the film progresses, Wanley understands that, despite all his efforts to the contrary, he is being trapped within a frame and turned into an object for someone else's (the law's) gaze.

Here we should register the presence of the Hitchcockian theme of the dead body that does not disappear (whose classic example is Hitchcock's *The Trouble with Harry*, 1955): The body as a signifier of the disturbing excess (*jouissance*) that always, dialectically speaking, also 'stains' the act of the murderer. Wanley's nightmare begins when he decides to follow Alice back to her apartment to 'see more art'. At this stage, Alice's ex-lover Claude Mazard (Arthur Loft) bursts in and attacks Wanley, who kills him in self-defence. Wanley's decision to dispose of the body rather than call the police drags him further into trouble, for he leaves many clues behind. Thus, the murderer and the dead body come to overlap in representing that surplus of subjectivity that qualifies, for us, the use of the term subject. It is difficult to resist the observation that this definition of bodily excess paradoxically fits Adorno's ruminations on the body as one of the last repository of subjective freedom. Indeed, if the category of the body, after Adorno, has become a central intellectual concern for Critical Theory and Cultural Studies, I suggest that we continue treating this term as we find it in film noir, preserving it from anodyne cultural gentrifications. The classic 'crime film' situation where we see the murderer attempting to dispose of the dead body, yet in doing so leaving traces of his guilty presence behind him, should alert us precisely to the inerasable weight of *jouissance*. Paranoia, in Lang, is the inevitable consequence of the awareness of one's *jouissance*. Indeed, the attempt to erase one's excessive presence is a constant feature in Lang's cinema, and the failure to do so eventually proves that the subject ultimately *is* its *jouissance*. The inerasable weight of the subject is inscribed in Wanley's every attempt at erasing evidence of his guilty presence, from his footprints in the mud to the threads from his suit. Evidence here is evidence of the subject's presence in its most radical guise, that is, as an embodiment of the power of negativity. This is best epitomized in the passage when Heidt (Dan Duryea), Mazard's former bodyguard, discovers traces of Wanley's guilt in the *absence* of fingerprints in Alice's apartment. Turning around the standard crime fiction procedure, *evidence of the subject's guilt here emerges where the successful erasure of evidence has taken place.*

We should also notice that, in a further cruel twist, the film turns the protagonist into the bearer of the gaze that frames him. Wanley is not merely chased by the police, or by Heidt, who soon begins to blackmail him (thus providing a dialectical image of the law's double); more significantly, he is compelled to become an impotent spectator of his own progressive demise. When, in the highly dignified framework of the club, his friend District Attorney Lalor, who has been assigned to the investigation of the murder, informs him of the latest news on the case, Wanley effectively becomes the object of his own gaze. The gaze, Lang tells us in an exemplary cinematic rendition of Lacan's theory of scopophilia, is that elusive/impossible point in the visual field where the subject recognizes his unbearably excessive presence qua real of *jouissance*. Wanley was initially looking at an external object, a portrait; eventually, we find him looking at a more disquieting object, the murderous kernel of his own being. Significantly, in fact, it is not the law that frames him, but his own gaze. While Lalor does not suspect him, he repeatedly betrays himself through either slips of the tongue, by showing physical evidence of his involvement (a scratch on his hand), or even by accidentally leading the police in the right direction when the body is being retrieved. Again, self-incrimination here is not merely a strategy to enhance suspense, but it materializes the unconscious in its radically antagonistic magnitude. Eventually, after the plan to kill Heidt fails miserably, Wanley is left with no other choice but to kill himself. He takes the same poison destined to Heidt and slumps into his armchair, ironically unable to answer the phone call from Alice that would free him, since it carries the message that Heidt has been killed and incriminated with the murder. A close-up of his face, signalling his death, turns seamlessly (no cuts) into the shot of his awakening, when an arm enters the frame and shakes him, followed by a voice reminding him that 'it is ten thirty, Professor Wanley'. A nicely accomplished shot, with plenty of technical trickery involved, to suggest that the nightmare is over. Again, beyond its strict narrative meaning, Wanley's meticulously taken decision to end his life is most important in locating for us the position of the subject. As Lacan famously claimed, 'suicide is the only completely successful act' (Lacan 1990: 66–7), inasmuch as, different from bungled actions or slips of the tongue, the choice of suicide (not its irrational accomplishment) demonstrates that the unconscious is consciously assumed.

Lang's world, then, is literally a world of frames – frames in which his characters find a world. No other director is perhaps as aware as he is of the productive potential of encounters with framed images. Such images, contrary to what normally happens in art cinema, do not point to a *hors champ*, to a reality beyond the frame, but instead are fully self-contained, perfectly self-sufficient in their substantial balance. This is why Lang can be taken as a paradigm in the debate on the question of the ideological dimension in cinema. The general critical view that condemns self-enclosed filmic narratives and visual styles as implicitly ideological, clearly misses the point about the functioning of ideology. Considering 'ideological' a cinema structured around consistently developed narratives which do not refer to either another dimension outside of themselves or their own incapacity to capture the truth about reality, such critical views remain caught in the false binary opposition of ideology and a supposedly non-ideological plane. Lang's cinema, however, knows better. It finds itself at home within the Hollywood continuity system precisely because it is aware that imbalance and difference will emerge through embracing a conclusive, even teleological and deterministic narrative scheme. Lang's cinematic gaze is locked in the mirror, in the framed reflection of reality that, in so far as it endorses its well-defined boundaries, paradoxically has a chance to capture the disruptive core of the real. As we have observed, although *The Woman in the Window* would seem to provide an ideological ending by relieving spectators of the weight of despair and allowing them to leave the cinema theatre with a 'healthy laugh' – as Lang (quoted in McGilligan 1997: 318) himself commented – to a more attentive analysis the film manages to reveal the crucially disavowed, split dimension of subjectivity (Wanley's waking reality is represented as a flight from the disturbing real of his desire). In this respect, let us recall the ambiguity of another classic noir like Nicholas Ray's *In a Lonely Place* (1950). Here we are dealing with a case of split subjectivity that reminds us of the mechanism of displacement used by Lang in *The Woman in the Window*. Although by the end of the film Dix Steele (Humphrey Bogart) is exonerated of the murder of Mildred Atkinson (Martha Stewart), he is nevertheless portrayed, throughout the whole film, as a potential murderer, a man whose furiously irrational, near-psychotic behaviour is *in itself* criminal. The fact that he did not commit the murder does not make him less guilty, as the ending, with his girlfriend Laurel Gray (Gloria Grahame) walking out on him, testifies.

If we consider the 'ideological danger' of Lang's *The Woman in the Window* (which the unhappy ending of *In a Lonely Place* manages to avoid), even more problematic must appear to critical ears the surprising finale of *Clash by Night* (1952), a realist melodrama and one of Lang's most unsuccessful and misunderstood films. The fact that he changed visual style, experimenting with a realism that was becoming popular in the Hollywood of the early 1950s, does not mean that he moved away from his main concerns. The plot consists of a few criss-crossing movements: A woman comes back to her humble home after failing in her pursuit of the high life; she half-heartedly starts a family with a good-natured fisherman, breaks out again when she falls for a rebellious type, and eventually, when on the point of leaving, repents and goes back to her husband and baby daughter. The logic is the usual one in Lang, focusing on the aforementioned necessity of frames. When, about to leave with her lover, Mae (Barbara Stanwyck) suddenly has a change of heart and runs back to her husband, Earl (Robert Ryan), her lover, shouts in frustration that she is going back into the trap (a marriage with a man that she never really loved) and that sooner or later she will feel the need to escape again. Her reply is telling: She had always thought that there was an outside, a better life away from self-restraint and responsibility, but now all of a sudden she had realized that she was wrong. So she darts to her husband, who in the meantime had absconded to his boat with newborn baby Gloria, fearing that his wife would take her away. Upon hearing of her intentions, the husband tells her that he can do nothing but *risk* trusting her, giving her another chance . . . 'until the next time'. They do not embrace or kiss, as a standard romantic finale would demand; he simply tells her to go and fetch the baby in the adjacent room.

The key metaphorical cipher in this underrated work is represented by the image of the sea. Lang was renowned for his terror of the elemental force of the ocean (see Gunning 2000: 394). Here, he associates images, even close-ups, of the tempestuous sea clashing by night against the rocks, with the suggestion of a recalcitrant feminine libido that refuses to be tamed, that is, to find satisfaction in marriage. The revealing sequence is that of Mae awake in the middle of the night, smoking furiously in her bedroom while gazing out at the stormy ocean. Her husband is a couple of feet away, sound asleep, while in another room lies Earl, unconscious from excessive drinking; in the morning, Mae and Earl will become lovers. However, Lang does not stop at this rather facile allusion to the metaphorical affinity between unruly feminine libido and the power of the sea. Much more interestingly, he transforms this classic image of an instinctual, untameable force of nature that breaks all constraints (woman), into an image of closure (the family) which however is internally traversed by the very antagonism assigned to femininity. In line with the main theme of the film, what was outside and dangerous to the peace of the family/community, is drawn in.[23] However, rather than either exploding the balance of the community or being digested and seamlessly integrated, this otherness persists as the dialectical core of the very notion of a closed (framed) structure. Eventually, then, the substantial unity of the family is not merely (ideologically) asserted, but it is shown as coinciding with its ontological inconsistency. It is therefore significant that the final sequence, which sanctions Mae's reunion with her husband, takes place on the sea (on the husband's boat), and not in the family house. The potentially destructive power of the sea (Mae's libido) is not domesticated; it is accepted as the inerasable foundation of a common existence. The ending of the film is thus profoundly Hegelian in the way it endorses the necessity of the (family) frame while presenting it as ontologically fractured, immensely fragile.

The art of excremental painting

Frames are also central to the follow-up to *The Woman in the Window*, the more acclaimed *Scarlet Street* (1945). The film's main character, Christopher Cross (Edward G. Robinson), immediately strikes us as a Kafkaesque type, leading a life divided between bureaucratic duty (his job as a clerk) and artistic ambition (his painting hobby). The first feature to note here is that the side of his personality that is presented as representative of his 'true self', as a sort of transgression to a life of routine and humiliation (especially from his tyrant-wife Adele, played by Rosalind Ivan), is associated by Lang, in a real stroke of genius, to the excremental dimension: Chris Cross's painting talent is forced to express itself in the bathroom/toilet, due to the lack of space within the small flat he shares with his wife. The link between the sublime and the excremental is indeed vital to grasp Lang's portrayal of subjectivity. That Chris is a repressed man, even more than Wanley, is self-evident. However, his split condition (between the office and the toilet) manages to capture the universal condition of humankind. At the start of the film, we see him veering off his normal route home (he lives in Brooklyn, New York) and meandering through Greenwich Village, until he comes across the scene of a man beating up a woman. The scene itself, we should add, is presented very much like a painting (we are, after all, in the 'artistic' part of New York), or at least as if it was staged. The fatal encounter with the *jouissance* represented in this scene is structurally identical to Wanley's encounter with the portrait in Lang's previous film. The effect, in both films, is to enhance the character's desire to rebel against his alienating, humiliatingly mechanical existence. In other words, it is a desire to exit the frame in which his life is imprisoned. What Chris does not realize, of course, is that the opportunity that destiny allows him is not just to 'exit the frame', but to enter a new, more dangerous, one.

Replicating the narrative mechanism of *The Woman in the Window*, the Robinson character here becomes involved in another, much darker, narrative which resembles, in its main traits, the dream text of the previous film. It is as if Lang was warning us that although we can try to escape our dull and alienating life, over which we have little to no command, our efforts will nevertheless result in a false escape, since our subjectivity can only find expression within a frame that we are condemned to experience as (at least minimally) alienating. Being split (again, between 'the office' and 'the toilet') is nothing less than the condition of possibility of being. Lang's treatment of alienation and manipulation here is, however, more complex than in other films such as the previously discussed *Clash by Night*, for it involves a self-reflexive meditation on the meaning of art and authorship. Let us first observe, however, that we are fully within Lang's element, namely the ontological role of fictions. The relationship between Kitty (Joan Bennett) and Chris, for instance, involves mutual deception. While the two are chatting in the bar on the night of their encounter, Kitty takes on the persona of an actress and Chris that of an artist (a rich painter). Lang's finesse in introducing these performances is, of course, that in a profound way, they both are what they pretend to be – once again, that is, Lang blurs the dividing line between (diegetic) reality and fiction. Kitty is constantly 'acting', and not only to deceive Chris, while the latter in actual fact is what he had always aspired to be, a talented painter (albeit, as we shall see, deprived of authorship).

But perhaps the most interesting insight into the foundational role of fictions and the inescapability of frames in *Scarlet Street* is offered by a third character, who once again first appears, as it were, locked within a frame, though rather ambiguously so. The person in question is Homer Higgins (Charles Kemper), Adele's former husband, a New York policeman who drowned heroically when trying to rescue a woman after her suicide attempt. His blown-up photograph hangs on the wall of Adele and Chris's flat as yet another humiliating apparatus for the poor clerk. His imposing, pompous patriarchal look, ennobled by his heroic sacrifice, effectively seems to function as a castrating gaze for a weakling like Chris (see Gunning 2000: 316). When, however, Homer (whose name now becomes revealing) unexpectedly reappears as a derelict old man, we realize that the film is again exploring the literal and metaphorical function of frames. Homer comes back in flesh and blood into the film's narrative and begins to blackmail Chris, threatening him with making his presence known to Adele and breaking down their marriage. What he does not know is that Chris cannot let such a golden opportunity slip by. Chris promises Homer access to Adele's bonds and invites him to the flat when the wife is out. Homer enters the apartment with Chris, only however to discover that Adele is actually at home. Chris's plan thus becomes apparent: He has tricked Homer back into the 'family frame', the very frame that he can now safely exit (even legally, the fact that Homer is alive means that his marriage with Adele does not stand, and he is 'free' to run to Kitty). The logic is once again a self-reflexive one: Homer wanted to manipulate Chris and ends up manipulated by him, turned into a puppet unwittingly playing in Chris's carefully staged narrative. He had parted with his role as husband with a bang, pretending to be the *ideal* husband (feigning self-sacrifice when, in truth, actually he had come across a hefty sum and the chance to leave the country unnoticed). Now that this subterfuge is uncovered, Homer stands for yet another example of a Langian character *who is what he pretends to be*, in this case a husband (though the attribute 'ideal' should be conveniently replaced by 'abject').

One can see how Lang here works on the template already examined apropos the family melodrama *Clash by Night*, since the final movement is the same (though different in tone): Not from the alienating closure of (family) fiction to an idealized external place where full self-realization can be achieved, but rather the opposite denouement whereby this 'better life' is shown to never have existed in the first place. The difference between inside (the family) and outside becomes, as in *Clash by Night*, the gap or inconsistency within the framed reality. As Homer comes back into the frame, then, Chris at last leaves it, becoming what we now understand Homer wanted to be – a man free from the noose of an unhappy marriage. However, Lang's inflexible dialectical logic immediately catches up with our hero. The illusion of being outside the fiction, for once actually master of his own actions (in an idealized romance with Kitty), lasts only a few minutes, the time it takes Chris to reach Kitty's apartment. As he walks in, ready to break the news of his newly acquired freedom, he comprehends with horror that he has been framed all the way, from the moment of his first chance encounter with the young woman. The shocking spectacle he is now forced to behold consists of Kitty being romantically entertained by Johnny (Dan Duryea), the very guy he thought he had saved her from at the start of the film. Significantly, Chris looks at the couple embracing in the living room through the frame of a partition glass that now functions reflexively, for the tableau he is beholding is the very picture in which his desire was always caught. In the 'screen' in front of him, he now sees, more than the two lovers, his own stupidly humiliated desire. More than the eyes of the two lovers discovered in the act, it is the picture that looks back at him, as it were, with his own detached eyes: He watches himself watching, thereby observing his desire in all its inane senselessness. The picture returns to the subject the devastating emptiness at the heart of his (scopic) desire.

This scene thus reminds us of the significance of Lacan's gaze qua *objet a*: When we encounter this impossible object, we effectively encounter the objectified, alien, residual excess constitutive of the kernel of our subjectivity. No wonder, then, that Chris runs away in disgust. Like Wanley looking at Alice's painting in *The Woman in the Window*, he finds out that the externality of his gaze was a pious illusion he needed in order to convince himself that he was the master of his own actions. This externality here reveals itself for what it always was, a perspectival error (notably, when commenting on his painting technique, Chris states that he could never quite master perspective): His act of looking was always-already short-circuited into a 'being looked at', a 'being framed'. However, this gaze looking back at him, including him in the picture, was not merely that of other empirical characters; it was the strictly speaking 'impossible' point of view embodying the radically disavowed subject in him – the unconscious otherness at the heart of his desire. Ultimately, this scene is shocking for Chris because there he encounters the core of what he is. This short-circuiting of the gaze sums up the paradox of subjectivity – with crucial implications for any theory of ideology – that Lang often tries to unravel in his American cinema. Chris's 'criss-crossing' in and out of his existential frame was always an illusion. In fact, it created in him the double illusion of being trapped and thereby deprived of his genuine potential for self-expression, and of being able to free himself of his alienating 'cage'. What he discovers as the narrative unfolds is that no matter how much effort he put into trying to exit, he always remained inside, following a path that is common to Lang's most accomplished characters.

The ultimate irony is that even his psychotic killing of Kitty with an ice-pick (almost too easy to read as a phallic symbol, along with the knife he holds in an earlier scene at home, when talking to her tyrannical wife) does not provide for him a way out of his frame. A self-destructive act, this murder is pinned on Johnny, who was returning to see Kitty, completely drunk, just after the killing had taken place. A classic example of a self-destructive return of the repressed – the truth of his absurd sublimation of Kitty – Chris's murderous act does not lead him out of his alienated condition. One thinks of the end of Martin Scorsese's *Taxi Driver* (1976), with Travis (Robert de Niro) back to his job after the self-destructive acting out. A psychotic *passage a l'acte* does not necessarily lead one out of a deeply ingrained neurotic condition. In this respect, the interesting aspect of Lang's film is that, at Johnny's trial, Chris is faced with two possibilities: If he confesses that he and not Kitty is the painter, he would regain full authorship but would end up in jail, and eventually would be executed; on the other hand, if he lies (the option he takes), he would walk out free. After Johnny's execution, however, even Chris's achieved freedom (he is no longer married to Adele, lives on his own, etc.) begins to revolt against himself, as he starts being tormented by guilt in the shape of voices and visions from his brief romance with Kitty. In other words, he falls into a state of chronic paranoia which culminates in an attempted suicide. The point to underline is once again the impossibility to exit the frame – or, to put it in a theoretically more stimulating way, *to relieve subjectivity of the burden of alienation*. Despite his empirical freedom, Chris is now at the mercy of his superego. In yet another cruel twist, then, even his suicide fails, for when he hangs himself in his room he is rescued just in time and survives.

In so far as we belong in a reality which is by definition fictional, Lang seems to tell us sardonically, our actions are part of a script we never have full control over. This is confirmed by the final images of Chris, which are those of a totally destitute, homeless man, wandering in abject poverty while claiming in vain that he was the actual murderer, not only of Kitty but also of Johnny. These final portrayal is ambiguous: While on the one hand it would seem that Chris has reached the paradoxical condition of freedom identified by Lacan as the space 'in between the two deaths', at the same time the frame he finds himself in torments him more than ever, precisely in the form of an unbearable superego pressure. The ultimate confirmation of Chris's impotence in relation to his attempt to move out of his existential frame is his loss of authorship as a painter – a loss that cruelly makes it impossible for him to occupy the position of an external creator of the frame itself. To explain this, we should consider the last sequence of the film, when a derelict Chris Cross sees his own painting of Kitty (the 'self-portrait') sold in a famous art gallery for 10,000 dollars. Here, we are reminded of Lang's coupling of artistic sublimation and its excremental dimension. Although Chris was not actually sitting on the toilet when painting in his flat, as some critics have incorrectly noted (see, for instance, McGilligan 1997: 318), the point is nevertheless accurate. The connection between art and shit – one which, of course, figures prominently in today's contemporary art – is based on the psychoanalytic notion that any act of sublimation, such as artistic creation, is of necessity dialectically linked with an act metaphorically describable as excretion, whereby a certain excess of meaning that cannot be integrated in the 'sublimated picture' drops off and is obliterated, relegated to an 'off-limits' dimension – while it does not disappear, it remains fundamentally repressed. Sublimation then does not occur without this desublimated remainder.

As Žižek has repeatedly argued (e.g. in his visual commentary of Francis Ford Coppola's *The Conversation*) excrements supply, in a richly suggestive metaphorical way, an image of what the core of subjectivity is, as well as a peculiar approach to the foreclosed side of artistic creation. The same rapport between sublimation and excretion is explicitly evoked by Pier Paolo Pasolini in his *Teorema* (1968). Here, after the shocking yet life-changing sexual encounter with the guest, the young painter Pietro finally leaves his bourgeois home to devote himself only to art. However, after composing an abstract blue canvas, he urinates on it. In relation to the final sequence of Lang's film, then, it can be argued that the author finds himself confronted with the excremental dimension of his work which he could not have recognized when making it (the 'toilet dimension' implied precisely this coincidence of the work with the foreclosed dimension of shitting). That such dimension coincides with a highly priced commodity is also far from accidental. As Marx had intuited, and as was developed later by Alfred

Sohn-Rethel through his notion of 'real abstraction',[24] and more recently by Žižek,[25] money, this mother of all commodities, incarnates the attitude of 'fetishistic disavowal' that sustains our rational, balanced existence in a capitalist society. In other words, we disavow our fetishistic attachment to money so as to be able to convincingly pretend to be rational and balanced individuals in our everyday life. Chris's paintings, then, are the product of a process of sublimation that has its obverse (the other side of the coin) in the excremental remainder, as well as in the Real dimension of sex (the flower he paints in the toilet, for instance, can be seen as functioning as a sublimated image of the vagina). In dialectical terms, the key point made by the film is that Chris is ultimately unable to connect with the traumatic Real of his desire: Whatever he does, he remains prey to symbolic fictions. His painting activity thus works very much like a mirror for his 'framed subjectivity'. Even the killing of Kitty, which clearly symbolizes his instinctive and intrinsically self-destructive attempt to violently exit the dimension of the mirror, only leads him back into the frame.

The film can therefore be seen as dealing with the failure of the act of liberation and the impossibility of sustaining freedom – otherwise put, with the subject's chronic inability to refashion his identity according to radically alternative values, a fundamental impotence that the film seems to relate to the pervasive presence of capitalist ideology. To put it more directly, Chris's project of personal happiness fails in so far as, like all forms of individualistic/romantic rebellions within late capitalism, it is unable to think a truly different symbolic framework that could accommodate an alternative regime of subjective desires. In fact, his naive chimera (the relationship with Kitty) turns into a form of self-manipulation, which provides a telling equivalence with regard to ordinary self-manipulation through money. His renunciation of authorship for his paintings, which he happily assigns to Kitty (with her full name of Katherine March), is functional to his desire for a relationship with an idealized other who, instead, is always-already framing him through the medium of money. The dream of a type of happiness external to the capitalist structure is completely debunked, shown as integral to the functioning of that very structure. The final shot of Chris passing by the Dellarowe Gallery where his 'masterpiece' has just been sold testifies very accurately to the condition of ideological captivity the film focuses on. Here Lang resorts to a crane shot of the street, which then dissolves into an overlapping shot of the same street where, however, all passers-by have disappeared apart from Chris. We are left with a high angle shot inexorably underlining the character's alienated position within the frame, isolating him within the imposing architectural configuration of the city. Adorno, one is tempted to surmise, would have appreciated this shot.

Notes

1 When asked to express his thoughts on the film, Fritz Lang replied: 'I don't like it at all. I made it, let's face it, because I was bound by a contract. I think it is impossible to place the audience in the presence of a hero for an hour and a half and then reveal in the last five minutes that he is an assassin' (in Grant 2003: 26). In my view, this statement demonstrates why one should never rely on directors explaining their films.

2 The wonderful insight of *Beyond a Reasonable Doubt* could be summed up with two of Jacques Lacan's best known mottoes: 'the unconscious (truth) has the structure of a fiction' and 'les non-dupes errent' (those who think they are not duped, are in the wrong).

3 Including Ophüls's great Hollywood films *Letters from an Unknown Woman* (1948), *Caught* (1949) and *The Reckless Moment* (1949). These works could be placed on a par with Lang's American films inasmuch as they draw their strength from the structural limitations imposed on them.

4 'Denotation is not the first meaning, but pretends to be so; under this illusion, it is ultimately no more than the last of the connotations (the one which seems both to establish and close the reading), the superior myth by which the text pretends to return to the nature of language, to language as nature' (Barthes 1974: 9).

5 Žižek, for example, aptly claims that 'deconstructionism involves two prohibitions: it prohibits the "naive" empiricist approach [. . .] as well as global non-historical metaphysical theses about the origin and structure of the universe. This double prohibition, which defines deconstructionism clearly and unambiguously, bears witness to its Kantian transcendental philosophical origins' (Žižek 2001c: 204–5).

6 As Ben Agger put it: 'I conceive of cultural studies in its best sense as an activity of critical theory that directly decoded the hegemonizing messages of the culture industry permeating every nook and cranny of lived experience, from entertainment to education' (Agger 1992: 5).

7 When trying to convince Garrett to go along with his plan, Spencer states: 'A fictitious story wouldn't prove anything: it could only be proven by a fact that no one could deny.' Ironically, of course, what he has in mind is a 'fact made of fiction'.

8 The closest he comes to the figure of the killer is the moment he receives (what we retrospectively understand to be) a phone call from Patty Grey, the dancer he subsequently murders. When he hangs up, however, he only looks slightly worried. It is indeed remarkable how, throughout the whole film, Garrett's identity remains consistent with what he is supposed to be, never giving away signs of a potential 'other side'.

9 Edgar Allan Poe's short story *The Imp of the Perverse*, published in 1845, popularizes the human tendency to act against one's own interests. As such, Žižek (2005: 98–9) links it directly to the problem of the formulation of freedom in German Idealism.

10 Perhaps, this is the reason why Lang's *Human Desire* (1954) – the third remake of Émile Zola's novel *La Bête Humaine* – should be counted among his failed films. The depiction of Carl Buckley's (Broderick Crawford) desperate, animalesque excesses, and specifically the stabbing to death of his rival on the train, are far too deeply grounded in sociological context to account for the real (unconscious and thus transhistorical) excesses of subjectivity proper.

11 The same romantic attitude is epitomized by his constant reminiscing of a trip to Rome, which represents for him the kind of Eldorado he aims to return to.

12 It is interesting that Lang's critical attitude towards the United States takes the form of a film that also signals his decline as a Hollywood director, also as a consequence of his involvement in McCarthy's witch-hunt. Perhaps, the two facts are not merely accidental. We should, in other words, ask the naive question: How come Lang started showing a critical attitude towards the American society and way of life the very moment he began losing prestige as a Hollywood director? Lang himself admitted this connection when, replying to a suggestion that his film depicted American society in a venomous way, he said: 'The only thing I can tell you about it is that it was the first picture after the McCarthy business and I had to shoot it in twenty days. Maybe that's what made me so venomous' (in Jenkins 1981: 166).

13 See Janet Bergstrom (1993), Lotte Eisner (1984) and Peter Bogdanovich (1967).

14 Jacques Lacan reverses this reading, attributing to the moral law precisely the character of an unbearable injunction comparable to an act of subversion (see, e.g. Lacan 1998a: 275–6).

15 The film is adapted from the eponymous novel by Graham Green published in 1943.

16 Commenting on Weimer cinema, Siegfried Kracauer had already discovered the sinister associations that fairgrounds can have (see Kracauer 1947: 73–4).

17 The speculative identity of law and crime, a fairly standard theme in noir, comes to the fore with particular brilliance in the underrated procedural noir *Illegal* (Lewis Allen, 1955), where Edward G. Robinson plays a DA who, after sending an innocent man to the chair, starts working as a criminal lawyer and develops ties with a powerful hoodlum. Eventually, he redeems himself by saving the life of his secretary (played by Nina Foch), but inevitably the ambiguity of his role as representative of the law remains central in the film. Another perfect example of this coincidence can be found in the excellent B-noir *The Man Who Cheated Himself* (Felix E. Feist, 1950), particularly in the scenes with the two brothers: on the one hand, the law as neutral, non-pathological instrument (the 'good cop' played by the younger brother); on the other hand, the law as crime (the older cop, played by Lee J. Cobb). The latter is not the generically corrupt cop but a detective who is driven, like few other noir detectives, by the femme fatale he is besotted by, to the extent that he even beats up his own beloved brother to defend her ('You said it, she's got under my skin' are his final words to his brother).

18 It is interesting to note that the title of the novel from which Lang's film is adapted is *Rogue Male* (1939), by prolific British novelist Geoffrey Household.

As the title seems to suggest, the emphasis of the source of Lang's film falls precisely on the class-related arrogance of the hero.

19 The scene towards the end when Thorndike, hidden in a cave, manages to kill the hunter Quive-Smith (George Sanders) thanks to the arrow-shaped pin he had bought for Jenny, works precisely as a reminder of the centrality of both femininity and class difference.

20 In this respect, let us not forget Lang's reflections on the ontological dimension of images in his German cinema, epitomized by the inanimate machinic figures that seem to come to life in *Metropolis* (1927).

21 As the title of the novel from which the film was adapted suggests, *Once Off-Guard* (1942), by J. H. Wallis.

22 A classic example of this type of hallucinatory reflection can be found in Jean Vigo's classic *L'Atalante* (1934), when the smiling image of Juliette (Dita Parlo) appears under the sea to Jean (Jean Dasté), the desperate husband she has left.

23 See the wonderfully ambiguous scene at the beginning of the film depicting the other couple (Joe and Peggy, played respectively by Paul Andes and a young Marilyn Monroe) as they quarrel about their own roles in the relationship. As they approach Joe's home, Mae's voice surprises them, as she stands just outside the door. After 10 years of travelling, she has returned home. Since we still do not know that she is Joe's sister, we initially suspect that she might be Joe's old lover. The ambiguity concerning this 'other' is thus emphasized from the very beginning.

24 The action of commodity exchange, Sohn-Rethel argues, is fetishistic in so far as it is *an abstract act of practical solipsism*, which on the one hand, automatically sets up the social order, and on the other, allows the exchanging agents to develop a private consciousness, confirming that the division between manual and intellectual labour has taken place: 'What enables commodity exchange to perform its socialising function – to effect the social synthesis – is its abstractness from everything relating to use' (Sohn-Rethel 1978: 29–30). Or, more comprehensively put: '*The* unvarying formal features of exchange [. . .] constitute a mechanism of real abstraction indispensable for the social synthesis throughout and supplying a matrix for the abstract conceptual reasoning characteristic of all societies based on commodity production' (p. 51).

25 'In this precise sense, money is for Marx a fetish: I pretend to be a rational, utilitarian subject, well aware how things truly stand – but I embody my disavowed belief in the money-fetish' (Žižek 2001b: 14).

Coda: The enjoyment of film in theory

Let us go back one more and final time to *Beyond a Reasonable Doubt*. Here Lang's attitude towards appearances comes with two crucial corollaries. First, there is the small but decisive issue of the difference between 'the truth of appearances' (the plan staged by Spencer and Garrett) and 'the appearance of truth within this realm of appearances', that is, the question concerning the actual assassination of the young dancer, whom we never see (apart from a couple of photographs of her dead body, which do not show her face). This gap coincides with the different degrees of awareness qualifying the positions of the publisher (Spencer, a victim of the plan despite knowing well that it was a plan) and of the killer (Garrett, the only one who knew that 'things were exactly as they seemed'). At this level, our point of view as spectators is aligned exactly with the point of view of liberal publisher Austin Spencer, who did not know that his 'noble lie' was literally framed by another (much less noble) lie. What we have is not just the subversion of the Hollywood narrative canon (the so-called three-act narration) but, much more significantly, a subtle denunciation of *the gaze that refuses to identify directly with what it perceives*. Lang tells us that truth lies on the surface of things. What we do not recognize as we watch is that our own gaze is itself the result of a distortion; in other words, it is taken over by another (invisible) gaze which deprives it of its autonomy of judgement. The effect of Lang's unexpected twist (although Garrett only *pretends* to be guilty, *he really is guilty*) is one of utter, almost shocking displacement of our faculty of seeing and judging, precisely because, like Spencer, we thought that objective reality was neatly divided between superficial appearances and deeper truths.

Here, one could argue that the film is indeed split between appearances and truth, since Garrett's 'plan within the plan' still belongs to the realm of appearances, of manipulation of reality. But is it really the case? Different from what takes place in most thrillers or 'whodunit' narratives, the whole point of Lang's radical displacement of truth is definitely *not* that of warning us about its shifting status (say, we are led to believe that someone is the killer and eventually, in a final twist, we are shown that we were wrong, that someone else is the culprit). If *Beyond a Reasonable Doubt* had developed as a standard thriller, Spencer would have been the most likely candidate for the role of the real killer (or perhaps even Susan, the potentially jealous girlfriend). What makes this a profoundly innovative film is precisely the fact that in it, the simulation of reality ultimately coincides with reality itself. The lesson is therefore that, just like the killer is the one who pretends to be the killer, *we are what we pretend to be* – our 'true' identity is the identity we stage, that we exchange in the social arena, and that we mistakenly consider to be a mask hiding our 'true self'. It is within the parameters of this radical correspondence of mask and self, fiction and reality, that the seemingly contradictory claim about the 'truth of appearance' should be placed. For the assertion that truth belongs to the illusory surface of things also implies that the very status of truth is purely formal, that it can only materialize as an utterly evanescent appearance devoid of any content. Beyond the coincidence of fiction (the staged plan) and truth (the identity of the killer), there lies the issue of truth as a non-symbolic event which can only be represented as a fleeting appearance – or, differently put, as the appearance of lack.

Where, then, can we identify such a truth in Lang's film? In the unseen murderous act committed by the journalist, around which the entire story is articulated. We should not overlook how the truth of this act comes briefly to fruition through the photographic (fictional) images of the girl's dead body, following a strategy that, as previously mentioned, is often put to work in noir and will be fully endorsed by a 'modernist noir' like Antonioni's *Blow-up* (1966). Photography in *Beyond a Reasonable Doubt* plays therefore a double role in relation to the claim that truth coincides with appearance. First, we have the photographs documenting the *fictional staging* of the event, which effectively confirm that reality has the structure of a fiction. Though these polaroids end up destroyed in Spencer's car crash, they nevertheless *tell the truth (about the killing) in the guise of lying*. Then we have the fleeting appearance of photos that capture the ultimate truth about the murder, namely a truth that disregards empirical questions concerning the identity of the killer and simply attempts to portray lack, absence, in the guise of a dead body.

With regard to the displacement of the spectators' gaze in *Beyond a Reasonable Doubt*, it is interesting to connect this issue with an observation made by Adorno, in his 1966 essay 'Transparencies on Film'. Here Adorno ponders the question of spectatorship in a way that risks undermining his own critique of the culture industry. He claims that there is a 'potential gap' between 'the intentions of a film' and 'their actual effect', adding that such a gap 'is inherent in the medium' (Adorno 2001: 181). If filmic intentions do not necessarily correspond to how spectators are affected, then the presupposition of a direct connection between mass-produced cultural artefacts and the people who consume them would seem to be invalidated. However, drawing on his knowledge of Freudian theory, Adorno clarifies that the ideological impact of film does not reside in the film's conscious intentions, but in the unconscious enjoyment it provides. Consumers are captured by the 'juicy' ideological excess of the culture industry. In what would seem to be a reference to Federico Fellini's *La dolce vita* (1959), he exemplifies as follows: 'While intention is always directed against the playboy, the *dolce vita* and wild parties, the opportunity to behold them seems to be relished more than the hasty verdict' (p. 181). Although Fellini *intended* to condemn the degeneration of the modern subject, the *effect* of his film is to encourage the imitation of such degeneration, since the spectator tends to identify less with the conscious message of the film than with the enjoyment it provides.

From my perspective, here some reflections immediately spring to mind. First, the gap identified by Adorno effectively problematizes all theories of spectatorship in so far as it makes any such theory dependent on unconscious mechanisms, both at the level of cinematic enunciation and cinematic reception. Secondly, it captures in a nutshell the irrational, blind trajectory of capitalist cultural production (the unconscious enjoyment of film). Thirdly – as a corollary of the previous point – it locates the formidable strength as well as the potential threshold of that 'cultural ideology'. It is this last reflection that is particularly urgent for a critique of the culture industry. The ideology in question, which, as Adorno acknowledges, is internally antagonized by its fundamental lack of control over its effects, is none other than the capitalist *ideology of enjoyment*. Capitalist ideology works precisely by constantly producing 'juicy excesses' that by definition defy not only conscious effects, *but also conscious intentions*. So what if, ultimately, the history of film as industry is the clearest example of how the success of what today we might call 'media commodities' hinges on the full endorsement of the splintering of any causal linkage? The productive function of antagonism within the culture industry cannot be underestimated. This is to say that what makes culture (and film) a successful industry under capitalist conditions is precisely its ability to generate ever new regimes of enjoyment that, precisely because not clearly integrated in consciousness, sanction the success of the film-commodity. The ultimate strength of the culture industry – or indeed of the media industry as a whole – is that *the surplus of sense it creates is what makes it work*. At a fundamental level, cultural production in a capitalist economy obeys *only* its drive, which is articulated around ever new 'shocks of enjoyment'. The culture industry thrives on this ceaseless injunction to enjoy which is constitutive of its own nature, to the extent that it is this very drive that, paradoxically, plays a synthetic role, functioning as ideology's *raison d'être*. The culture industry is at its strongest when it encourages us to identify with what seems to work against it. Cinema is no exception. Rather, it is the most obvious incarnation of that ideological ruse. My wager, which aims to provide new analytical parameters to the Critical Theory of film, is that to actually move beyond the ideological ruse through which the film industry, and more generally today's media, 'defuse and recycle' just about any potentially explosive excess (in Adorno's terms, any 'preponderance of the object'), we need to abandon the illusion that spectatorship might finally yield a subversive or even a reliable descriptive formula; instead, we need to turn to theory. In the specific context of this book, we need to look for filmic symptoms which, irrespective of spectators' identification, might point to a different scenario than that embraced by the explicit symbolic dimension of film. We need to work along the thin and blurry line between ideological enjoyment and a disruptive surplus to be theorized beyond enjoyment, for only the latter approach opens the door to the possibility of injecting new meanings into given filmic contexts.

This insight proves crucial when attempting to link culture to politics. Since today's politics comes more and more to coincide with its medialization, that is, with an 'industry of images', one should not be afraid to draw the most depressing conclusion: The strategy of unveiling the scandalous excesses of power is not only a weak weapon against power, but ultimately serves the purpose of strengthening the hold of power on us by perpetuating the current conditions of its existence. Here it is not just a matter of lamenting the ubiquitous presence of the media in our postmodern world: Images are everywhere and desensitize us as to what really matters. Rather, one should insist on the specific ideological 'colouring' of images: They are produced by the contemporary capitalist media industry and as such obey its iron law, the commodification of excess. The very engine of the media industry is the commodification of potentially disruptive messages.[1] We should reiterate that it is not simply an issue of our being overwhelmed by images, by different forms of representation. On this point, we should fully endorse the most radical psychoanalytic thesis that *ordinary reality itself is a medium* – it is the medium, the screen, through which we keep at bay destructive (unconscious) drives, the excess produced by our necessary symbolization of reality. In Lacanian terms, symbolic castration (the mechanism of repression enabling us to relate to reality) amounts to nothing but the acceptance of the fact that reality is ultimately a screen for us. Precisely because images are always with us, always supporting us in our relation to the world – as they always were, even in pre-technological times – then it is obvious that they are not, in themselves, the problem. What constitutes our 'slavery to images', rather, is their specific use by the media industry. More to the point, the trump card in the hands of such industry is its full identification with what is in excess of the message. Herein lies the main weakness of Guy Debord's *The Society of Spectacle*, first published in 1967. What Debord rejects is the (psychoanalytic) view that representations are the ultimate horizon of human existence. Already in the first short thesis of his book, which sounds like one of Adorno's aphoristic remarks, Debord makes his key point: 'All that was once directly lived has become mere representation' (Debord 1995: 12). For a Lacanian, on the contrary, all that is directly lived is the result of an act of symbolic representation, of fictionalization even. It is not merely that images have supplanted genuine human interaction, since images and representations have *always* been the only way for man to relate to the external world. Representations enable man to experience life. What one should add to Debord's stance is that the commodification of images in mass culture is synonymous with the commodification of the enjoyment of the image that drives capital forward, quite irrespectively of any sense that one might wish to attach to what is being represented.

More and more in our capitalist universe, the meaning or content of a given representation is being fragmented and colonized by the mediatic enjoyment it carries over. In this sense, we need to take seriously, that is, radicalize, Marshall McLuhan's legendary claim that 'the medium is the message' (including the other version 'the medium is the *massage*'). Today we have reached a stage where the message is totally absorbed and annihilated by its specific mediatic enjoyment, which effectively is also a massage since it 'gentrifies' enjoyment, depriving it of its subversive sting. We live in a world in which, to put it simply, meaning tends more and more to seamlessly pass into enjoyment the very moment it emerges through the media image. Take McLuhan's own example when commenting on the 1976 television debate between Jimmy Carter and Gerald Ford. In relation to the technical hitch that suddenly interrupted the debate, McLuhan famously remarked that it was 'the rebellion of the medium against the bloody message', claiming that the two politicians did not have a clue about how to use the TV medium itself. Later, he added that although Carter was advantaged by the medium, the simple operation of obscuring the TV screen while listening to the debate as if on the radio would have given Ford a clear lead. In this respect, the passage from radio to TV necessarily implied a transformation in the way messages are delivered, received and, more specifically, enjoyed. What one should note is the shift from a logic where enjoyment secretly sustained representations (where therefore representations still retained a precise symbolic value), to a logic where representations, texts, images themselves, coincide more and more with their enjoyment. 50 years ago images of political leaders retained a symbolic weight that images of today's political leaders have completely lost, as they increasingly coincide with the way we enjoy them. This shift has occurred as a consequence of the changed role of enjoyment in our lives, namely the fact that it has established itself as the explicit core of capitalist ideology. If even in a recent past the libidinal connection with a given symbolic representation could be regarded as the *secret* anchoring point that conferred symbolic dignity upon that representation, today there is nothing but libidinal connection, which implies that the domain of the symbolic itself is withering away. But how does all this impact on cinema?

What I have argued throughout this book is informed by the overarching premise that, given the current levels of cultural commodification, the critical dimension of cinema can only be located in its alliance with theory. The theoretical analyses that I have proposed here stem from an understanding of the dialectic that harks back to Critical Theory's dialectical method in the attempt to redefine its scope. On today's evidence, Adorno and his fellow critical theorists were absolutely right: Culture (film) is thoroughly commodified, and as such it is the backbone of capitalist ideology. What they missed, however, is equally evident: The only hope for a critical response to today's universal cultural commodification resides not in an uncompromising rejection of culture and retreat into 'high art', but in a dialectical analysis of cultural commodities aimed at identifying their intrinsic and symptomatic self-division, their radically inconsistent constitution. The future of Critical Theory depends on our ability to make the cultural commodity (film) speak against its pervasive ideological character.

Note

1 For this reason, a phenomenon like wikileaks should perhaps be renamed *weak*leaks: Its lack of subversive political impact is the measure of the fundamental (theoretical) weakness of Julian Assange's strategy of releasing secreted information. What he has not fully taken into consideration, it seems, is the extent to which the contemporary media industry *enjoys* revealing power's dirty secrets, in so far as it recycles its potentially subversive content into commodified 'images'. This strategy then does not hurt capital as it does not hurt the political power that supports capital. At most, it can promote a transfer of power between people supporting the same ideological framework, always on condition that such process does not damage capital.

References

Aaron, Michele (2007) *Spectatorship. The Power of Looking On*. London and New York: Wallflower.

Adorno, Theodor (1964) 'Chaplin in Malibu', *Chaplin Times Two*, in *Yale Journal of Criticism*, vol. 9, no. 1 (1996): 57–61.

— (1992 [1974]) *Notes on Literature*, vol. 2. New York: Columbia University Press.

— (1993 [1963]) *Hegel: Three Studies*. Cambridge (MA) and London: MIT Press.

— (1994 [1950]) *The Authoritarian Personality*. New York: W. W. Norton & Co.

— (1998) *Critical Models. Interventions and Catchwords*. New York: Columbia University Press.

— (1999 [1970]) *Aesthetic Theory*. London: The Athlone Press.

— (2000 [1966]) *Negative Dialectics*. London and New York: Routledge.

— (2001) *The Culture Industry*. London and New York: Routledge.

— (2005a [1951]) *Minima Moralia: Reflections on a Damaged Life*. London and New York: Verso.

— (2005b [1952]) *In Search of Wagner*. London and New York: Verso.

Adorno, Theodor and Benjamin, Walter (1999) *The Complete Correspondence 1928-1940*, edited by Henri Lonitz. Cambridge: Polity Press.

Adorno, Theodor and Eisler, Hanns (2005) *Composing for the Films*. London and New York: Continuum.

Adorno, Theodor and Horkheimer, Max (1997 [1947]) *Dialectic of Enlightenment*. London and New York: Verso.

Agger, Ben (1992) *Cultural Studies as Critical Theory*. London and Philadelphia (PA): The Falmer Press.

Anderson, Perry (1976) *Considerations on Western Marxism*. London and New York: Verso.

Auerbach, Jonathan (2011) *Dark Borders: Film Noir and American Citizenship*. Durham (NC): Duke University Press.

Badiou, Alain (2007 [2005]) *The Century*. Cambridge: Polity Press.

Barthes, Roland (1973 [1957]) *Mythologies*. London: Paladin.

— (1974 [1973]) *S/Z*. London: Cape.

Basinger, Jeanine (2007) *Anthony Mann*. Middletown (CT): Wesleyan University Press.

Benjamin, Walter (1992) *Illuminations*. London: Fontana Press.

Bergstrom, Janet (1993) 'The Mystery of *The Blue Gardenia*', in Joan Copjec (ed.), *Shades of Noir*. London and New York: Verso, pp. 97–120.

Bloch, Ernst (1988) 'A Philosophical View of the Detective Novel', in Ernst Bloch (ed.), *The Utopian Function of Art and Literature*. Cambridge (MA): The MIT Press, pp. 245–64.

Bogdanovich, Peter (1967) *Fritz Lang in America*. London: Studio Vista.

Bonitzer, Pascal (ed.) (1985) *Michelangelo Antonioni: Identificazione di un Autore*. Parma: Pratiche editrice.

Borde, Raymond and Chaumeton, Etienne (2002 [1955]) *A Panorama of American Film Noir 1941-1953*. San Francisco (CA): City Lights Books.

Bordwell, David and Caroll, Noël (eds) (1996) *Post Theory: Reconstructing Film Studies*. Madison (WI) and London: The University of Wisconsin Press.

Bordwell, David, Staiger, Janet and Thompson, Kristin (1985) *The Classical Hollywood Cinema: Film Style & Mode of Production to 1960*. London: Routledge.

Bottomore, Tom (1984) *The Frankfurt School*. Chichester: Ellis Horwood.

Brommer, Stephen Eric (1994) *Of Critical Theory and Its Theorists*. Oxford and Cambridge (MA): Blackwell.

Buckland, Warren (2009) *Film Theory and Contemporary Hollywood Movies*. London and New York: Routledge.

Buck-Morss, Susan (1977) *The Origin of Negative Dialectics: Theodor W. Adorno, Walter Benjamin, and the Frankfurt Institute*. New York: The Free Press.

Cantor, Paul A. (2007) 'Film Noir and the Frankfurt School: America as Wasteland in Edgar G. Ulmer's *Detour*', in Mark Conard (ed.), *The Philosophy of Film Noir*. Lexington: University Press of Kentucky, pp. 139–61.

Casetti, Francesco (1999 [1993]) *Theories of Cinema, 1945–1995*. Austin: University of Texas Press.

— (2007) 'Theory, Post-Theory, Neo-Theories: Changes in Discourses, Changes in Objects', in *Cinémas*, 17 (2–3): 33–45.

Claussen, Detlev (2008) *Theodor W. Adorno: One Last Genius*. Cambridge (MA) and London: The Belknap Press of the Harvard University Press.

Cohan, Steve (1997) *Masked Men: Masculinity and the Movies in the Fifties*. Bloomington and Indianapolis (IN): Indiana University Press.

Comolli, Jean-Luc and Narboni, Paul (1969) 'Cinema/Ideology/Criticism', reprinted in Leo Braudy and Marshall Cohen (2004) *Film Theory and Criticism* (6th edn). Oxford: Oxford University Press, pp. 812–19.

Conard, Mark T. (2007) 'Nietzsche and the Meaning and Definition of Noir', in Mark Conard (ed.), *The Philosophy of Film Noir*. Lexington (KY): The University of Kentucky Press, pp. 7–22.

Cowie, Elizabeth (1993) 'Film Noir and Women', in Joan Copjec (ed.), *Shades of Noir*. London: Verso, pp. 121–65.

Debord, Guy (1995 [1967]) *The Society of Spectacle*. New York: Zone Books.

Deleuze, Gilles (2005 [1985]) *Cinema 2. The Time-Image*. London and New York: Continuum.

Demonsablon, Philippe (1981 [1959]) 'The Imperious Dialectic of Fritz Lang', in Jenkins (ed.), *Fritz Lang: The Image and the Look*. London: BFI, pp. 18–25.

Eisner, Lotte (1984) *Fritz Lang*. Paris: Cahiers du Cinéma/Cinémathèque Française.

Elsaesser, Thomas (2004) *Weimar Cinema and After: Germany's Historical Imaginary*. Oxford and New York: Routledge.

Fink, Bruce (1995) *The Lacanian Subject. Between Language and Jouissance.* Princeton: Princeton University Press.
Finlayson, James Gordon (2009) 'The Work of Art and the Promise of Happiness in Adorno', *World-Picture 3.* http://www.worldpicturejournal.com.
Frank, Nino (1946) 'Un Nouveau Genre "Policier": L'aventure Criminelle', *L'Écran Français*, 61 (28 August): 14–16.
Grant, Barry Keith (ed.) (2003) *Fritz Lang: Interviews.* Jackson (MS): University Press of Mississippi.
Gunning, Tom (2000) *The Films of Fritz Lang: Allegories of Vision and Modernity.* London: BFI.
Haller, Robert (ed.) (2000) *Fritz Lang 2000.* New York: Anthology Film Archives.
Hegel, Georg Wilhelm Fredrick (1977 [1807]) *Phenomenology of Spirit.* Oxford: Oxford University Press.
— (1969 [1812–16]) *Science of Logic.* New York: Humanity Books.
Held, David (1980) *Introduction to Critical Theory: Horkheimer to Habermas.* Berkeley (CA): University of California Press.
Horkheimer, Max (1978) *Dawn & Decline: Notes 1926–1931 and 1950–1969.* New York: Seabury Press.
— (1992) *Critical Theory: Selected Essays.* New York: Continuum.
— (1995) *Between Philosophy and Social Science: Selected Early Writings.* Cambridge (MA): MIT Press.
— (2004 [1947]) *Eclipse of Reason.* New York and London: Continuum.
Hutchings, Kimberly (2006) 'Hegel, Ethics and the Logic of Universality', in Katerina Deligiogi (ed.), *Hegel: New Directions.* Chesham: Acumen Publishing, pp. 105–23.
Jacobs, Lea (1992) 'The B Film and the Problem of Cultural Distinction', *Screen,* 33(1) (Spring): 1–13.
Jameson, Fredric (2007 [1990]) *Late Marxism: Adorno or the Persistence of the Dialectic.* London and New York: Verso.
Jay, Martin (1996 [1973]). *The Dialectical Imagination. A History of the Frankfurt School and the Institute of Social Research, 1923–1950.* Berkeley (CA) and London: University of California Press.
Jenemann, David (2007) *Adorno in America.* Minneapolis (MN) and London: University of Minneapolis Press.
Jenkins, Stephen (ed.) (1981) *Fritz Lang: The Image and the Look.* London: BFI.
Kant, Immanuel (1933 [1781]) *Critique of Pure Reason* (trans. Norman Kemp Smith). London: Macmillan.
Kellner, Douglas (1989) *Critical Theory, Marxism and Modernity.* Cambridge: Polity Press.
Kluge, Alexander (1988) 'On New German Cinema, Art, Enlightenment, and the Public Sphere: An Interview with Alexander Kluge' by Stuart Liebman, *October,* no. 46 (1988): 23–59.
Kracauer, Siegfried (1947) *From Caligari to Hitler: A Psychological History of the German Film.* Princeton (NJ): Princeton University Press.
— (1960) *Theory of Film: the Redemption of Physical Reality.* Oxford: Oxford University Press.
Krutnik, Frank (1991) *In a Lonely Street: Film Noir, Genre, Masculinity.* London: Routledge.

Lacan, Jacques (1990 [1973]) *Television: A Challenge to the Psychoanalytic Establishment*. New York: Norton.
— (1993 [1955–56]) *The Seminar, Book III: The Psychoses*. New York: Norton.
— (1998a [1964]) *The Seminar, Book XI: The Four Fundamental Concepts of Psychoanalysis*. New York: Norton.
— (1998b [1972–73]) *The Seminar, Book XX: Encore, On Feminine Sexuality, The Limits of Love and Knowledge*. New York: Norton.
— (2006) *Écrits*. New York and London: W. W. Norton.
Lazaroff Alpi, Deborah (1998) *Robert Siodmak: A Biography, with Critical Analyses of His Films Noirs and a Filmography of All His Works*. Jefferson: McFarland & Co.
Leslie, Esther (2002) *Hollywood Flatlands: Animation, Critical Theory, and the Avant-Garde*. London and New York: Verso.
Lindlof, Thomas R. and Taylor, Bryan C. (2002) *Qualitative Communication Research Methods* (2nd edn). Thousand Oaks (CA): Sage.
Lukács, Georg (1975 [1920]) *History and Class Consciousness: Studies in Marxist Dialectics*. London: The Merlin Press Limited.
Marcuse, Herbert (1973 [1941]) *Reason and Revolution: Hegel and the Rise of Social Theory*. London: Routledge and Kegan Paul.
Marx, Karl (1990 [1867]) *Capital. A Critique of Political Economy*, vol. 1. London: Penguin Books.
McElhaney, Joe (2006) *The Death of Classical Cinema: Hitchcock, Lang, Minnelli*. New York: SUNY Press.
McGilligan, Patrick (1997) *The Nature of the Beast*. New York: St Martin's Press.
Metz, Walter (2006) 'Modernity and the Crisis in Truth: Alfred Hitchcock and Fritz Lang', in Murray Pomerance (ed.), *Cinema and Modernity*. New Brunswick (NJ): Rutgers University Press, pp. 74–89.
Morrison, James (1998) *Passport to Hollywood. Hollywood Films, European Directors*. Albany: SUNY Press.
Mulvey, Laura (1992 [1975]) 'Visual Pleasures and Narrative Cinema', in *The Sexual Subject: A Screen Reader in Sexuality*, edited by Mandy Merck. London: Routledge, pp. 22–34.
Naremore, James (1998) *More Than Night. Film Noir in its Contexts*. Berkeley, Los Angeles and London: University of California Press.
— (2002) 'A Season in Hell or the Snows of Yesteryear?', in Raymond Borde and Etienne Chaumeton (eds), *A Panorama of Film Noir 1941–1953*, 2002 [1955]. San Francisco (CA): City Lights Books, pp. vii–xxi.
Pahl, Katrin (2011) 'The Way of Despair', in Slavoj Žižek, Clayton Crockett and Creston Davis (eds), *Hegel and the Infinite: Religion, Politics and Dialectic*. New York: Columbia University Press.
Pasolini, Pier Paolo (1967) 'Ora tutto è chiaro, voluto, non imposto dal destino', *Cineforum*, no. 68 (October): 609–10.
— (1995) *Empirismo Eretico*. Milano: Garzanti.
Rancière, Jacques (2006a) *Film Fables*. Oxford and New York: Berg.
— (2006b) *The Politics of Aesthetics: The Distribution of the Sensible*. London and New York: Continuum.
Rivette, Jacques (1957) 'La Main [The Hand]', in *Cahiers du Cinéma* 76 (November 1957), reprinted in Jim Hillier (ed.) (1985), *Cahiers du Cinéma. The 1950s: Neo-Realism, Hollywood, New Wave*. London: BFI, pp. 140–4.

Rush, Fred (ed.) (2004) *The Cambridge Companion to Critical Theory.* Cambridge: Cambridge University Press.

Russell, Catherine (1995) *Narrative Mortality: Death, Closure, and New Wave Cinemas.* Minneapolis (MN) and London: Minnesota University Press.

Sanders, Steven M. (2007) 'Film Noir and the Meaning of Life', in Mark Conard (ed.), *The Philosophy of Film Noir.* Lexington (KY): University Press of Kentucky, 2007, pp. 91–105.

Sarris, Andrew (1968) *The American Cinema: Directors and Directions, 1929-1968.* New York: Da Capo Press.

Schnauber, Cornelius (1997) *Hollywood Haven: Homes and Haunts of the European Émigrés and Exiles in Los Angeles.* Riverside (CA): Ariadne Press.

Schrader, Paul (1986) 'Notes on *Film Noir*', in Barry Keith Grant (ed.), *Film Genre Reader.* Austin (TX): University of Texas Press.

Slater, Philip (1977) *Origin and Significance of the Frankfurt School.* Pyrmont: Law Book Co of Australasia.

Sohn-Rethel, Alfred (1978) *Intellectual and Manual Labour. A Critique of Epistemology.* London: Macmillan.

van Reijen, Willem and Bransen, Jan (2002) 'The Disappearance of Class History in *Dialectic of Enlightenment: Philosophical Fragments*', in Max Horkheimer and Theodor W. Adorno (eds), *Dialectic of Enlightenment* (2002 [1947]) Stanford: Stanford University Press, pp. 248–52.

Telotte, Jean-Pierre (1989) *Voices in the Dark: The Narrative Patterns of Film Noir.* Urbana and Chicago (IL): University of Illinois Press.

Vighi, Fabio (2006) *Traumatic Encounters in Italian Film: Locating the Cinematic Unconscious.* Bristol: Intellect.

Žižek, Slavoj (1989) *The Sublime Object of Ideology.* London and New York: Verso.

— (1992) *Looking Awry. An Introduction to Jacques Lacan through Popular Culture.* Cambridge (MA) and London: MIT Press.

— (1993) *Tarrying with the Negative. Kant, Hegel, and the Critique of Ideology.* Durham: Duke University Press.

— (1999) *The Ticklish Subject: The Absent Centre of Political Ontology.* London and New York: Verso.

— (2001a [1992]) *Enjoy Your Symptom! Jacques Lacan In and Out of Hollywood.* London and New York: Routledge.

— (2001b) *On Belief.* London and New York: Routledge.

— (2001c) *Did Somebody Say Totalitarianism? Five Interventions in the (Mis)use of a Notion.* London and New York: Verso.

— (2005 [1994]) *The Metastases of Enjoyment: Six Essays on Women and Causality.* London and New York: Verso.

— (2006) *The Universal Exception: Selected Writings.* London and New York: Continuum.

— (2010) *Living in the End Times.* London and New York: Verso.

Žižek, Slavoj; Crockett, Clayton and Davis, Creston (2011) *Hegel and the Infinite: Religion, Politics and Dialectic.* New York: Columbia University Press.

Index